man's quest

In Search of a Quantum God

Copyright © 2015 by John Luckey

All rights reserved.

Cover design by Ignite Design and Advertising

No part of this publication may be reproduced, distributed, or transmitted in any form or by any means, including photocopying, recording, or other electronic or mechanical methods, without the prior written permission of the author, except in the case of brief quotations embodied in critical reviews and certain other noncommercial uses permitted by copyright law.

Ordering Information: Special discounts are available on quantity purchases by corporations, associations, and others. For details, contact the author at: http://insearchofaquantumgod.com/

Dedication

For anyone and everyone who seeks the truth.

Testimonials

"Finding God using today's modern physics is quite a task. The author makes a valiant attempt in this book."

~ Dr. Fred Alan Wolf, PhD, aka Dr. Quantum ® physicist, bestselling author, including *The Spiritual Universe, Time-loops and Space-twists: How God Created the Universe.* http://www.fredalanwolf.com

"The Copernican Revolution and the Great Reformation occurred in the same era in history, and both had their roots in the Church. Science and the Spirit cannot be separated. For the Creator, the secrets of the universe are no mystery. God delights in hiding things so that we might delight in searching them out. From the days of the Copernican Revolution to the days of Newtonian physics, and on to the days of Quantum Physics, great clues to the mysteries of the Universe continue to unfold. How all of it connects to our journey in and with God is the 'stuff' of Dr. John Luckey's *In Search Of A Quantum God*. Enjoy the journey John takes you on as you begin with the original explosive Big Bang to the creative, profound, mysterious explosions of God's presence in your own life."

~ Dr. Mark Chironna, bestselling author, including *Beyond the Shadow of Doubt, Stepping into Greatness, Life Quest.* http://www.Markchironna.com

Contents

Dedication 3
Introduction 6
Chapter 1: The God Particle? 9
Chapter 2: Quantum Physics—What's That? 25
Chapter 3: DNA—Your Personal Computer Code Inside 40
Chapter 4: The "God Code" Within our DNA 65
Chapter 5: Conscious Cells & the Intergalactic Tagger, Fibonacci 92
Chapter 6: Ancient Aliens—our Gods or Parents or ? 126
Chapter 7: Flood Gates, Star Gates, and Genetics 170
Chapter 8: Sir Isaac Newton's Secret Code Found? 208
Chapter 9: The Shroud of Turin... a Quantum Event? 231
Chapter 10: Astrology of Origin - A Code in the Stars, and More? ...255
Chapter 11: Man's Ability to Conceptualize a Quantum God 297
Chapter 12: Black Holes, Ten Dimensions, Old Codes, New Codes 335
Epilogue 376
Bibliography 380
About the Author 382

Introduction

One must be truthful and honest in his approach; a constant independent inquiry and not blindly following a certain blue print laid down by others.
~ Bruce Lee

What if long ago and far away… there was nothing. You could sense "everything" out there somewhere… everywhere… yet it was nowhere. You could feel a presence, a pure potentiality of everything, just beyond your reach.

Suddenly you're struck with a powerful concussion, but just before it hits you, you catch sight of what appears to be a giant sphere of energy and light, and then you are sent reeling head-over-heels through an ever expanding universe. Galaxies appear all around you as you are swept through the rapidly expanding Cosmos.

What was that loud noise? What or who was that ball of energy and light, that field of pure potentiality that you saw for a moment? That moment just before the great concussion hit you as it expanded and transformed the energy into mass throughout the ever-growing Cosmos. What was that?

This is a story of my personal search for a quantum God. Not in the classic sense of exploring religion, but through examining science and the codes and clues it give us and the statistical probabilities that first life was designed and put in motion at the Big Bang by an all-powerful energy source… or …

In the search for truth, our perceptions can be accurate or inaccurate. It is imperative that we continually check the source of our perceptions and run impartial updates for accuracy on a regular basis! It is the foundational step in ANY search for truth!

Ask any pilot. Your instruments must be telling you the truth, they must be properly calibrated. If not you may fly the perfect approach, following their direction's accurately and still end up short of the runway... short of your desired destination!

As I searched for the ultimate truth I felt the pull of extremism from religion and from science. I know that I am not the only one who has felt this. The superstitious and narrow minded on both sides do great damage to the search for truth. It is no wonder that elements from both extremes seek to align themselves with a great scientist like Einstein, who is universally admired. It is an attempt to wrap their extremism in the reputation of a man who was not and to find credibility by associating themselves with the reputation of a great man who lived outside the box.

I have always admired Albert Einstein and refuse to be part of that. I will not, however, stay away from this great man's approach to science because others have misquoted or misrepresented his words, which at times admittedly do seem contradictory regarding religion.

May I submit that is because, religion is not God. Religion is what man does with spirituality and a genuine seeker of truth cannot ignore the hypocrisy that is found in anything that men touch, including science and religion. The spirit of truth is a double-edged sword that cuts away the lies that have boxed us in. It frees us from the lies of religion and the lies of science and will eventually reunite both as they really are two halves of a whole... try bouncing half a ball. You need both halves functioning as designed to play the game as intended.

Join me in my search for truth, as I press for a healing of the artificial man-induced schizophrenia that has affected the subjects of God and science. Sadly, it is as if we have been trying to solve the mysteries of the Cosmos with a brain that has been lobotomized. I, for one, need both halves to see the whole picture!

While examining Einstein's brain, post mortem, one thing stood out—the well-developed corpus callosum—where the left and right hemispheres communicate. Balance and communication is what we need in the search for truth!

A man should look for what is,
and not for what he thinks should be.
~Albert Einstein

Chapter 1
The God Particle?

This is your last chance. After this, there is no turning back. You take the blue pill - the story ends, you wake up in your bed and believe whatever you want to believe. You take the red pill - you stay in Wonderland and I show you how deep the rabbit hole goes.
~ Morpheus, *The Matrix*

Let others be concerned with the details, I just want to learn to think like God thinks.
~ Albert Einstein

One hundred meters deep below Cern, Switzerland is a giant manmade cave extending eighteen miles in circumference through parts of France and Switzerland. It is filled with some of the most complex equipment, computers, and instruments ever built by man. That's where you will find the LHC or Large Hadron Collider.

Throughout the month of June 2012 scientists fought to contain their excitement as teams worked underground on the LHC buried beneath the French and Swiss countryside. Many environmental activists had fought to prevent their project, fearing that because the Collider would simulate conditions they theorized were present at the Big Bang, it might trigger another Big Bang and thus threaten the stability of not only our planet, but perhaps the known universe. In other words, they were afraid that if the scientists found what they were looking for we all might go out with a BIG BANG!

Every great new idea meets with resistance, sometimes even fear, but this project had more than its share. It was an ambitious attempt to speed up two protons to as near the speed of light as possible. They were traveling in opposite directions and, yes, the plan was to crash them into each other! Many were concerned. After all, that was close to what we did to create the hydrogen bomb: speed up particles, then crash them into each other, the resulting fusion releasing the most powerful force of nature man had seen to date.

What if it created a chain reaction that could not be stopped? The scientists knew they were on the verge of one of the greatest discoveries of their lifetimes. The data had to be analyzed. Had they found the missing link in quantum physics, the so-called God particle? Or did the Higgs boson particle even exist outside of the quantum particle theory?

On the morning of July 4th, 2012, scientists all over the world collectively held their breath, waiting for an announcement that could confirm or deny the existence of the God particle. The world waited to hear.

It was about 10:30 a.m. local time in Geneva.

Dr. Fabiola Gianotti was the head of the ATLAS collaboration, a group of about 3,000 or so scientists who work on a giant detector at the LHC. Her talk that morning at Cern, the particle physics lab near Geneva, came directly after another presentation by Joe Incandela, head of the CMS detector group, which also saw the particle. However, everything rested on her talk; had the

ATLAS group seen nothing, the lab could hardly claim a discovery.

It was an incredibly tense and exciting time. They were so focused on producing the long awaited results. The month of June flew by as the team collected evidence that pointed to a Higgs-like particle. Nearly every week there was another step forward. They all agreed that it was a time of great team spirit, everyone working toward a common goal. People at all levels of the LHC were working around the clock.

Dr. Gianotti was in mid-sentence when her audience spotted the result they had so long hoped for and rose to their feet to whistle, cheer, and roar their approval. She tried to calm them down, asked them to wait, that there was more.

But the result they had spied, a simple number five followed by the Greek letter sigma in a little red box was all the hundreds gathered needed to know. It told them that the Higgs boson, or at least a particle that looked suspiciously like it, had been found at last. Nothing was going to delay their celebration. After more than two decades of research, it appeared that the God particle existed and the planet was still in one piece! Frontiers of science had been pushed back and some dark corners of the unknown had just been illuminated. Many of those in attendance had spent their entire careers in this search for proof of the so-called God particle.

The Higgs boson particle did not get the nickname—God particle—because of the beliefs of the scientists involved. Some were atheists and even called it the "God damn" particle because it was so hard to find. A book written in 1994 by Leon Lederman coined the phrase and it stuck. He actually wanted to call it the God damn particle but his publisher convinced him otherwise. But whether it was called God or God damn, didn't that imply the presence of a supreme being?

The existence of the Higgs boson seems to verify the theory envisioned by the British physicist Peter Higgs as he hiked through the Scottish highlands and later drew up with a pencil and paper in his office at Edinburgh University nearly half a century ago. The theory says that elementary particles, like the quarks and electrons inside atoms, get their masses from an invisible field that stretches through all of space. Without something to give particles mass, there would be no stars, planets, or life as we know it!

Higgs, now 83, was in the audience on the fourth of July. At the end of Gianotti's talk, when the crowd stood for a second standing ovation, he drew a handkerchief from his pocket and wiped tears from his eyes, overwhelmed by their reaction to the news. Gianotti went to greet him and to offer congratulations. She respected Higgs enormously, not only for his genius and insight, but for his deep-seated modesty.

Dr. Higg's boson or God particle seemed to be the missing piece of a jigsaw puzzle that physicists had pieced together since the 1970s to explain how the known particles in nature behave.

As I watched the news conference I heard one reporter ask her about the discovery of the Higgs boson, *Would that be good news for her?*

Wisely she replied something to the effect, It's not about good or bad news, it's about what nature has chosen. It's always good news when you're closer to the truth!

So, just what is this Higgs field-God particle theory all about?

Well, as we just discovered, it started in an attempt to explain where the expected mass for elementary particles was. It was in the math but not in the experience. They couldn't find it in the lab. Enter the Higgs field theory. Imagine for a minute that the mass wasn't in the particle but in the resistance to the movement of the particle... through, you guessed it, the unseen Higgs field.

Visualize this: you have a large cookie pan the size of your kitchen table and in this pan you have a few pounds of sugar spread out evenly an inch deep. In that field of sugar you drop in some ping pong balls and for contrast, some golf balls. Now imagine that the table is rocking back and forth slowly like a rocking chair. The particles move through the field but with resistance from the field of sugar. The resistance is their mass and the resistance is contained in the field of sugar. I admit that's an over simplified view, but you got to admit—it's sweet.

The electrons and protons and ping pongs traveling through this field meet with different levels of resistance, and hence, mass.

At least now the physicists had a plausible explanation for the lost mass that the folks over in the math department said was there.

To prove the theory, scientists built the Large Hydron Collider, an eighteen-mile race track, (the sugar field) where protons were accelerated to nearly the speed of light so that they traversed the eighteen miles 11000 times a second! Then they aimed these tiny particles right at each other until they collided! The resulting energy of the collision was thought to disturb the Higgs field, dislodging one of the grains of "sugar," which was moved out of its place for a moment in time and measured by the detectors surrounding the collider at the point of impact. It was called the Higgs boson. Highly unstable and hard to find, it was postulated that the Higgs particles quickly degraded into electrons, neutrinos, photons, etc. Scientists hoped by measuring the quantity of these particles, they could then back track to prove the Higgs state or field that gave rise to them.

Why is this important to physicists? Why did they convince governments around the world to contribute ten billion dollars to build it? Symmetry, just symmetry; Einstein said every valid theory must have it. If the chaotic data could come together into a pattern with symmetry—all parts of a unified whole—they might be able to approach the Theory of Everything! (That's the Big T.O.E., as I call it.) If they could just find the missing mass. The problem on the mathematical level was that symmetry worked until mass was assigned to the particle; there must be mass, because it was proven in the laboratory. But where was it? If not in the particle, where?

This is what Peter Higgs was thinking about as he walked through the Scottish highlands that day. His imagination was looking for a way to explain what they saw in the laboratory without unbalancing the equation that mathematically explained it. This is the challenge that spawned the Higgs field theory.

The theory he came up with that day provided a solution that in a manner of speaking allowed them to have their cake and eat it, too! The Higgs field allowed the preservation of the delicate symmetry and then balanced the mathematical equations for the missing mass of the particles.

The Higgs field theory says that every particle in the universe passes through this field, and by communicating with the field, some particles—like quarks and electrons—acquire mass. Some mass-less particles don't interact with the Higgs field and just pass right through the universe at the speed of light. (I guess they are just not in the "mood" to communicate. Sorry, that's probably humor only fans of Sheldon from the TV program *The Big Bang* will appreciate.)

Scientists also discovered that the Higgs particle had fundamentally different characteristics when compared to other particles. (It should, right? It's the God particle!) All other particles spin at their appropriate rates. It seems, however, that the God particle in the Higgs field is the first nonspining particle we have discovered.

Why should you care about all this quantum mumble jumble? Well, for starters, a lot of really cool things have come from practical applications of quantum physics. For instance, cell phones, computers ... anything that works with integrated circuits came about through practical application of quantum mechanics, allowing us to move tiny little electrons through small circuits. Can you imagine what lies ahead? Think of the speed of computing when we learn how to operate effectively in the "Higgs Field," where it seems things can exist in two places at once... even though they are light years apart. Is it an illusion or a magic trick, or is it really named the God particle for a reason?

In this age of hi-tech supercomputers and graphics, seeing isn't always believing. In fact, has it ever been? There always seems to be more than we see. Take for instance the TV series the *Masked Magician.* He routinely risks the anger of his fellow magicians as he reveals how illusion is used to produce some seemingly miraculous events.

The eye of the needle is a well-known magician's trick that has perplexed me for years. The name of the trick clearly invokes the statement made by Jesus that it was easier for a camel to go through the eye of a needle than for a rich man to enter heaven. In Biblical times, the eye of a needle was a small opening in the city wall that would allow entrance but only if you unloaded your camel and had it crawl through on its knees. It was designed to protect the occupants of the city from a mass attack and yet allow after-hours access to the city. It provided a chokepoint and a challenge to get in without making it impossible.

The Eye of the Needle, the illusion that every magician since Houdini has performed in one form or another, has two seemingly magic pillars. One, a beautiful assistant moves magically and unseen from one place to another through what seems to be an impossibly small opening. Two, during the trick the assistant appears to be in two places at once! Watch the masked magician's program and you will see how it is really done. Here is a hint: it's science, not "magic."

Speaking of being in two places at the same time... some very real scientists have been working with the concept of moving faster than the speed of light for some time now and not just on the set of *Star Trek*. It seems that numerous different experiments have been and are currently being conducted where not only does it seem they have broken Einstein's speed limit but they have also observed a subatomic particle existing in two places at once! Now, is that scientific prestidigitation or the next step in expanding our boundaries of the new normal or abnormal in quantum physics?

Get ready for the yoga of time travel. Besides sounding really cool, that is the name of an interesting book by Dr. Quantum himself. Dr. Quantum is actually the quantum physicist, Dr. Fred Alan Wolf. You may remember him from the movie *What the*

Bleep do We Know? I had the honor of sitting and talking with Dr. Wolf in San Diego a few years back. Even after all this time, I am still trying to digest everything he said! What a genius. For the moment, I invite you to wrap your mind around this: Scientists claim they have broken the ultimate speed barrier: the speed of light. In research carried out in the United States, some particle physicists have shown that light pulses can be accelerated to up to 300 times their normal velocity of 186,000 miles per second. The implications, like the speed, are mind-boggling. In one interpretation it means that light will arrive at its destination before it has started its journey. In effect, it is leaping forward in time. Exact details of the findings remain confidential, but the original work, as far as we know was carried out by Dr. Lijun Wang of the NEC research institute in Princeton, who transmitted a pulse of light toward a chamber filled with specially treated Caesium gas.

Before the pulse even fully entered the chamber it had gone right through and travelled on farther, sixty feet across the laboratory. In effect, it existed in two places at once, a phenomenon that Wang explained by saying it travelled 300 times faster than light.

As you might have guessed, the research caused controversy among physicists. What bothered them is that if light could travel forward in time it could carry information. This would breach one of the basic principles in physics—causality—which says that a cause must come before an effect. It would also shatter Einstein's theory of relativity, since it depends in part on the speed of light being unbreachable.

But wait, aren't we forgetting something? What do we really know about this Higg's field and the so-called God particle or particles. Could it hold the answer?

Dr. Wang seemed excited, proud, and even a bit confused that his results confirmed that their light pulses did indeed travel faster than the accepted speed of light. Professor of physics at the University of California at Berkeley, Dr. Raymond Chiao, and others were impressed by the findings. Many found it an extremely fascinating, if not perplexing experiment.

In Italy, another group of physicists also succeeded in breaking the light speed barrier. In a newly published paper, physicists at the Italian National Research Council described how they propagated microwaves at 25 percent above normal light speed. The group speculated that it could be possible to transmit information faster than light.

Dr. Guenter Nimtz, of Cologne University, an expert in the field, agreed. He believed that information could be sent faster than light and gave a paper describing how it could be done at a conference in Edinburgh. He believed, however, that this would not breach the principle of causality because the time taken to interpret the signal would fritter away all the savings.

The majority of scientists agreed that the most likely applications for this new find were not in time travel but in speeding up the way signals move through computer circuits.

Wang's experiment was the latest and possibly the most important evidence that the physical world might not operate according to any of the accepted conventions. Just when we had it all figured out!

Clearly, or maybe not so clearly, there is a field surrounding the subatomic particles connecting everything everywhere. Is it the Higgs Ocean? Can a stimulus somewhere in that field or ocean create a simultaneous response far away, defying the speed of light? Or even deeper into the rabbit hole, what about the concept of causality? Could one's intention to do something create a reaction somewhere far away, even before the action occurs? The quantum world is indeed intriguing! What is science and what is consciousness?

In the new world that modern science is beginning to perceive, sub-atomic particles can apparently exist in two places at the same time—making no distinction between space and time. Separate experiments carried out by Chiao illustrate this. He showed that in certain circumstances photons—the particles of which light is made—could apparently jump between two points separated by a barrier in what appeared to be zero time. The process, known as tunnelling, has been used to make some of the most sensitive electron microscopes.

The implications of Wang's experiments have aroused fierce debate. Many question whether his work can be interpreted as proving that light can exceed its normal speed—suggesting that another mechanism may be at work.

Neil Turok, professor of mathematical physics at Cambridge University, seemed to doubt these new findings would change the view of the fundamental laws of physics. *They always say that until it does.*

Wang emphasized that his experiments are relevant only to light and may not apply to other physical entities. Nevertheless, scientists are beginning to accept that man may eventually exploit some of these characteristics for inter-stellar space travel.

Like a speeding vehicle on the Autobahn, scientists discovered a fast moving particle they called a neutrino. Just like the cars on the Autobahn, Neutrinos come in a number of different types or models, like hard tops and convertibles, even hardtop convertibles.

Some, like the hardtop convertible, have recently been seen to switch spontaneously from one type to another. The Cern racing team prepared a beam of just one type, muon neutrinos, and sent them through the Earth to an underground laboratory at Gran Sasso half way down the boot of Italy, to see how many showed up as different types, tau neutrinos.

In the course of doing experiments, researchers noticed that the particles showed up sixty billionths of a second earlier than they would have if they were travelling at the speed of light!

This is a tiny fractional change—just twenty parts in a million—but one that occurs consistently.

The team measured the travel times of these 'fast and furious' neutrinos some 16,000 times, and reached a level of statistical significance that in scientific circles would count as a formal discovery.

This has motivated them to publish their measurements with the disclaimer that they hoped others in the scientific community would help them understand their results because it all just seemed too crazy to be true.

Since then, scientists at Cern posted new results that confirm measurements made in September 2012. A beam of subatomic particles has indeed travelled faster than the speed of light.

The initial result caused widespread debate as it appeared to break the speed limit again, the one that says that nothing can travel faster than the speed of light.

The findings have proved troubling for scientists as it goes against Dr. Einstein's law of special relativity and opens up the possibility of being able to send information back in time. There's that causality clause again!

The researchers behind the experiments, which involved sending neutrino particles 450 miles through the ground from the CERN facility in Geneva to the Gran Sasso laboratory in Italy, have now attempted to rule out at least one possible source of error.

By tweaking the experiment in an attempt to address a potential flaw in their original experiment, they again showed that the neutrons arrived at the Italian site some 60 billionths of a second faster than if they had been travelling at the speed of light. Wow! It would seem that this is not just an error in measurement. It seems we really have broken or found a way around the intergalactic speed limit!

The Higgs field theory provided physicists with a mechanism whereby some particles could obtain mass, simply by passing through a field. It made sense. It also makes sense that it could explain these greater-than-the-speed-of-light events. When the teams at Cern verified the existence of the God particle, they gave great crediblity to Higgs field theory. It seems that all other fields had verifiable particles associated with them, with the glaring exception of the equally elusive graviton, the tiny chap allegedly associated with gravitational fields.

But there was one big difference! This field was larger than an electromagnetic field, larger than the gravitational fields of the earth and other celestial bodies; in fact, it existed throughout the universe.

Higgs' idea holds promise to unite theories, standard and quantum, particles and waves by sweeping them into an omni-present universal field. Omni-present, now that sounds interesting and familiar at the same time.

That reminds me of something that Dr. Wolf said to me: "A quantum mechanic might not be able to fix your car, but he could fix your time machine… if you don't mind waiting."

So throw off the bowlines, sail away from the safe harbor.
Catch the trade winds in your sails. Explore. Dream. Discover.
~ Mark Twain

Chapter 2
Quantum Physics—What's That?

Einstein was among the group that first proposed the quantum mechanics theory, but we also know it troubled him. He once said his uncertainty was due to its uncertainty. "God doesn't play dice," he said, to which Niels Bohr is reported to have replied with a smile, "Don't tell God what He does."

There aren't many ideas so widely discussed and just as widely misunderstood as quantum theory. If there is a quantum God it sounds like He is the only one who really understands it!

The history of the quantum theory goes back to between 1801 and 1900 when Max Planck introduced the term 'quanta' to describe an exotic and bizarre subatomic entity, much to the dismay of many classical physicists. The scientists had discovered another box within the box, another "Russian doll within the doll," another level down the rabbit hole that had not yet been recognized by classical physics. There were particles and waves smaller than what physicists at that time believed existed. Suddenly electrons and protons were not the smallest particles "known"… they were the big kids on the block in this quantum neighborhood. There were a variety of other smaller quantum particles. They couldn't see them yet, though the math was predicting them. But as they developed experiments to identify them they found that sometimes the particles disappeared into waves. They were confused and a multitude of new theories emerged.

I am not an Einstein or Niels Bohr but I had to know what they found when they got down to the lowest common denominator. After all, I was in search of a "quantum God," so I jumped in to try and understand it all. This new branch of physics focused on the quantum realm, which met with skepticism, as most new theories do, but it eventually became accepted and then the search for a link that would unite the General Theory of Physics with the quantum theories became intense. It has remained so since. The discovery of the Higgs boson represents a giant step in explaining how and why the old theories worked and made sense to the degree they did and why, and how the "new" quantum physics does, too. The discovery of the quantum God particle—the Higgs boson—was a result of scientific diplomacy, a detente, a marriage of "old physics" with new, and the promise of much more to come.

What is the difference between quantum physics and quantum mechanics? Here is one explanation that helped me.

Quantum physics is a branch of science that deals with discrete, indivisible units of energy called quanta as described by the quantum theory, while quantum mechanics is the study of mechanical systems (things like this computer, highly advanced electronics and pretty much all of Silicon Valley) whose dimensions are close to or below the atomic scale (things like molecules, atoms, electrons, protons, and other subatomic particles). The basic difference is that the former is a branch of science while the latter is the study of the mechanics of its operation.

So what is quantum physics anyway and why is it so weird?

That's an easy one: it's the science of things so small that the quantum nature of reality has an effect. Some say at this level it's like a consciousness affecting the physics. If indeed it is, whose is it...the scientists or something or someone more? The observer or the observed?

If you begin to feel a bit like Alice down the rabbit hole, don't be afraid; you're not alone and we won't stay here too long.

Quantum means 'discrete amount' or 'portion.' In 1900 Max Planck discovered that you couldn't get smaller than a certain minimum amount of anything. This minimum amount is now called the Planck unit. By definition it is the lowest common denominator.

Why is it weird?

Niels Bohr, the father of the orthodox 'Copenhagen Interpretation' of quantum physics once said, "Anyone who is not shocked by quantum theory has not understood it."

Dr. Quantum (Wolf) said that to understand the weirdness completely, you just need to know about three experiments: Two Slits, the Light Bulb and Schrödinger's Cat.

Two Slits

The simplest experiment to demonstrate quantum weirdness involves shining a light through two parallel slits and looking at the screen. It can be shown that a single photon (particle of light) can interfere with itself, as if it travelled through both slits at once.

Light Bulb

Imagine a light bulb filament gives out a photon, seemingly in a random direction. Erwin Schrödinger came up with a nine-letter-long equation that correctly predicts the chances of finding that photon at any given point. He envisioned a kind of wave, like a ripple from a pebble dropped into a pond, spreading out from the filament. Once you look at the photon, this 'wave function' collapses into the single point at which the photon really is.

Schrödinger's Cat

In this experiment, we take your cat and put it in a box with a bottle of cyanide. (I know, I was about to call PETA, too, but this is just hypothetical.) We rig it up so that a detector looks at an isolated electron and determines whether it is 'spin up' or 'spin down' (it can have either characteristic, seemingly at random). If it is 'spin up', then the bottle is opened and the cat gets it. Ten minutes later we open the box and see if the cat is alive or dead. The question is: what state is the cat in between the detector being activated and the box being opened? Nobody has actually done this experiment (to my knowledge) but it does show a paradox that arises in certain interpretations.

If you dare to think about it (you're not really supposed to), you have to believe one of the following things: your consciousness affects the behavior of subatomic particles; particles move backward as well as forward in time and appear in all possible places at once; the universe is splitting every Planck-time (10 E-43 seconds) into billions of parallel universes; or the universe is interconnected with faster-than-light transfers of information.

Perhaps an inter-dimensional model would work to explain this mystery or a Higg's field or ocean reaction where a particle enters in one spot but instantly has a reaction elsewhere. Like putting your feet in the water in California and a small wave disturbance simultaneously arrives on the shore in Japan. No one knows yet, although many think they do.

These different options are the results of the different interpretations of quantum physics. The interpretations all compete with each other. Otherwise respectable physicists can get quite heated about how sensible their pet interpretation is and how crazy all the others are. At the moment, there's about one new interpretation every three months, but most of them fit into these categories.

What does it mean?

The *meaning* of quantum physics is a bit of a taboo subject; to make it all a bit more respectable, it is better to say 'ontology' than 'meaning,' though it's the same thing. There are several competing interpretations and the one thing they all have in common is that each of them explains all the facts and predicts every experiment's outcome correctly.

Copenhagen Interpretation (CI)

This is the granddaddy of interpretations, championed by the formidable Niels Bohr of Copenhagen University. He browbeat all dissenters into submission (with the notable exception of Einstein) at a Brussels conference sponsored by a man called Solvay in 1927. Bohr thereby stifled the debate for a generation or two.

The CI has a bit of nerve calling itself an interpretation, because it essentially says "thou shalt not ask what happens before ye look." He pointed out that the Schrödinger equation worked as a tool for calculating where the particle would be, except that it 'collapsed' as soon as you took a peek.

When you do try to take Copenhagen seriously you come to the conclusion that consciousness and particle physics are interrelated, and you rush off to write a book called The Dancing Wu-Li Masters. Some will welcome it but most physicists will not.

More recently, Henry Stapp at the University of California has written papers such as "On Quantum Theories of the Mind" [1997]. Stapp's central thesis is that the synapses in your brain are so small that quantum effects are significant. This means that there is quantum uncertainty about whether a neuron will fire or not—and this degree of freedom that nature has allows for the interaction of mind and matter.

What happens to the cat? You're not allowed to ask.

Many Worlds Interpretation (MWI)

The various paradoxes that the Copenhagen Interpretation gave rise to (famously Schrödinger's cat, and Einstein's dislike of "spooky action at a distance") led others to keep on trying to find a better interpretation.

The simplest was put forward by a student, Hugh Everett, in 1957. He said that the Schrödinger equation does not collapse. Of course, everyone laughed at him, because they could see that the photon, for example, was in just one place when they looked, not in all possible places. But after a couple of decades, this issue was resolved with the concept of decoherence—the idea that different universes can very quickly branch apart, so that there is very little relationship between them after a fraction of a second.

This has led to what should strictly be called the 'post-Everett' Interpretation, but is still usually called MWI. It is now one of the most popular interpretations. Unfortunately, it means that billions of you are splitting off every fraction of a second into discrete universes and it implies that everything possible exists in one universe or another. This comes with its own set of hard-to-digest concepts, such as the fact that a 500-year-old you exists in some universes, whereas in others you died at birth.

In 1997, Max Tegmark at Princeton University proposed an experiment to prove that MWI was correct. It involved pointing a loaded gun at your head and pulling the trigger. Of course, you will only survive in those universes where the gun, for whatever reason, fails to go off. If you get a misfire every time, you can satisfy yourself—with an arbitrarily high level of confidence—that MWI is true. Of course, in most universes your family will be weeping at your funeral (or possibly just shaking their heads and muttering).

What happens to the cat? It's dead in half the subsequent universes and alive in the other half.

Pilot Waves, Hidden Variables and the Implicate Order

Because David Bohm [1917-1992] was a brilliant physicist, people went along with him when he came up with an elegant but more complicated theory to explain the same set of phenomena (normally, more complicated theories are disqualified by the principle known as Ockham's Razor). It sounds like a subtitle to a *Star Trek* episode, right?

Bohm's theory follows on some original insights by Prince Louis de Broglie [1892-1987], who first studied the wave-like properties of the behavior of particles in 1924. De Broglie suggested that, in addition to the normal wave function of the Copenhagen Interpretation, there is a second wave that determines a precise position for the particle at any particular time. In this theory, there is some 'hidden variable' that determines the precise position of the photon.

Sadly, John von Neumann [1903-1957] wrote a paper in 1932 proving that this theory was impossible. Von Neumann was such a great mathematician that nobody bothered to check his math until

1966, when John Bell [1928-1990] proved there could be hidden variables after all—but only if particles could communicate faster than light (this is called 'nonlocality'). As we saw in the last chapter that is a possibility! In 1982 Alain Aspect demonstrated that this superluminal signaling did appear to exist, although David Mermin then showed that you could not actually signal anything. There is still some argument about whether this means very much.

Bohm's theory was that the second wave was indeed faster than light, and moreover it did not get weaker with distance but instantly permeated the entire universe, acting as a guide for the movement of the photon. This is why it is called a 'pilot wave'.

This theory explains the paradoxes of quantum physics perfectly. But it introduces a new faster-than-light wave and some hidden mechanism for deciding where it goes—to create an 'implicate order'. Worse still, to the purists, Bohm went on to become a mystic, identifying his 'implicate order' with Eastern spirituality and spawning books like Fritjof Capra's *The Tao of Physics*. That's heretical behavior in the eyes of any 'decent' physicist.

What happens to the cat? It's either dead or alive, of course!

Consistent Histories

The Consistent Histories interpretation, put forward by Robert Griffiths in 1984, works backward from the result of an experiment, arguing that only a few possible histories are consistent with the rules of quantum mechanics. It's an interesting idea, but not very popular because it still doesn't explain how a particle can go through two slits and interfere with itself. In *The Interpretation of Quantum Mechanics* [1994], Roland Omnès wrote down eighty equations in a single chapter and came to the conclusion that the 'consistent histories' interpretation was pretty much the same as Copenhagen, with a few bells and whistles and knobs on.

What happens to the cat? You're not supposed to ask.

Alternate Histories

The Alternate Histories Interpretation is quite different, being similar to the Many-Worlds Interpretation, but with the insistence that only the actual outcome is the real world and the ones we're not in don't actually exist. Unfortunately this gets us right back to their being some kind of 'collapse'.

What happens to the cat? Again, you're not supposed to ask.

In the movie, *Men In Black III*, Will Smith, playing Agent J, meets with an alien named Griffen who has the ability to see all of these alternate histories at once. The scene is at once hilarious and quite informative. You can see it online or on a DVD, if you have one. Either way, thank quantum physics for the video; you couldn't watch it without it.

Time Reversibility

Richard Feynman [1918-1988] was a genius who developed a new approach to quantum mechanics. He formalized its crowning achievement, quantum electrodynamics, which is the most accurate scientific theory ever devised. He also developed the Feynman Diagram, which represents the interaction of two particles at the exchange of a third particle. This diagram has time on one axis and space on the other and the interaction can be viewed as happening in both forward and reverse time.

An electron, on its way from point A to point B, can bump into a photon. In the diagram this can be drawn as sending it backward not just in space, but also in time. Then it bumps into another photon, which sends it forward in time again, but in a different direction in space. In this way, it can be in two places at once.

There is little doubt that a Feynman diagram offers the easiest way to predict the results of a subatomic experiment. Many physicists have seen the power of this tool and have taken the next step, arguing that reverse time travel is what actually happens in reality.

And what happens to the cat? It is both dead and alive simultaneously. We don't see this because of the macroscopic 'measurement problem'.

Transactional Interpretation

John Cramer's Transactional Interpretation relies on the fundamental time-symmetry of the universe. He argues that particles perform a kind of 'handshake' in the course of interacting. One sends out a wave forward in time, and another sends one out backward in time.

What happens to the cat?

In the early days of quantum mechanics, Albert Einstein suggested that if it were right, then quantum mechanics would mean that there would be "spooky action at a distance." It turned out that quantum mechanics was right, and that what Einstein had described as spooky action at a distance actually happened. This kind of "spooky connection" between certain quantum events is now called "quantum entanglement."

On the subject of "spooky action": another magic trick I have always wondered about was levitation. We have all heard of gurus of mystical religions who claim they can levitate. I even read a book by a former Satanist who said they did it routinely, conjuring spirits to move ceremonial altars too heavy to lift to the exact spots they wanted them secured. I would call that spooky action!

When the masked magician promised to reveal the science behind the trick of levitation, I had to be there to see how it was done. In his case, it was done with sleight-of-hand, lighting, and wires… and two beautiful assistants who served as additional distractions. The magic was really an illusion with a practical application of science behind it!

So are there practical applications for quantum mechanics? As a matter of fact… yes!

Let's start with the laptop I typed this on. It is a result of advances in our understanding of quantum physics. Quantum mechanics has also made possible technologies such as: spectroscopy, lasers, MRIs, CDs and DVDs, smart phones, etc.

Here is sort of how it works: electrons surround every atom's nucleus. Chemical bonds link atoms to form molecules. A chemical bond links two atoms when electrons are shared between those atoms. Thus QM (quantum mechanics) is the physics of the chemical bond and of chemistry. QM helps us understand how molecules are made and what their properties are.

QM can also help us understand big things, such as stars and black holes and even the entire universe. QM is a very important part of the theory of how the universe began what we call the Big Bang.

Everything made of matter is attracted to other matter because of a fundamental force called gravity. Einstein's theory that explains gravity is called the theory of general relativity, although a problem in modern physics is that some conclusions of QM do not seem to agree with the theory of general relativity. We'll come back to that. This is the area where outstanding minds are, as we speak, attempting to find the equation that will connect the dots between the two. The Higgs field, and what it implies promises to do just that.

QM is the part of physics that can explain why all electronic technology works as it does. Thus QM explains how computers work, because computers are electronic machines. But the designers of the early computer hardware of around 1950 or 1960 did not need to think about QM. The designers of radios and televisions at that time did not think about QM either. However, the design of the more powerful integrated circuits and computer memory technologies of recent years does require QM. The smaller and more compact we make our devices the more we encroach on and rely on the fundamentals of the Quantum kingdom.

Remember those speed demons on the European autobahn? They arrived in their "hardtop" convertible neutrinos in Sasso without a ticket, breaking Einstein's speed limit... quantum nonlocality is their excuse.

Basically, quantum nonlocality is the phenomenon by which microscopic objects seem to interact instantaneously (or nearly instantaneously) at a distance without any apparent intervening force. The phenomenon violates the common notion that an object may be directly influenced only by its immediate surroundings (the principle of locality).

This would seem to allow for faster-than-light communication! Very interesting, don't you think? One of the main reasons the theory of quantum nonlocality is of so much interest is because of its potential practical applications, such as quantum computing and faster-than-light communication.

In other words, before I finished typing this sentence and emailed it to myself, it was already in my inbox.

Softly the evening came… seemed all on fire at the touch,
and melted and mingled together
~ Henry Wadsworth Longfellow

Chapter 3

DNA—Your Personal Computer Code Inside

Human DNA is like a computer program but far, far more advanced than any we've ever created
~ Bill Gates

Late one night two snowmen are standing in the falling snow.

One says to the other, "How did we get here?"

The other one says, "The children in that house built us yesterday."

The first snowman replies, "Don't be absurd! Nobody made us! We evolved by chance from snowflakes."

After all the invisible quantum particles and waves and mysterious fields extending throughout the universe, then considering the possibility of an infinite number of parallel universes, with crazy quantum particles breaking the laws of non-locality and the convertible hardtop neutrinos breaking Einstein's speed limit, I needed to exit the rabbit hole and fast. As I did, I caught sight of myself in a mirror and peered into my confused face, remembering the words from the Bible: "in his image He created them, Man and Woman." I felt a few quantum particles short of the image of a quantum God!

As I stared at myself in the mirror like a deer in headlights, I also remembered what some spiritual leaders have said: that God is Omnipotent and Omnipresent, all powerful and everywhere. I had to admit that sounded like an echo from the rabbit hole that I had just escaped and I wanted to connect with "reality" again, for a little bit anyway. However, as I looked again in the mirror I was drawn into another incredible voyage, the one within. In my search for a quantum God I escaped, if only for a moment, from the rabbit hole only to be drawn into the Matrix!

I began to study the science and mystery of human life with all of its complexities, as found in our DNA—the very code of human life—I remembered a street magician who claimed to have the power of life that the masked magician exposed. Not surprisingly, his abilities were based on illusion. Then I wondered, what illusions are we falling for in real life? For that matter, what is real life? Quantum physics seems to offer an infinite number of options...

But what about the quantum world within our own bodies? Are there answers there or only more questions? Did we descend from apes, were we genetically engineered by a visiting alien race, or as the Bible says, were we amazingly and carefully made by a Creator?

If we did evolve from apes ... where did they come from? There is ample evidence that our bodies can adapt to our environments, but what does that prove? Is it even statistically possible that original life, whatever form it took, actually evolved from the randomness of an amino acid rich environment; if so, where did the amino acids come from?

With questions circling my head like a digital halo, I chose to continue my search for some code or proof that there was a designer or that we actually evolved from randomness, and DNA was my next stop.

Our DNA is an elegant example of a supercode. The interesting truth is that we haven't even known of its existence for that long. When Darwin was postulating his theory, the common belief was that the cell was simply filled with jello, well not the Jell-O or pudding pops Bill Cosby loves so much, but just an empty protoplasmic gel that filled the space.

In the 1950s we realized that was a colossal mistake, as scientists discovered that there actually was a lot more than jello in the cells; in fact, it was like a burgeoning metropolis inside with streets and stores and factories and this really cool spiral staircase called DNA or "Jacobs Ladder" as I sometimes call it…

It wasn't just a rickety old spiral staircase with double rails to hang on to, either. It was a vibrant, dynamic structure with at least three billion rungs on it. Then we found out that this DNA ladder contained a digital code! A what? A digital code like computers use and like almost everything electronic now operates on.

It turns out that we seem to consist of a series of biometric computers, and that our internal computers are running on a self-correcting code something that is extremely rare even with our best engineers and computers and software!

A digital error detecting code is something that perhaps only one in twelve engineers could produce. Our DNA is an error detecting code, but more than that, it is an error detecting and self-correcting code. Our bodies seem to be a complex matrix of interrelated computer systems.

That advanced code design written into our DNA is the same design that occurs in all life! This would imply design, and a designer, and that whomever, or whatever made us also made the plants and trees and flowers and animals etc.

There is a factory within each of our cells and this self-correcting code is designed to keep the master blueprint, the DNA, in ideal order. Using the DNA master blueprint, the cellular factory then translates this into proteins, which build the machines within the cell that make life happen on a cellular level. There are hundreds of amino acids that we know about but only twenty are used by the body to build these proteins that build our cells. During this assembly process, you have messenger RNA, yes running on another code, that come down the factory assembly line and customize the amino acid sequences to fit the body's needs.

One example often used to show how complex our bodies are is the construction of the human hemoglobin molecule—the one that carries the oxygen in our blood to every cell in our body—which the cells then use to "keep us alive."

Hemoglobin (abbreviated Hb or Hgb) is the iron-containing oxygen-transport metalloprotein in the red blood cells of all vertebrates (with the exception of the fish family Channichthyidae.) It is also found in the tissues of some invertebrates as well. Hemoglobin in the blood carries oxygen from the respiratory organs (lungs or gills) to the rest of the body (i.e. the tissues and on down to the cellular factories) where it releases the oxygen to burn nutrients to provide energy to power the functions of the organism AND collects the resultant carbon dioxide to bring it back to the respiratory organs to be expelled from the organism. It's a great multi-tasker. It brings in the fuel and removes the exhaust, so to speak.

In mammals, this protein makes up about 97 percent of the red blood cells' dry content, and around 35 percent of the total content (including water). Hemoglobin has an oxygen-binding capacity of 1.34 mL O2 per gram of hemoglobin, which increases the total blood oxygen capacity seventy-fold compared to dissolved oxygen in blood. The mammalian hemoglobin molecule can bind or carry up to four oxygen molecules.

Hemoglobin is vital to life and as we discovered a great multitasker. It carries at least 10 percent of the body's respiratory carbon dioxide as carbaminohemoglobin, in which CO_2 is bound to the globin protein. The molecule also carries the important regulatory molecule nitric oxide bound to a globin protein thiol group, releasing it at the same time as oxygen.

There is a sequence of 574 amino acids that make up the hemoglobin molecule, which must occur in the proper sequence or what brings life could instead bring death!

This proper sequence exists as one possibility in ten to the 650th power, which means it is absurd to believe that it could occur by chance. Let's get a picture of what this extreme number is. If you believe that the universe is fourteen billion years old, then there have been ten to the eighteenth power seconds since the Big Bang fourteen billion years ago. Let's expand our minds with another quantum leap... there are only ten to the 66th power atoms in our entire galaxy. To believe it just happens by chance seems absurd.

A leading authority on the probability theory, Emile Borel, states in his book *Probabilities and Life* that once we go past one chance in ten to the fiftieth power the probabilities are so small it's impossible to think they will ever occur. Seems to me this is so far beyond coincidence that it defies explanation!

It now seems quite absurd to believe the equation mass plus energy plus entropy equals life. Really? In what universe? Certainly not a parallel one, maybe in a reverse universe.

Mass plus energy plus information and you have a chance, however remote, at life!

But if you have information, does it not imply a source of that information? It appears that randomness is not a statically realistic source for that information. New information demands new paradigms and understanding. Like the way we adapted and changed our opinions to reflect the facts when we exchanged our Jell-O pudding pops for DNA in the fifties.

The discovery of truth demands intellectual honesty and the ability to adapt to new facts and alter our set opinions in accordance with those new facts, wherever they take us.

Imagination is invaluable in the search for truth. With it we imagine and form theories, or enlightened preconceived ideas, and then we set about proving them or disproving them, right? We hold on to what we prove and we discard what is disproved. Right? Or do we? Sometimes working hypotheses seem to take on a life of their own, even after the facts show them to be false.

Let's take a quick high school science refresher course. Remember the four forces that exist? There is the force of gravity, electromagnetic force, and two nuclear forces—the strong nuclear force and the weak nuclear force. Gravity keeps the Earth and the planets in their orbits. It also keeps the solar system in its alignment and our feet on the ground. The electromagnetic force can overcome the power of gravity on Earth. It holds the atoms together, it determines the orbits of the electrons in the molecule, and governs the laws of chemistry. X-rays, radio waves, and light are all electromagnetic phenomenon. It dominates down to the nucleus of the atom where the week and strong nuclear forces take over.

The strong force binds the protons and the neutrons in the nucleus of the atom. Positive and negative force tend to repel each other but the strong force holds them in place; the balance between the strong force and the electromagnetic force together limit nuclei to around 100 protons. If it didn't, the periodic table of elements would be larger than we have today. As we have seen with the development of the nuclear bomb, the strong nuclear forces can generate great power, substantially more than with the electromagnetic forces. The strong nuclear force is also the magic potion that causes the stars to shine.

The weak nuclear force governs the disintegration of the heavier nuclei, atomic instability, and radioactivity and it can create heat, such as at the earth's core or in a nuclear power plant.

As I reviewed these fundamental forces it brought about another moment of truth! What an incredibly delicate balance exists to allow life on our planet. What are the chances that this balance occurred through randomness? The entire premise of order out of disorder went against the second law of thermodynamics and just plain common sense. It seemed to me that could only occur with information and a source of information and an application of that information! Random style was rapidly falling off my list of favorites.

So many ratios must be exactly as they are or life could not exist in so many areas. If any of the four forces were off by a proverbial hair, life would not exist on Earth. Interesting!

Let's take another quick high school review of terms that will help us in our journey back inside the human matrix.

DNA: Deoxyribonucleic acid is the chemical that stores genetic information in our cells. Shaped like a double helix, DNA passes down from one generation to the next.

RNA: Ribonucleic acid is a type of molecule used in making proteins in the body.

Genome: The complete genetic makeup of an organism, which contains all the biological information to build and keep it alive.

Gene: A stretch of DNA that tells a cell how to make specific proteins or RNA molecules.

Enzyme: A molecule that promotes a chemical reaction inside a living organism.

Stem cell: A biological master cell that can multiply and become many different types of tissue. It can also replicate to make more stem cells.

For years, the vast stretches of DNA between our 20,000 or so protein-coding genes—more than 98 percent of the genetic sequence inside each of our cells—was written off as "junk" DNA. But just recently this "junk DNA" has been found to be crucial to the way our genome works. An international team of researchers have been working on this for a decade, but even now with these new discoveries, they say they are just beginning to touch the magnitude of the complexity in our DNA. New information, new paradigms!

Their discovery is the most significant shift in scientists' understanding of the way our DNA operates since the sequencing of the human genome in 2000, when it was discovered that our bodies are built and controlled by far fewer genes than expected. Now the next generation of geneticists have updated that picture.

The results of the international Encode project will have a huge impact for geneticists trying to work out how genes operate. Until now, the focus had largely been on looking for errors within genes themselves, but the Encode research will help guide the hunt for problem areas that lie elsewhere in our DNA sequence. The findings will also provide new leads for scientists looking for treatments of conditions such as heart disease, diabetes, and Crohn's disease that have their roots partly in glitches in the DNA.

Our DNA is an error detecting and self-correcting digital program but as we know, it does not always pick up all the errors or at least does not always correct all of the errors found in the code. Why is that? Is it due to environmental damage caused by diet, chemical or radiation damage, or what? These are questions scientists hope to answer, but first there are still fundamental questions to be answered about the very nature of our DNA. At the very least, it is complex and in my humble opinion less and less likely that it could have ever randomly evolved without direction, a source of information and a designer. Even given more than twenty billion years, it appears to be statically impossible for that to have occurred. At this point in my quest, my search for a quantum God began to evolve from whether there is an intelligent force behind creation to who, what, when, where and why?

Dr. Ewan Birney of the European Bioinformatics Institute near Cambridge, was one of the principal investigators in the Encode project, that in 2000, published the draft human genome and in 2003, published the finished human genome. They always knew that was going to be a starting point. They knew that protein-coding genes were not the whole story.

When Bill Gates remarked that our DNA is a digital code more complex than any software we have produced, it was an understatement!

Encode is the largest single update to the data from the human genome since its final draft was published in 2003 and the first systematic attempt to find out what the DNA, outside protein-coding genes does. The researchers found that it is far from useless: within these regions they have identified more than 10,000 new "genes." They produce codes for components that control how the more familiar protein-coding genes work. Up to 18 percent of our DNA sequence is involved in regulating the less than 2 percent of the DNA that code for proteins. In total, Encode scientists say about 80 percent of the DNA sequence can be assigned some sort of biochemical function. It seems there is less and less "junk" in our DNA every day.

Scientists know that while most cells in our body contain our entire genetic code, not all of the protein-coding genes are active. A liver cell contains enzymes used to metabolize alcohol and other toxins, whereas hair cells make the protein keratin. Through some mechanism that regulates its genes, the hair cell knows it should make keratin rather than liver enzymes, and the liver cell knows it should make the liver enzymes and not the hair proteins. How random is that? Not!

The results of the five-year Encode project were published recently across thirty papers in the journals *Nature*, *Science*, *Genome Biology* and *Genome Research*. The researchers have mapped four million switches in what was once thought to be junk DNA, many of which will help them better understand a range of common human diseases, from diabetes to heart disease, that depend on the complex interaction of hundreds of genes and their associated regulatory elements.

It appears the regulatory elements are the things that turn genes on and off, and Professor Mike Snyder of Stanford University, who was another principal investigator in the Encode consortium, believed that many of the differences between people were actually due to the differences in the efficiency of these regulatory elements. They believe that there are more variants in the regulatory elements than in the genes themselves.

Wow. Regulatory elements—another piece of the puzzle that looks like us! That's just so random. Right?

Now we know that genes cannot function without these regulatory elements. If regulation goes wrong, malfunctioning genes can cause diseases including cancer, atherosclerosis, type 2 diabetes, psoriasis, and Crohn's disease. Errors in the regulation of a gene known as Sonic Hedgehog, for example, are thought to underlie some cases of human polydactyly in which individuals have extra toes or fingers.

Professor Anne Ferguson-Smith of Cambridge University, believes that they also have important implications for the growth and development of embryos and fetuses during pregnancy. These appear to be the kind of elements that make your tissues and organs grow properly, at the right time and place, and containing the right kinds of cells.

Encode scientists found that 9 percent of human DNA is involved in the coding for the regulatory switches, although Birney thinks the true figure may turn out to be about 20 percent.

The project has identified about 10,000 stretches of DNA, which the Encode scientists have called non-coding genes, that do not make proteins but, instead, a type of RNA, the single-stranded equivalent of DNA. There are many types of RNA molecules in cells, each with a specific role such as carrying messages or transcribing the DNA code in the first step of making a protein. These 10,000 non-coding genes carry instructions to build the large and small RNA molecules required to regulate the actions of the 20,000 protein-coding genes.

The results have already shed light on previous, massive studies of genetic data. In recent years, scientists have compared the genetic code of thousands of people with a specific disease (such as diabetes, bipolar disorder, Crohn's disease or heart disease) with the DNA code of thousands of healthy people in an attempt to locate mutations that could account for some of the risk of developing that disease. These so-called genome-wide association studies (GWAS) have identified scores of locations in the DNA that seem to raise a person's risk of developing a disease, but the vast majority are nowhere near protein-coding genes. That makes sense if regions previously thought of as "junk" are actually vital for controlling the expression of protein-encoding genes.

Indeed, there is a big overlap between the locations identified by GWAS and the regulation switches identified in Encode.

Understanding some of these regulatory elements could help explain some of the environmental triggers for different diseases.

Crohn's disease, for example, is a long-term condition that causes inflammation of the lining of the digestive system and affects up to 60,000 people in the UK, (where this research was done), but scientists cannot fully explain why some people suffer from it and others do not, even when they all have the genetic mutations associated with an elevated risk. One hypothesis is that the disease could be triggered by a bacterial infection. Perhaps there's a place in the middle of what we previously thought to be 'junk DNA,' not close to a protein-coding gene, that if you have one variant you're more sensitive to this bacterium; if you have another variant you're less sensitive. It is possible that you get Crohn's disease because you have the more sensitive type of regulatory elements and that a particular bacterial infection occurred at a time when you were vulnerable.

The Encode consortium's 442 researchers, situated in thirty-two institutes around the world, used 300 years of computer time and five years in the lab to get their results. They examined a total of 147 types of tissue including cancer cells, liver extracts, endothelial cells from umbilical cords, and stem cells derived from embryos and subjected them to around a hundred different experiments, recording which parts of the DNA code were activated in which cells at which times.

The current and future phases of Encode will prove useful not only for scientists, but also for you, if you desire to have a more personalized approach to medicine in the years to come. We have entered an era where people are starting to get their genomes sequenced. With Encode data we could start mapping regulatory information as well.

This means that the individual differences in people's diseases can be more effectively targeted for treatment. For the last several millenia diseases have been identified and defined by the medical profession as they observed symptoms. Now we know, for example, that the symptoms of breast cancer are not simply one disease but that there are multiple types of breast cancer with all sorts of different mechanistic processes going wrong.

A given drug only works in about a third of the people it is given to, and the catch is, we don't know which third. That could change with a greater understanding of genomics. In other words, if we knew the relationship between people's genomes and which drugs work for them and which ones they shouldn't take because they suffer from side effects, medicine would be improved exponentially.

Understanding exactly how each type of cell in the body works—in other words, which genes are switched on or off at different stages of its function—will also be useful in future stem cell therapies. If doctors want to grow replacement liver tissue, for example, they will be able to check that it is safe by comparing the DNA functions of their manufactured cells with data from normal liver cells.

The decade since the publication of the first draft of the human genome has shown that genetics is much more complex than anyone could have predicted. Deeper and deeper into the Matrix we go! Some felt that when we first sequenced the genome we had arrived, but if we did we switched flights and off we went again on another incredible journey. What we thought was junk DNA, simply wasted space, now turns out to be vital in understanding why the same gene can act differently in different people. That wasted space isn't wasted after all; it is full of "Regulatory Elements." We're losing some of our ignorance and each time we do, understanding ourselves gets more complicated. Remember, these genomes comprise one of the most complicated things we know: ourselves. Dr. Birney still thinks we're at the start of this journey, just warming up for the marathon ahead.

Just a few years back Charles Darwin thought that the content of our cells was merely protoplasm—a nonfunctional jello that simply filled space. With new information comes the need for new paradigms, new hypotheses, new theories, right?

Some used to feel that Darwin was able to explain away all traces of intelligent design. Today with our growing understanding of our own complexity that's much harder to do with a straight face. Then there is the glaring question, the critical problem unsolved by evolutionary theory and that is… first life! Where did it come from?

In Darwin's time, they believed life was a simple thing and that the cells were just jelly-filled mini donuts with nothing but protoplasm inside. Today's science proves that naive and dramatically wrong! New information requires new paradigms!

In 1869 T.H. Huxley wrote, "The cell is a simple homogenous globule of plasm."

And he was considered one of the greatest biologists of the nineteenth century! He was just limited to the information he had and that formed his hypothesis. We, on the other hand, would be the foolish ones if we simply buried our heads in the sand and stayed with it in light of new information.

Perhaps it is way past time to update our paradigms to include modern science and new information.

The discovery of protein building blocks in the body in the fifties was the beginning of the end for this belief in randomness; we discovered they were very complex and specific. In fact, specific proteins in enzymes are designed to digest food like a glove fits to a hand. This specificity is due to the fact that they are microscopically shaped so that only a certain substrate molecule will fit into it! They have to match the food they digest spatially in three dimensions. The shape of the specific protein is determined by the specific alignments of the amino acids. This sequence determines the protein which determines its function. Like written languages and computer codes! Those are all created by a programmer, by design, with intelligence, with intention. Oh, the power of intention! Is that laughter I hear coming from the rabbit hole again?

We learned this in 1952. Then in 1953 we discovered the double helix of DNA. Four years later Francis Crick proposed that the arrangement of the characters of the DNA form a digital code. Now we know that messenger RNA carry and edit the information from the blueprint DNA at the ribosome—the cellular factory where it is assembled for its specific task—then released out through the cell to its cellular destiny. It's like CAD CAM technology! Digital information directing machines to create mechanical parts!

It seems that it can work both ways. In fact, one could ask the question, "Are we human or machine?" Whatever we are we are not the product of a random style event!

Art often reflects real life, sometimes before the majority is aware of it. Could it be that this quote from the movie *The Matrix* reflects the reality we are just now discovering inside our human matrix? "Throughout human history, we have been dependent on machines to survive. Fate, it seems, is not without a sense of irony." ~ Morpheus

The question then turns to the origin of life. Sure our system is working now, but what or who gave us our first codes that our digital biological CAD CAM-run cellular factories now produce day in and day out? If you want a new function for your computer… you need a new code. If you want a new biological life form... you need a new code! It is the same process coded through the DNA with its protein sequences. Like the chicken or egg dilemma; for the DNA you have to have the proteins and to have the proteins you must have DNA programmed with the correct code to produce them with the proper amino acid sequence. Which came first and where did it get its information for its code?

Richard Dawkins said, "The machine code of the genes is uncannily computer-like. Apart from differences in jargon, the pages of a molecular biology journal might be interchangeable with those of a computer engineering journal." [*River out of Eden: A Darwinian View of Life,* Harper Collins, 1995]

As a matter of fact, scientists have just recently recorded MP3 files onto our DNA, according to a report published in the journal *Nature*. The data that can be written isn't limited to just audio files. It is achieved using trinary encoding. In this particular experiment, the researchers encoded all of Shakespeare's sonnets, as well as a part of Martin Luther King's "I have a dream" speech, a photo, a PDF, and the binary-to-trinary algorithm used for encoding.

The computer data had to be converted from binary to trinary because of the number of bases in a DNA molecule. While there are four bases, the researchers utilized one of the bases to avoid straight sequences of a single base, resulting in a total of three bases for data. This was done in order to avoid the errors that would result from utilizing the single base sequences.

The encoded data was split into sections, tagged with an ID, and marked to indicate its position within the overall file. In most of the instances, the files were then reconstructed correctly, with only one having a mistake in the sequence, although the mistake wasn't so severe that the researchers weren't able to recover the missing data.

The team responsible for the project stated that the storage density per gram was an astounding 2.2 petabytes.

In this project, the DNA used was dried before being sent out, but for the purpose of long-term data storage, the DNA can be chilled, which will have longer lasting results. Estimates say that DNA can be used to archive data for 5,000 years, with it becoming economically viable for shorter term duration (fifty years) within the next decade.

Random style—chance—is just not a serious explanation for the origin of the code. Even if you had twenty billion years your DNA codes are "simply" too statistically complex for that to have happened. New information demands new paradigms for everything it affects!

Natural selection and chance are not statistically possible either, and I have to ask, natural selection of what? We are speaking of origin, not adaptation. Prebiological natural selection is a contradiction in terms.

To have natural selection you must have sequence specific DNA and proteins that are self-replicating to give rise to natural selection.

If you buy prebiological natural selection, then you also have to buy the story of the philosophy professor who on his walk home stumbled and fell into a construction ditch so deep he was unable to get out. He tried various means of escape and could not find any way out. Then he had a brilliant idea: he would go home and get his ladder and use it to climb out!

Henry Quastler said, "The Creation of new information is habitually associated with conscious activity."

Charles Darwin said, "if you're trying to explain an event in the remote past you should be looking for a cause that is now known to produce the effect in question." That makes perfect sense: if you have volcanic ash on your car in the morning don't look for an earthquake to explain it.

Put those two thinkers together and you have intelligent design. Information always comes from an intelligent source. We know of no other source that produces information in a digital form than intelligence.

Ironically, using the methods espoused by Darwin with the knowledge we now have, it is impossible to come to any conclusion other than he was wrong. Not in his approach, but in his conclusions, as seen clearly now with the information we have today. When he said there was not enough evidence of intelligent design, it may have been true, but not today.

Darwin's mentor, Charles Lyell, said: "Principles of geology: Being an attempt to explain the former changes of the Earth's surface by reference to the causes now in operation."

Clearly if Mr. Darwin were to continue to follow the rules of investigation that he and his mentor established with the "causes now known to be in operation," a different conclusion would result: source is intelligence. They didn't even dream of the complexity and intelligence demonstrated by our own DNA!

But even now in the face of the unbelievable complexity of our DNA, those who bought into the theory of evolution and its "random style" dance for the origins of life refuse to relent. They have more faith, if you want to call it that, than my religious friends who simply believe what Genesis 1:1 says.

It seems obvious to me that those who follow Darwin's old theory rather than his rules for acceptance of theories are frozen in time. Many of them try and slip the entire issue of randomness and the statistically impossible situation it puts them in by simply drawing parallels of how close our DNA is to other creatures like apes etc. The fact that there are physical and DNA similarities between human and other living organisms has been interpreted as evidence for the theory of evolution.

Since apes and humans are both mammals, with similar shapes, they should have similar DNA. We should expect humans to have more DNA similarities with another mammal like a pig than with a reptile like a rattlesnake. And this is so. And while humans are very different from yeast, they do have some biochemistry in common, however we should expect human and yeast DNA to be only slightly similar. And this is so.

Proper statistics applied to the data show that there is about 96 percent similarity between human and ape DNA through a technique called DNA hybridization. In this technique, single strands of human DNA were combined with DNA from chimpanzees and other apes. Actually, even if we grant that degree of hybridization entirely correlates with similarity, there are flaws. Another interpretation of the same data is the theory of a common designer. In the automotive world, different vehicles can use the same parts, so it isn't surprising that a designer for life uses the same biochemistry and structures in many different creatures. Frankly, the fact that all living organisms are not totally different adds validity to this theory.

An interesting point about the common biochemistry is that we can gain nourishment from other living things. Our digestive systems can break down food into its building blocks, which are then used either as fuel or for our own building blocks.

For example, our hemoglobin molecule found in vertebrates is also found in some earthworms, starfish, crustaceans, mollusks, and even some bacteria. The α-hemoglobin of crocodiles has more in common with that of chickens (17.5 percent) than that of vipers (5.6 percent), their fellow reptiles. An antigen receptor protein has the same unusual single chain structure in camels and nurse sharks, but this cannot be explained by a common ancestor of sharks and camels. No common ancestry, but perhaps they share a designer?

Alternating a few simple building blocks can result in big differences in the end result or life form. Good! Sounds intelligent and efficient with less to design.

> *I feel we are all islands… In a common sea.*
> ~ Anne Morrow Lindbergh

Chapter 4
The "God Code" Within our DNA

"Does that mean the war is over?"

"It does, Mr. Pepper."

"I sure hope so," says the lady.

"I wouldn't be so sure, ma'am," replies Mr. Pepper. "There's an old saying: 'There's no law west of Dodge, and no God west of the Pecos.' Right, Mr. Chisolm?"

"Wrong, Mr. Pepper, 'cause no matter where people go, sooner or later there's the law, and sooner or later they find out God's already been there."

~ John Wayne, from the movie *Chisolm*

There has long been a war in the world of science between the disciplines of physics, the rabbit hole, and biology which I call the matrix. Biologists seek to make biology preeminent and physicists have always said, "it's all about the physics." Biocentrism, which leans toward a biology first approach, does promise to end the war between the two with a peace treaty that includes everyone and, in fact, promises a theory of everything, if honored. My head is still spinning because of my encounter with the rabbit hole, so I choose to spend some more time in the matrix, admittedly that might be influenced by the fact I was a biology major in college.

The human body is a universe of its own. It is a strange at times, yet beautiful place, that leaves one in awe of the complexity that is hidden within. Far from the rabbit hole of the quantum world, system after system works in perfect harmony to support human life as we know it.

At the National University of Singapore, Elisabeth Rieper and several of her colleagues have asked "what role might quantum entanglement play in DNA." To find out, they constructed a simplified theoretical model of DNA to work out their theory.

There was a time, not so long ago, when biologists swore that quantum mechanics could play no role in the field of biology. Since then the two sciences have settled on an uneasy truce.

But recently the rabbit hole has expanded and the discipline of quantum biology has emerged as one of the most exciting new fields in science. It's beginning to look as if quantum effects are crucial in a number of biological processes, such as photosynthesis and avian navigation, and now even in the formation of our own DNA building blocks. Is there no end to this quantum world?

Now a group of physicists say that the weird laws of quantum mechanics may be more important for life than biologists could ever have imagined. Their new idea is that DNA is held together by quantum entanglement. Only time will tell if they are right or just encroaching on biology's "sacred space." Like a rabbit hole popping up in the matrix! Quantum tunnelling, I guess.

Recently a Russian scientist conducted an experiment with photons in a vacuum chamber, measuring their order or lack of order (randomness) on a collection screen on one end of the vacuum chamber. As expected, they formed a random arrangement on the screen.

In the second part of the experiment the doctor introduced a single strand of human DNA into the equation and into the vacuum chamber with the photons. This time the photons formed an orderly pattern mimicking the outline and shape of the DNA!

Were they communicating? If so, how were they communicating? I suggest it was through a field, one with the ability to communicate the information from the DNA to the photons through "space," yes, a vacuum, that allows them to act on or align themselves with that information. So the vacuum—space—isn't empty after all! Is there a consciousness involved as well? If so, whose? Is it the so-called observer effect, or is it simply another level of a complex software program in action on "auto pilot?" If so, who is the software engineer?

Physicists have always said all science is just physics. Well, maybe they were at least partially correct. Perhaps there is entanglement or perhaps there is a field that not only spans the external universe but also connects to and expands through the internal universe as well.

Over a decade ago I was referred to a wonderful occupational therapist by the name of Lilly Fuller. She is also a doctor of holistic medicine, a wonderful unique blend of conventional and alternative medicine. One treatment modality that she uses to bring the body back into balance and give a patient great pain relief is called myofascial release. It was developed by her mentor, John Barnes PT. PhD, a man I was honored to spend a week with in Sedona, Arizona, at one of his teaching seminars.

To understand the theory of myofascial release requires an understanding of the body's fascia system. When I was back in school dissecting human cadavers I remember that there was a large amount of connective tissue to get through wherever you were going. That's where we start.

Fascia is a tough three-dimensional connective tissue that spreads throughout your body like a spider web. From your head to your toes this fascia permeates every system of your body without interruption, like a knitted sweater. Trauma or inflammation can create a binding down of fascia, resulting in excess pressure on nerves, muscles, blood vessels, the skeletal system, and the vital organs. Through hands-on therapy, the goal of myofascial release is to release the pressure, undo the restrictions, and restore the individual's freedom so that he or she may return to a pain free active lifestyle. From personal experience, I can say it often works when other treatments don't!

The reason I bring this up is that I see a distinctive correlation between the Higgs field theory and the myofascia theory.

Both are three dimensional and permeate their universe. What if the myofascia theory is simply a larger, yet smaller version of the Higgs field, like the larger Russian doll that contains many other smaller identical ones. But how can it be smaller and larger at the same time? Good question. I used that for a lack of better terms.

The myofascia is larger in the sense that we can actually see parts of it upon dissection, but smaller in the sense that it is contained within our bodies. The Higgs field is smaller in the sense that it is subatomic and invisible—not only to the naked eye but to any microscope we have yet invented—yet it is larger in the sense that it is universal. There is no end to it or beginning to it; for that matter it is everywhere and in everything, here and across the Cosmos... like an Omnipresent Quantum God might be.

Now I can see one reason they might call the Higgs boson particle the God particle. It comes from a field flowing throughout all of Creation connecting all matter and energy.

Perhaps the Higgs field is simply a field of pure potentiality, a high potential-low level energy field holding together the fabric of the Cosmos, both internal and external. When a demand is placed on it, a frequency of some sort is released to transform the energy into the matter needed. It exists in the form of small potential matter particles manifesting as needed in and from a field of energy. It's still hypothetical but it could exist, for what if all matter is really... well... just energy with a frequency applied to it, as Einstein and Tesla often said? Different frequencies, different forms of matter, different amplitudes, different volumes of matter.

Wouldn't it be cool, though, if there is a God and He left us some code, some secret message that says yes, I am real... I exist?

Something to prove an intelligent being is behind all this that we live and breathe every day? Well, that's what I am looking for; let's see what we can find. I certainly have my doubts about the statistical possibility of our random evolvement at this point of my search. I am impressed with the complexity and the beauty of the universe within. It's science at its best and really a work of art!

What would you say if I told you that not only is each cell of your body a work of art, but that the artist himself signed each one? If you find that hard to believe, well, buckle up; it is quantum leap time!

By now you know I like exposing illusions and finding out how things really work. As a child, that used to drive my mom crazy as I went around taking things apart to see how they worked. The problem was I would then get distracted and go outside to play football or baseball and forget about putting them back together again.

The question occurred to me again… if a designer is at work, did he drop us a clue, leave us a trail of bread crumbs to follow? Did he leave us a code or something to let us know He had been here and could return whenever He wanted? If He did, it could be called the God Code!

Interestingly enough, a few years back I came across a book by that very name, written by Gregg Braden. I encourage you to get a copy and read it.

Gregg asks, what would it mean to find a principle, a message, a code (you know that got my attention) that touched the life of every thinking human in the world today with a single unifying—not divisive—message so deep, so powerful, and so personal that it could not be denied? Something that would cut through the outward differences that divide us as families, nations, races and religions? We can only imagine how differently we would live our lives and build our world if we were confident in the knowledge that our existence stems from a Creator whose name is literally encoded into each cell of our bodies. At the very least, a discovery like this could become the beginning of a new era clarifying our relationship to one another and our surrounding world. Gregg feels that even if this message fell short of identifying precisely "who" the God of creation is, it would still be valuable. But if we found a code with a name that is consistent with the historical records of the universal nature of one of God's ancient names; if we found this ancient name hidden within our very own DNA the very code of life; if this name could be confirmed as it is now through twentieth-century science and ancient records as presented in Gregg's book, it certainly would add to a growing body of evidence suggesting that something more than a chance combination of chemicals and evolution is responsible for our being here. Enough of the random style!

In my opinion, at its best, revealing the name of God imprinted within all life would provide powerful new evidence that we are here on purpose, sharing our world as one family, one tribe! This discovery could offer a much-needed reason for hope in a time when our differences are increasingly viewed as insurmountable and become reasons to separate us further, rather than being recognized as the diversity that strengthens us. A code, an extraterrestrial message discovered within the chemistry of the cells of everybody, regardless of religion, lifestyle, race, or belief, would be a sign so universal in nature that it could transcend any differences in our past!

I believe what Gregg has found has the potential to do so… if we let it. The question is, will we?

I believe modern science has already shown that the random style theory of evolution is statistically impossible. I also believe that the code Gregg discovered corroborates that! It seems to stand in defiance of Darwin's theory of evolution that postulates we evolved simply by chance into the complex homo sapiens we are today. It is important to track the facts, wherever they lead us.

In researching a story that Charles Darwin recanted his theory of evolution just before his death, I found the story of "Lady Hope" (her real name) who claims to have been with Darwin when he was near death and found him reading the Bible, the book of Hebrews to be exact. She claims that he had returned to his childhood upbringing and his faith in God. It may be true; however, there is not enough evidence to convince me of that, and in fact, his surviving daughter said she never knew of anything he said or did that would confirm that he had changed his mind on any of his work. I asked myself who would benefit from this story (or the truth being covered up if it were truth) and reasoned the answer could be both sides in the court of public opinion. So in the absence of evidence I discarded it from my search. Perhaps it is time that all of science and religion use this approach. There is still room for faith on both sides, but a faith based on facts must be better than a blind faith, I think!

What real difference would it make anyway? His ideas were just that! Ideas that became theories and if the story were true, it would only mean he changed his mind, hardly anything to cause me to change mine either way. His theory has been the most accepted theory of evolution, but it is just that, a theory.

Others postulate theories for why we evolved into our present state, such as the Ancient Alien Theorists, which we will look into in depth later. No search for a quantum God or gods would be complete without it.

So what is Gregg Braden's remarkable discovery? Nothing less than the very name of God hidden deep within each of us! Every human being who has walked this planet has, or had within his or her cells the ancient name of God encoded across each cell! Coded into our very DNA, waiting the day we would have the ability to discover it! It appears to be the signature of the Master Artist who created us.

Yes, created us! Did I say that out loud? What we have is scientific evidence of a hidden code in our very DNA, a DNA that Darwin and other scientists of his era were not even aware of!

The *Mona Lisa* is signed by Leonardo, *The Night Watch* signed by Rembrandt. An artist always signs his masterpiece in one form or another.

Now consider the words of the co-discoverer of DNA, Dr. Crick, who said: "For all of the factors to be in the right place, at the perfect time, and for life to arise by chance, borders upon the miraculous." In light of what Gregg has discovered, his statement makes even more sense!

The paradigm busting discovery that the very chemistry of our DNA contains an ancient code in an ancient language spelling out the message: "God Eternal within" is not something some dead old religion, or religious group brought to you. It is science! And a search for truth! I respect that!

When student Phyllis Wright asked Albert Einstein in 1936 if scientists pray, he replied, "Everyone who is seriously involved in the pursuit of science becomes convinced that a spirit is manifest in the laws of the universe a spirit vastly superior to that of man."

Science and spirituality together unlock the mysteries of the universe. When I referred to a dead old religion above, I referred to my belief that it is man's religion that does more damage to the truth about spirituality than all the atheists put together. Charles

Darwin, who many don't know trained for the clergy, agreed. His path may have taken him down a rabbit trail, but it also may have looked to be truth to him at the time. I have no reason to believe he was less than intellectually honest in his theories and beliefs. But honestly believing something doesn't make it the truth. It may be, or the facts that come to light later may prove you dead wrong. One thing is clear to me; over time, truth can stand the test of time.... and science and even religion.

I find it sad that so often man takes a truth, a spiritual law, and wraps it in his own laws and regulations and it becomes a burden at best and lethal at its worst. In my journey, I have come to the conclusion that there is a "God" and He hates religion! He loves relationships but detests what man does to try and control those relationships and limit the access of others to them. It seems as rapidly as some discover truth, others endeavor to bury it so they can control and profit from it. Thus I have come to this conclusion: relationship with Creator is good; religions controlled by man, not so much.

In his book *The God Code*, Gregg asks the question: Is it possible that in our rush to advance our civilization from campfires to microwaves, we inadvertanly left behind some profound truths? Gregg asks: "Could the clues for surviving the greatest threats to our existence be buried within the oldest records from our past? If so, then discoveries of science and technology, in combination with the recovery of such ancient records, have placed the wisdom of the heavens within our reach for the first time in a very long time. Now our job is to understand the messages left by those who have come before us."

He has found that spiritual traditions and manuscripts of ancient science reveal:

"A common theme in the ancient stories of human origins states that we are created from the dust or clay of the earth. All life comes from the same dust. The secrets of our creation and our ability to transmute life's circumstances (bridge Heaven and Earth) are preserved through the hidden traditions of ancient alchemy. Within those traditions, the keys state that our world and our bodies are made of the elements: fire, water, and air. A detailed account of the alchemy leading to the creation of the universe and the origins of humankind is also revealed through the mystical Hebrew Book of Creation, the *Sepher Yetzirah*. The book is available today and, in its completeness, offers a detailed account of a higher power forming the universe and our world. New discovery: Modern science confirms the ancient models, revealing that the alchemical elements of fire, air, and water actually represent three of the most abundant elements of our bodies: hydrogen, nitrogen, and oxygen, respectively. What are the Hebrew symbols or letters for these elements?"

Gregg also quotes from *The Lost Gospel of Thomas*. In my opinion, it is a profound quote, no matter who said it:

"Let those who seek, continue seeking until they find. When they find, they will become troubled, when they become troubled they will be astonished and recognize what is in your sight, and that which is hidden from you will become plain to you."

Gregg does some incredible work with ancient manuscripts and modern science and mathematical formulas, and as a result, comes up with a secret code hidden in the base pairs of our DNA sequence. The odds of this code occurring are about 250,000 to 1, statistically improbable.

When this code is de-coded and with varying degrees of repetition 50 percent of the message within our cells translates literally to God/Eternal. The remaining 50 percent of our genetic code translates to "within the body," thus describing where we may find God's eternal nature in this world. "God Eternal within the Body," that's what it says!

In mankind's most cherished writings and traditions, we are reminded of our relationship to a greater power and the lasting nature of that relationship. And now science has allowed us to look within ourselves, to our very essence and discover a hidden message from "Him." At the very least, the discovery of God's name within each cell of all life reveals a message, as well as a promise, that transcends any of the differences that we could use as excuse to go on fighting and killing one another. We just discovered that in a very real sense, the very cells of our bodies... all of our bodies... contain an extraterrestrial message from a source that claims to be the artist that created us as "His" crowning achievement! We are connected to a power that is outside time and space and left His message with His name in every cell of our bodies to be discovered when He knew we would. It is this spark of creation that texts such as the Sepher Yetzirah and the Bible equate to the Creator.

God Eternal within the Body. Think of it! Every cell in your body is carrying that message... whether you believe the message or not, you are a piece of artwork (some of us are just a piece of work), but all of us have the signature of a supernatural extraterrestrial creator written all over us. Doesn't it give you hope and courage that no matter what conditions you face in your life, no matter what challenges confront you, you are Highly valued by a supernatural source?

You choose to believe whichever one fits your paradigm... and you can change your paradigm and hopefully you will do so often to reflect new information! It is a message that is shared by every man, woman, child, and ancestor of our global family! It is the living message coded within each cell of our bodies.

Here is how Gregg Braden sums it up:

"Replacing the four elements of our DNA with the letters represented by their ancient and hidden number code reveals that the basis of all life is made of various combinations of God's ancient name, YH, meaning Eternal. In addition to the name itself, the letters VG, meaning within the body, are encoded into the remaining building blocks of life. The message is a reminder that human life specifically, and all life in general, is united through a common heritage.

"The message within our DNA reads precisely the same in both the Arabic and Hebrew languages. These relationships graphically show us what we already sense on an intuitive level. The letters of God's name within our bodies are universal, regardless of our differences. Within each cell of every body, we find the same code, yielding the same message; and transcending the language, faith, and race of the individual without bias, prejudice, or exception."

How powerful is that? It seems the artist has signed His name to His crowning achievement ... you and me!

I think you would have to agree that even though Gregg stops short of explaining exactly how the code within our cells originated, the very fact of its existence, against overwhelming odds, more than suggests an intelligence and intention behind our origins here on planet Earth.

So, it seems we have found a code, a paradigm-busting code, right within our own cells! Actually a code within a code as it is contained in our DNA, which is a super code as Bill Gates has said.

In computer languages, certain commands exist with which values in an existing or running computer system can be changed. In older computer systems, for example, the commands Peek and

Poke were used: Peek would allow the programmer to "look at" a certain location, while Poke allowed him or her to change something in that location.

Even in the early days of the home computer (in the early 80s), the thought of having 65,000 of such locations (or "addresses") available for manipulation was exciting and fascinating. Some addresses defined the color of the screen, while others produced a beep. Assigning a "bad value" to some locations would cause the computer to freeze. Pretty soon it became clear that it was not easy to be productive without a good "directory" of the available addresses: the user guide for the computer. The manufacturer of the computer created the address list and knew where each function resided.

In a general sense, a comparison can be drawn between DNA and the computer memory. Functions are stored in DNA similar to the way functions are stored in computer memory. Both DNA and computer memory have "home addresses" for each function. In many respects such an analogy is deficient, for example because DNA plays a role in the production of cells and because DNA, for "real-time" processing, first has to create copies of certain parts of a chain (RNA) which then are used for the real-time processing itself. Another example is the limited number of addresses (65,000) of the computer in the example, compared to the 220,000,000 gene pairs in the first chromosome of the human DNA alone! That means 3300 times as many addresses! And, of course, those gene pairs are far more complex and diverse than a memory address in a computer. All together the base pairs in the human genome contain more than 23 billion DNA base pairs!

Perhaps it is time to reconsider the theories we have been working with. Even Mr. Darwin would agree with that:

"I test this hypothesis, (common decent) by comparison with as many general and pretty well established propositions as I can find in geographical distribution, geology, history, affinities… and it seems to me that supposing that such a hypothesis were to explain such propositions, we ought, in accordance with the common way of following all sciences, to admit it until some better hypothesis be found out."

Hidden codes aside, Darwin's Theory of Evolution is a theory in crisis in light of the tremendous advances we've made in molecular biology, biochemistry, and genetics over the past fifty years. We now know that there are in fact tens of thousands of irreducibly complex systems on the cellular level. Specified complexity pervades the microscopic biological world. Molecular biologist Michael Denton wrote, "Although the tiniest bacterial cells are incredibly small, weighing less than 10 to the negative 12 grams, each is in effect a veritable micro-miniaturized factory containing thousands of exquisitely designed pieces of intricate molecular machinery, made up altogether of one hundred thousand million atoms, far more complicated than any machinery built by

man and absolutely without parallel in the non-living world."
[*Evolution: A Theory in Crisis*, 1986, p. 250]

I found this secret code to be paradigm-busting information, but as you may have guessed, I wasn't willing to stop here on my search for hidden truth. I kept thinking, are there other codes or clues that this quantum God left behind for us to find? Is there more evidence of an outside designer? Are there other extraterrestrial messages waiting for us to discover and decode?

If we can find a hidden mathematical code in our DNA, I have to wonder what else is waiting for us to find down the rabbit hole of quantum physics. Are there other mathematical codes or clues left for us in the form of some type of math by this quantum artist? Perhaps still other codes might suggest just who this "originator" is?

I did find another unique phenomenon that is a design based on a mathematical sequence found in nature. You can see it repeated through the entire universe. It is found in animal and plant life and if you had access to the Hubble telescope you would see it painting the night skies across the Cosmos. You can also see it repeated through the eyes of the most powerful electron microscopes as we peer into our universe within, and guess what? It is also in our very DNA as well! Another code that starts or ends or at least passes through our DNA! What are the chances of that?

I keep hearing the phrase Fibonacci, Fibonacci, Fibonacci, repeated over and over again. What is that all about? Is that where we are headed? Well, Fibonacci is not a place; it is a phenomenon! It seems to occur and even connect the Cosmos from the inside out with a unique order that both internal and external microsystems and macrosystems all operate on—another super code!

In mathematical terms, the sequence Fn of Fibonacci numbers is defined by the recurrence relation

$$F_n = F_{n-1} + F_{n-2},$$

with seed values[3]

$$F_0 = 0, \ F_1 = 1.$$

By definition, the first two numbers in the Fibonacci sequence are 0 and 1, and each subsequent number is the sum of the previous two. Basically, you add the last two numbers and you get the next number in the parade of numbers like 1+2=3, 2+3=5, 3+5=8. You see it?

I don't know why, but there is a sweet intimate relationship between this logical progression, this math, and the structure of the Cosmos! Let's look at some examples.

First we have a giant galaxy, much larger than our own, in fact. Next, back here on Earth you see the only view you would ever want to see of a very powerful hurricane, again displaying the classic Fibonacci sequence. If you were able to peer through the clouds of the storm into the sea below you might see the classic sea shell, the chambered nautilus, again displaying the Fibonacci spiral. Fibonacci numbers appear in nature often enough to prove that they reflect some naturally occurring patterns... or do the naturally occurring patterns actually reflect Fibonacci? That is a question!

You can easily spot these patterns by studying the manner in which various plants grow. Here are a few examples:

The seed heads of many plants, pinecones, fruits, and vegetables. Look at the array of seeds in the center of a sunflower and you'll notice what looks like spiral patterns curving left and right. Amazingly, if you count these spirals, your total will be a Fibonacci number. Divide the spirals into those pointed left and right and you'll get two consecutive Fibonacci numbers. You can decipher spiral patterns in pinecones, pineapples, and cauliflower that also reflect the Fibonacci sequence in this manner.

The Fibonacci sequence connects the external universe with the internal universe from galaxies to DNA; yes, DNA! It leaves a consistent code, a ratio, a sequence in its path. Is this evidence of an intelligent designer, an engineer at work throughout the quantum world? Perhaps. Maybe the Fibonacci sequence emerges from the Higgs field as a template for matter to organize around?

But wait, there is more! There is math within the math here! If you look at the ratio of each successive pair of numbers in the sequence it approximates the mathematical constant phi (1.618.), as 5 divided by 3 is 1.666 and 8 divided by 5 is 1.60. Phi (pronounced Fi) is the mathematical constant of 1.618. This ratio has been used by mankind for thousands of years. The Egyptians used it in the design of the pyramids, the Greeks in the Parthenon, and on and on. It is called the Golden Ratio. You are surrounded by it; in fact, you are constructed by it!

Let me explain. The Golden Mean (1.618) is found in everything within nature! Within everything in the universe! The human body is based on the mathematics of the golden mean... storms... the galaxies... flowers, leaves, DNA, music... everything.

No doubt you see it all the time without even noticing. Take a good look at yourself in the mirror. You'll notice that most of your body parts follow the numbers one, two, three and five. You have one nose, two eyes, three segments to each limb and five fingers on each hand. The proportions and measurements of the human body can also be divided up in terms of the golden ratio. DNA molecules follow this sequence, measuring 34 angstroms long and 21 angstroms wide for each full cycle of the double helix.

Let's look a little closer at the DNA molecule, the program for all life. As we just learned it contains a mathematical code or message, a signature as it were, from our designer. Now we see that it is based on the golden section, too—something it shares with the external universe!

It measures 34 angstroms long by 21 angstroms wide for each full cycle of its double helix spiral. 34 and 21, of course, are numbers in the Fibonacci series and their ratio, 1.6190476 closely approximates Phi, 1.6180339. The DNA cross-section is also based on Phi. A cross-sectional view from the top of the DNA double helix forms a decagon. A decagon is in essence two pentagons, with one rotated by 36 degrees from the other, so each spiral of the double helix must trace out the shape of a pentagon. The ratio of the diagonal of a pentagon to its side is Phi! So, no matter which way you look at it, even in its smallest element, DNA, life, is constructed using phi and the golden section!

From the microscopic to the telescope, Fibonacci is there, and maybe someone else, too?

Leonardo da Vinci [1451-1519] was one of the greatest inventor-scientists of recorded history. His genius was unbounded by time and technology, driven by his insatiable curiosity and his intuitive sense of the laws of nature. Da Vinci was dedicated to the discovery of truth and the mysteries of nature, and his insightful contributions to science and technology were and are legendary. As the archetypical Renaissance man, Leonardo helped set an ignorant and superstitious world on a course of reason, science, learning, and tolerance. He was an internationally renowned inventor, scientist, engineer, architect, painter, sculptor, musician, mathematician, anatomist, astronomer, geologist, biologist, and philosopher in his time.

Ever the perfectionist, Leonardo turned to science in the quest to improve his artwork. His study of nature and anatomy emerged in his stunningly realistic paintings, and his dissections of the human body paved the way for remarkably accurate figures. He was the first artist to study the physical proportions of men, women, and children and to use these studies to determine the "ideal" human figure. In so doing he discovered and worked with the "Golden Mean."

Other artists of the Renaissance like Michelangelo [1475-1564] and Raphael [1483-1530] also constructed their compositions on the golden ratio. The proportions of Michelangelo's David conform to the golden ratio from the location of the navel with respect to the height down to the placement of the joints in the fingers.

Is there yet another meaning hidden in Phi, the symbol for the golden number? I dug for a deeper meaning and discovered that there was at least some symbolism here that pointed toward a Creator, a designer, a mathematical genius! The symbol for Phi is a circle—a zero with a one through it. It is the first two numbers of the Fibonacci sequence 0 and 1. 0 represents nothing. It is interesting that the major religions of the world say that from nothing the ONE (true God) created everything. It could be said that Phi symbolizes that out of nothingness the One created it all and this ratio, this golden number found throughout the Cosmos is the signature of the One God in math! Thus, this God code also found within all DNA is also a math code. It starts in the DNA and extends out throughout the entire Cosmos.

Recently I was reading an article by Dr. Chuck Missler, whom I admire greatly and had the opportunity to meet about fifteen years ago in Anaheim, California. The article reminded me of our conversation about hidden math codes in the text of the Bible, both Old and New Testaments. Dr. Missler said there was a wealth of math in the Bible, enough to teach a course in higher math.

Don't you find it interesting that there is a course on math in the Bible? Dr. Missler shared this with me:

Both the Hebrew and the Greek languages have numerical values to their letters. It is the science of gymatria where words and math overlap. You might say it's a place where some of man's languages overlap with the universal language math!

Chuck showed me two specific texts in the Bible—one in the Old and one in the New Testament—that contained a hidden mathematical meaning; well, a mathematical constant at least. Both of these texts shared something else in common; they both pointed to a supreme being as the source of all… all energy, frequencies, and matter. The origin of first life.

A hidden message from the Originator; I was all ears!

The first text in the Bible is Genesis 1:1 translated from Hebrew:

"In the beginning God created the Heaven and the Earth."

The second text is near the beginning of the New Testament John 1:1 translated from Greek:

"In the Beginning was the Word and the Word was with God and the Word was God."

Now consider this, both Greek and Hebrew alphabets have assigned numerical values for each letter, which allows for the study of gymatria. And hidden codes and meanings. That is just what was found in these two verses! A mathematical constant from "old math" in the Old Testament and a mathematical constant from "new" math in the New Testament!

When we do the math as described below there is a stunning find: these two hidden mathematical codes in the two most direct and powerful statements of authorship in both the Old and New Testaments are dimensionless constants. They express the vast expanse of the time/space dimension always constant, but yet at the same time dimensionless in nature. The incredible number Pi (pie) 3.1416... in the Old Testament-Genesis 1:1 and a Napaerian logarithm "e", 2.718281828... in the New-John 1:1; clearly this is not the result of randomness. It is statistically impossible! A complex mathematical signature in Hebrew in the Old and Greek in the New! Fascinating, don't you think?

The formula is: the # of the letters x the product of the letters, divided by the # of the words x the product of the words! It is the same formula for both verses. Of course you would have to study some Greek and Hebrew and gymatria to do it by yourself but it does pen out as advertised!

Mathematics has become our way of explaining the chaotic world around us with a system of numbers. You may be surprised to learn just how many mathematical concepts are abundant in nature. But which is the case? Does math mimic nature or does nature mimic math?

Two key verses in the Bible—one in the Old Testament, one in the New Testament—that on the surface address the order and the mystery of creation and the extraterrestrial nature of the communication found within the Bible. It seems to imply that these are not all just stories... there are hidden messages of authentication there, even in the universal language of math! Genesis 1:1 and John 1:1. Both are speaking of our origins and first life, a hidden message from the Originator Himself for those with wisdom to find.

A Parrot sways upon a tree,
Raging at his own image in the enameled sea.
~ William Butler Yates

Chapter 5

Conscious Cells and the Intergalactic Tagger, Fibonacci

Now this is not the end. It is not even the beginning of the end. But it is perhaps the end of the beginning.

~ Sir Winston Churchill, 1942

In the beginning of my serious search for truth, I was an atheist, though I was not raised as one. But I had seen and lived through enough unfair and painful life experiences that I had determined the conditions I witnessed and experienced did not support the belief in a loving Diety that I had been taught as a child. I felt if by chance there was a god... that he was more of a devil than anything, so I chose the belief of unbelief at that season of my life.

Soon I was moving toward a position of agnosticism, neither believing or disbelieving in a diety, but admitting something was going on that science couldn't totally explain. In retrospect, I was actually beginning to engage and use the other side of my brain again, and look at the total picture—as my hero Einstein had—and encouraged others to do. My search for truth was honestly entering the phase of the "end of the beginning." I was just getting started, but I was willing to admit that there was an order and a super intelligence involved in the external and internal worlds. It was evident and undeniable in every discipline of science I explored.

Who or what was responsible for that order, I was still not sure. I was sure, though, that my old paradigms were destroyed and some new ones were taking shape. It was just a bit too soon to discern what shape was emerging. One thing I knew, as Winston Churchill said, "It was the end of the beginning" of my search.

I had discovered that there was a hidden code within our very cells that spells out the message, God Eternal Within. That shuffled my deck and rearranged my most fundamental beliefs, and that paradigm busting code appears not just in our cells but in the DNA of all living things! I also discovered how the mathematical Fibonacci sequence permeates all of nature with its order from within our own DNA to the far side of the most distant galaxy. Then, of all things, I discovered that there was another code hidden in two Bible texts that "just happen" to claim God created all things and all things are of Him, two hidden mathematical constants: $Pi = 3.1416$ etc. in Gen 1:1, and the Napaerian Logarithm, $e = 2.7182$ in John 1:1!

My mind was blown, but open enough to go where the facts led me. When I began my search for the ultimate truth, I made a commitment to myself to simply "let the chips fall where they may." No one was more surprised than I where these facts were leading me now. Were there more hidden math formulas and codes concealed in the Bible? What about other spiritual writings?

In fact, I found there was more math in the Bible. Look at Noah's ark in Genesis 6:15. God commands Noah to build an ark saying,

"And this is the fashion which thou shalt make it of: The length of the Ark shall be three hundred cubits, the breadth of it fifty cubits, and the height of it thirty cubits."

The breadth versus the height of the ark was 50 by 30 cubits, the ratio of 5 to 3, or 1.666… a part of the Fibonacci sequence as it approaches Phi. Another interesting fact is that Noah's ark was built in the same proportion as ten Arks of the Covenant placed side by side. Can you see the pattern here?

Following the instructions God gave Moses, the Ark of the Covenant was constructed using the Golden Section, or Divine Proportion. This ratio is also the same as 5 to 3, again numbers from the Fibonacci series, resulting in Phi.

The question then arises: is Fibonacci another name for God? Well, not really. It actually is one of many names used by a Leonardo Pisano Bigollo of Pisa.

He was considered by some "the most talented western mathematician of the Middle Ages." Ironically, he actually did not even develop the sequence named after him. He discovered it when traveling with his father who was a merchant. It appears to be of Indian Hindu origin, and in 1202, at age thirty-two, he published it along with his math, and all that he had learned in Liber Abaci in English *Book of Calculations.*

It seems there is a connection between this historical math made famous by the man from Pisa and our modern day science, extending from the study of the stars right down to the incredibly delicate science we are now involved in as we explore inner space. Now we are decoding the genome, working with DNA, and exploring ways to re-engineer our programming to eliminate disease, etc. Could it be that this mathematical phenomenon discovered by Fibonacci back at the end of the dark ages is another code or mathematical signature of a cosmic consciousness, a designer, even our Creator?

The avalanche of information in the various fields of science grows daily! The study of genomics has revealed the focus on the static sequences of genes and proteins. Now that focus has shifted to their dynamic functions and interactions with each other. The new challenge is to learn how to use this vast amount of data to discover how the DNA and proteins work with each other and the quantum world to create complex living systems. Do they know what they are doing? Are they conscious?

Dr. Bruce Lipton believes they are.

In his book, *The Biology of Belief,* Dr. Bruce describes his personal life experiences that transformed him from an agnostic scientist to an enlightened scientist, embracing the "New Biology" that unites spirit and science, or rather, "reunites spirit and science."

In truth, spirit and science can never be separated, except arbitrarily in one's mind. Who we are is much more than our genetic programming. I now believe that it is possible for every living person to not only "change," but to consciously direct the subconscious and the cellular systems of our bodies into a creation of our own making. We are no longer victims of bad parenting or bad religion or bad genes or bad theories. We are not static; we are constantly evolving creatures. As "good" religion would say "from glory to glory," translation: "from revelation of new truth to the revelation of new truth, or from enlightenment to enlightenment." We have moved past the protoplasm of the cells and the survival of the fittest of Darwin to cellular cities containing DNA and the cooperation and consciousness of our cells with ourselves. A fully integrated, fully conscious enlightened mind-body and spirit can do this.

I call it the MBSM, the Mind-Body-Spirit-Matrix! When it's in alignment, I think the "Big Field"—that is, the external Cosmos—connects to the Little Big Field, the internal universe. In those connections we will find God. The God particle must be part of a God field, right?

Dr. Lipton used to teach cellular biology to medical students. He noticed that among cells, there was much more cooperation than competition and wondered if that would work in his class as well. He purposely threw out the old Darwinian approach of grading on the curve and survival of the fittest and brought about a spirit of cooperation and revolutionized his classes. Everyone did better!

He demonstrated that when the trillions of cells of the human body worked together in unity it was strong and healthy, even though each still maintained its individuality and assignment; they all worked together to benefit each other. There was also an intelligent pattern at many different levels, just like we found in the Fibonacci sequence from our DNA to the galaxies and beyond!

Dr. Lipton refers to the life-saving miracle for millions that is best exemplified by Jonas Salk and his development of the polio vaccine. While not without problems, vaccines closely duplicate what our cells do naturally... that is, react to a viral invader by calling an immature cell in to create a protective protein antibody against that virus. In the process, the cell must create a new gene to serve as a blueprint in manufacturing the antibody protein.

The new antibody gene can also be passed on to all the cell's progeny when it divides. In this process, not only did the cell "learn" about the virus, it also created a "memory" that will be inherited and propagated by its daughter cells. This amazing feat of genetic engineering is profoundly important because it represents an inherent "intelligence." Who designed that— or is it statistically possible that this ability occurred randomly?

Say, are those designer genes you are wearing, or did they self-evolve?

Well, from what Dr. Lipton was finding, it seems to me that the answer is yes to both. Initial life questions aside, they have the ability, a form of consciousness perhaps, that allows them to self-evolve and adapt to new challenges! So where is the cellular brain that directs all these actions? Most would say it must be the DNA in the nucleus! Most would be wrong!

Darwin suggested with some accuracy that hereditary factors were responsible for traits being passed on from one generation to another. Darwin's influence was so great that even after his belief that the cell was filled with simple protoplasm was proved incorrect, scientists still sought to fit the facts into his incorrect paradigm. Even when DNA was discovered, they focused myopically on it as the hereditary material that controlled all life. That turns out not to be entirely true. We gazed at the stunning new discoveries of DNA, RNA, etc. and through the false filters of an old paradigm, we made some false assumptions. That's how most learning takes place. Hence the need for constant review with a routine that includes viewing what we think we know and what we know we don't know from every different perspective possible.

To this day some still use genetics as an excuse for dysfunctional behavior of every kind. A wonderful scientific discovery was quickly sullied by those who wanted a ready excuse to be victims of heredity. I was one until I knew better. There are at least three things that affect who we are. We'll consider environment next. But first consider what Dr. Lipton says about genetics:

"Since the dawning of the Age of Genetics, we have been programmed to accept that we are subservient to the power of our genes. The world is filled with people who live in constant fear that, on some unsuspecting day, their genes are going to turn on them. Consider the masses of people who think they are ticking time bombs; they wait for cancer to explode in their lives as it exploded in the life of their mother or brother or sister or aunt or uncle. Millions of others attribute their failing health not to a combination of mental, physical, emotional, and spiritual causes but simply to the inadequacies of their body's biochemical mechanics. Are your kids unruly? Increasingly, the first choice is to medicate these children to correct their "chemical imbalances" rather than fully grappling with what is going on in their bodies, minds, and spirits."

I couldn't agree more! There is no question that some diseases, like Huntington's chorea, beta thalassemia, and cystic fibrosis, can be blamed entirely on one faulty gene. But single-gene disorders affect less than two percent of the population; the vast majority of people come into this world with genes that should enable them to live a happy and healthy life. What we are finding now is that the diseases that are today's scourges, such as diabetes, heart disease, and cancer are not the result of a single gene, but of complex interactions among multiple genes AND environmental factors.

What about all those headlines trumpeting the discovery of a gene for everything from depression to schizophrenia? If you read those articles closely, you'll see that behind the breathless headline is a more sober truth. Scientists have linked lots of genes to lots of different diseases and traits, but scientists have rarely found that one gene causes a trait or a disease. There is a difference between causing and being associated with a disease.

Environment has its place, too, as Dr. Lipton discovered when he was cloning stem cells. (He was one of the first to do that.) When he maintained a healthy environment for them, they thrived and when it was less than optimal, they didn't, and when he reestablished a healthy environment, the "sick" cells revived.

In an 1876 letter to Moritz Wagner, Darwin wrote, "In my opinion, the greatest error which I have committed has been not allowing sufficient weight to the direct action of the environments, i.e., food, climate, etc., independently of natural selection. When I wrote the *Origin*, and for some years after, I could find little good evidence of the direct action of the environment; now there is a large body of evidence." [Darwin, F 1888]

There is an outside influence on our genes. Now we have proof that environmental factors have a cause and effect on the genes we inherit, and as we now understand, we can cause mutations in those genes by altering our environment!

Perhaps even our own beliefs can activate or suppress those genes! Consider this again from Dr. Lipton: "The confusion occurs when the media repeatedly distorts the meaning of two words: correlation and causation. It's one thing to be linked to a disease; it's quite another to cause a disease, which implies a directing, controlling action. If I show you my keys and say that a particular key "controls" my car, you at first might think that makes sense because you know you need that key to turn on the ignition. But does the key actually "control" the car? If it did, you couldn't leave the key in the car alone because it might just borrow your car for a joy ride when you are not paying attention. In truth, the key is "correlated" with the control of the car; the person who turns the key actually controls the car."

Scientists have found that when a gene product is needed, a signal from its environment, not an emergent property of the gene itself, activates expression of that gene." In other words, when it comes to genetic control, "It's the environment, stupid."

It appears one can make a case for a form of consciousness found in a design pattern that allows the body to intelligently respond to its environment. Without going into the complexity that Dr. Lipton could, let's review how our cellular cities function.

It is easy to understand how genetic control became a metaphor as scientists with ever-greater excitement zeroed in on the mechanisms of DNA. Organic chemists discovered that cells are made up of four types of very large molecules: polysaccharides (complex sugars), lipids (fats), nucleic acids (DNA/RNA), and proteins. Though the cell requires each of the four molecular types, proteins are the most important single component for living organisms. The brain of the cell was thought to be in the long threadlike nucleic acid, DNA, found in the nucleus. You'll remember from the last chapter that to make DNA it required four, (another 4) nitrogen-containing chemicals called bases (adenine, thymine, cytosine, and guanine, or A, T, C, and G). The sequence of the A, T, C, and G bases in DNA spells out the sequence of amino acids along a protein's backbone. Those long strings of DNA molecules can be subdivided into single genes or segments that provide the blueprint for specific proteins. The code for recreating the protein machinery of the cell has been cracked! You know how I like breaking codes. Not only that, as we just saw it also contains the hidden message God Eternal, Within. Pretty cool!

With all we have discovered about the complexity of DNA, how could they now say that protein is the most important component for living cells? How so?

Well, each protein is a linear string of linked amino acid molecules. It sounds simple, but it isn't. For one thing, it takes over 100,000 different types of proteins to run our bodies.

These twenty amino acids that make up the 100,000 different proteins are linked together by peptide bonds, and like pearls on a string they are flexible so that they can move about. There are two factors that determine the shape that they will take. One is the amino acid sequence, and the second is the electromagnetic charge. Most of our amino acids have positive or negative charges, which act like magnets; like charges cause the molecules to repel one another, while opposite charges cause the molecules to attract each other.

The final shape of a protein molecule reflects a balanced state among its electromagnetic charges. However, if the protein's positive and negative charges are altered, the protein backbone will dynamically twist and adjust itself to accommodate the new distribution of charges. The distribution of electromagnetic charge within a protein can be selectively altered by a number of processes including the binding of other molecules or chemical groups such as hormones; the enzymatic removal or addition of charged ions; or interference from electromagnetic fields such as those emanating from cell phones and other electromagnetic "helpers." That list is growing daily, just something to stay up on and think about.

These shape-shifting proteins are an impressive engineering feat because their precise, three-dimensional shapes also give them the ability to link up with other proteins. When a protein encounters a molecule that is a physical and energetic complement, the two bind together like man-made machines with interlocking gears like a fine Swiss watch. It is the electromagnetic charges that are responsible for the behavior generating movements of the protein gears, not the DNA, but you need DNA to create proteins, right? Is this another chicken or the egg conundrum?

So just where is the "brain" on the cellular level? For a long time we thought that would be the nucleus of the cell, but yes, you guessed it, that has changed. Dr. Lipton describes an experiment where a lone cell is enucleated (the nucleus removed). If this is the brain of the cell, it should result in death, but what happens is that the cell recovers and heals and goes on living, eating, and producing what it is supposed to produce. These poor enucleated cells maintain their coordinated ability to function and communicate with other cells for months until they die. Why do they die then? Because they no longer have the DNA in the nucleus to reproduce.

If it's not the brain, then what does that make it? Here is how Dr. Lipton puts it: the nucleus is the cell's gonad!

Okay, so if the nucleus with its RNA and incredible DNA, is not the brain of our cells, where is it? I have a hint for you. Perhaps the there is another code here… a name within the name. Let's look at the list of different parts of the city that make up our cells and see if one stands out.

Cell membrane: the thin layer of protein and fat that surrounds the cell. The cell membrane is semipermeable, allowing some substances to pass into the cell and blocking others.

Centrosome: (also called the "microtubule organizing center") a small body located near the nucleus; it has a dense center and radiating tubules. The centrosomes is where microtubules are made. During cell division (mitosis), the centrosome divides and the two parts move to opposite sides of the dividing cell. The centriole is the dense center of the centrosome.

Cytoplasm: the jelly-like material outside the cell nucleus in which the organelles are located.

Golgi body: (also called the Golgi apparatus or golgi complex) a flattened, layered, sac-like organelle that looks like a stack of pancakes and is located near the nucleus. It produces the membranes that surround the lysosomes. The Golgi body packages proteins and carbohydrates into membrane-bound vesicles for "export" from the cell.

Lysosome: (also called cell vesicles) round organelles surrounded by a membrane and containing digestive enzymes. This is where the digestion of cell nutrients takes place.

Mitochondrion: spherical to rod-shaped organelles with a double membrane. The inner membrane is infolded many times, forming a series of projections (called cristae). The mitochondrion converts the energy stored in glucose into ATP (adenosine triphosphate) for the cell.

Nuclear membrane: the membrane that surrounds the nucleus.

Nucleolus: an organelle within the nucleus; it is where ribosomal RNA is produced. Some cells have more than one nucleolus.

Nucleus: spherical body containing many organelles, including the nucleolus. The nucleus controls many of the functions of the cell (by controlling protein synthesis) and contains DNA (in chromosomes). The nucleus is surrounded by the nuclear membrane.

Ribosome: small organelles composed of RNA-rich cytoplasmic granules that are sites of protein synthesis.

Rough endoplasmic reticulum: (rough ER) a vast system of interconnected, membranous, infolded and convoluted sacks that are located in the cell's cytoplasm (the ER is continuous with the outer nuclear membrane). Rough ER is covered with ribosomes that give it a rough appearance. Rough ER transports materials through the cell and produces proteins in sacks called cisternae (which are sent to the Golgi body, or inserted into the cell membrane).

Smooth endoplasmic reticulum: (smooth ER) a vast system of interconnected, membranous, infolded and convoluted tubes that are located in the cell's cytoplasm (the ER is continuous with the outer nuclear membrane). The space within the ER is called the ER lumen. Smooth ER transports materials through the cell. It contains enzymes and produces and digests lipids (fats) and membrane proteins; smooth ER buds off from rough ER, moving the newly-made proteins and lipids to the Golgi body, lysosomes, and membranes.

Vacuole: fluid-filled, membrane-surrounded cavities inside a cell. The vacuole fills with food being digested and waste material that is on its way out of the cell.

Yes, this and more exist in each of your several trillion cells!

I hear MemBRANE. Is that your final answer? It is, if you are Dr. Bruce Lipton! That's a bit counterintuitive to those of us that were once biology majors and were perhaps taught a well-meaning non-truth. The idea that the membrane was the cell's brain back in the seventies would have been laughable. The membrane was described then as a three-layered saran wrap with holes that held the cytoplasm together, but then again, it wasn't so far back that Darwin thought the entire cell was filled with simply cytoplasm. Seasons change, science advances, sometimes in spite of itself.

It really wasn't until after WWII when we had electron microscopes to actually see the thin membrane that is said to be seven millionths of a millimeter thin (I really can't say "thick," can I?) Now with the aid of the electron microscope scientists have found out that every living cell has a membrane and that they all share the same three-layered structure. Cell biologists gained insight into the amazing abilities of the cell membrane by studying the most primitive organisms on this planet: the prokaryotes.

Prokaryotes, which include bacteria and other microbes, consist only of a cell membrane that envelops a droplet of soupy cytoplasm. Though prokaryotes represent life in its most primitive form, they have purpose. A bacterium does not bounce around in its world like a ball in a pinball machine. A bacterium carries out the basic physiologic processes of life like more complicated cells. A bacterium eats, digests, breathes, excretes waste matter, and even exhibits "neurological" processing. They can sense where there is food and propel themselves to that spot. Similarly, they can recognize toxins and predators and purposely employ escape maneuvers to save their lives. In other words, prokaryotes display intelligence!

So what structure in the prokaryotic cell provides its "intelligence"? The prokaryotes' cytoplasm has no evident organelles, such as the nucleus and mitochondria that are found in more advanced, eukaryotic cells. The only organized cellular structure that can be considered a candidate for the prokaryote's brain is its cell membrane.

Certainly the extremely complex DNA, RNA and genes that exist in the cell nucleus contains incredible amounts of information that can and does sustain carbon-based life. But could it perhaps be analogous to our memory and the non-conscious functions of our brain, while the membrane actually acts as the source of conscious action on the cellular level? Consider that when you destroy a cell's membrane, the cell dies just as you would if your brain were removed. Unlike what happens when you remove the nucleus. If you leave the membrane intact, destroying only its receptor proteins, which can easily be done with digestive enzymes in the lab, the cell becomes "brain-dead." It is comatose because it no longer receives the environmental signals necessary for the operation of the cell. The cell also becomes comatose when the membrane's receptor proteins are left intact and its effector proteins are immobilized. To exhibit "intelligent" behavior, cells need a functioning membrane with both receptor (awareness) and effector (action) proteins. These protein complexes appear to be the fundamental units of cellular intelligence. I think that answers the question why protein is the most important component of the cell!

There appear to be several levels of cellular intelligence and function. Remember that recently they used human DNA to store huge volumes of mp3s and pictures and Shakespeare's sonnets? I can't help but see the comparison on the cellular level to the functions of a computer. We have talked about software and programs like DNA but now let's look at the living cell from another perspective. Consider that the membrane is your semiconductor with gates and channels for the flow of information. The cell membrane is a structural and functional equivalent of a silicon chip, the processor portion of the brain within your PC. The keyboard is equivalent to the membrane receptors. Receptors trigger the membranes, effector proteins which could be analogous to the CPU. The effector proteins in the cell convert the environmental information into action in the cell, just as the receptor functions of the keyboard create effector functions in the PC involving the software, and the hard drive working as directed all being processed through the microchip.

Cells and PCs are programmable with hardware and software, and respond to environmental input. We are made up of trillions of subminiature computers!

What a concept that our cells have a consciousness. It gives new meaning to the litany of poets who have attributed the variety of human emotions literally to the heart. In his book, Dr. Lipton quotes several people who have had heart transplants and have had what could be called cellular memory feedback from the transplanted organs. I understand that it is very rare at best. I have known several heart transplant surgeons and none of them have reported any cases like this.

I also spoke about this subject with our former Senate Majority leader Senator Bill Frist, M.D. Not many people know that Dr. Frist is quite a humanitarian who travels the world donating his medical services for free. Before he served in the US Senate, he was a renowned heart transplant surgeon. I was honored to have dinner with him in Southern California in 2005 where I asked him if he had ever had a transplant patient experience unexplained memories. Not to his knowledge, he replied; if they had, they had not shared it with him. It may occur more than we are aware simply because we are not looking for it. Or not. Perhaps this level of consciousness is not so easily perceived on the conscious level.

Dr. Lipton reported that a conservative, health-conscious New Englander, Claire Sylvia, was astonished when she developed a taste for beer, chicken nuggets, and motorcycles after her heart-lung transplant. After talking to the donor's family, Claire found she had the heart of an eighteen-year-old motorcycle enthusiast who loved chicken nuggets and beer. In her book called *A Change of Heart,* Sylvia outlines her personal transformational experiences, as well as similar experiences of other patients in her transplant support group. [Sylvia and Novak 1997]

Paul P. Pearsall presents a number of other such stories in his book, *The Heart's Code: Tapping the Wisdom and Power of Our Heart Energy* [Pearsall 1998]. "The accuracy of memories that accompany these transplants is beyond chance or coincidence. One young girl began having nightmares of murder after her heart transplant. Her dreams were so vivid that they led to the capture of the murderer who killed her donor."

It seems that science is in the process of a deep revolution. When you look at the growing body of evidence that consciousness and what we call the mind is not simply confined to the skull, the horizons of research expands. Many people are now realizing the ways in which we have been limited by the assumptions of science. Some are even talking about it.

As I was writing this chapter I came across an article in *PT Today* by John Barnes. In the article, John talks about how science is catching up with his theories. For years he has taught about the fascia on the microscopic level and how it is actually a three-dimensional web of tiny, hollow tubules filled with fluid carrying information throughout the body. When there are physical scars from injury or surgery, or even emotional scars, they can block the flow of energy through the body and manifest in pain, muscle tightness, and tension. The blocked energy, i.e. information, can be unblocked and released via myofascial release for healing on the deepest levels. Then the information in the form of thermal, electromagnetic and mechanical energy is transmitted to all aspects of the mind/body complex.

In his article, Dr. Barnes states:

"Two of the leading researchers on consciousness, mathematical physicist Roger Penrose and Stuart Hameroff, have stated that past brain/consciousness research had been severely limited by scientists not looking deeper than the synapse of the nervous system.

With the help of new, sophisticated electronic microscopes capable of incredible magnification, Penrose and Hameroff have discovered microtubules filled with fluid within the cytoskeleton of the cell." This discovery validates the theories that Dr. Barnes postulated many years ago.

The famous neuroscientist C.S. Sherrington has further observed that the cytoskeleton may act as the nervous system of single-cell organisms. Synaptic connections are formed and regulated by cytoskeletal polymers, including microtubules.

After confirming their theories with new microscopes, Penrose and Hameroff speculated that the cytoskeleton is like a micro-myofascial system within each cell. This micro-myofascial system is made up of a skeleton of tubules filled with fluid and surrounded and interconnected from cell to cell by a viscous ground substance.

They go on to suggest that using the quantum field theory, that ordering of the water molecules and the electromagnetic field confined inside the hollow microtubules core manifest a specific collective dynamics called "super radiance." Accordingly, each microtubule can transform incoherent, disordered energy (molecular, thermal or electromagnetic) into coherent photons within its hollow core.

Dr. Barnes says that this new information supports his theory of the continuity of the myofascial system from the inside of the cell to the very periphery of our being and the holographic model of reality where photons (light) are transmitted as information throughout the mind/body complex. He further contends that Consciousness (information) is necessary for healing and that Consciousness may emerge as a macroscopic quantum state from a critical level of coherence of quantum-level events in and around a specific class of neurobiological micro-structures: the cytoskeletal microtubules within neurons."

Can you visualize that? Microscopic myofascial type tubules so small, smaller than capillaries with one molecule of water passing through them at a time, but having a quantum effect on the entire system? I can and I'll tell you why. It's due in part to some research accomplished by a Japanese gentleman with water. It can exist as a solid in the form of ice cubes in our drinks. It can exist as a liquid in the form of our drinks... and as rain and lakes and oceans, etc. We are, after all, a water planet! Then there is the gaseous state of steam from your tea kettle or your hot Jacuzzi. It is an interesting molecule.

A researcher by the name of Mr. Emoto discovered an interesting phenomenon that is currently undergoing further verification and research. Mr. Emoto would subject water to various sounds and frequencies, then freeze the water, and then prepare it for viewing under the microscope. What he found fascinated me. Water subjected to rap music and other discordant music such as heavy metal, etc. produced chaotic disfigured crystalline shapes, while water subjected to classical music demonstrated beautiful crystalline shapes well-ordered and symmetrical like snowflakes.

He published a book with pictures contrasting and comparing different frequencies. I look forward to seeing more scientific research on this. Our bodies are 70 to 80 percent water! Seems like it is something we should be interested in! Is there a consciousness demonstrated by the water molecule? If so, seems we ought to know! Do attitudes and negative words and frequencies have a negative effect on it, as it appears? If so, this would be another good reason to avoid negativity in general, considering our bodies are largely water and if there are things that distort and disrupt water, we might want to consider the possibility that it could penetrate into our bodies systems and have a deleterious effect. My Jacuzzi already provides me good therapy, but what if certain sound frequencies were sent through it that could induce relaxation or healing? Worth looking into!

We have come a long way from the "old science" that treated us simply as machines. We know that our bodies on the cellular level are incredible computers with hardware and software etc. but now we can see the "new" science of consciousness as well. Is that consciousness the proof of a connection to God, the Higher consciousness, or is it simply a trip deeper into the matrix that is the human being?

In her book *The Heart Speaks*, Dr. Mini Guarneri, certified in Internal Medicine and Cardiology, and founder and medical director of Scripps Center for integrative medicine in La Jolla, California, shares numerous amazing stories of the mind-body-spirit connection that she has seen in her patients. When she was just eight-years-old she lost her vivacious forty-four-year-old mother to a heart attack. She says she found that in healing the hearts of her patients her own broken heart was healed. She began to see that the lessons of the heart were as much about forgiveness and gratefulness as they were pharmaceuticals and surgery. She now speaks about knowing and treating the whole heart, mind, body, and spirit and in so doing it can truly become whole, in a way that surgery and pharmaceuticals alone cannot deliver.

Perhaps knowing how powerful negative emotions and the energy they create can be, will act as an eye opener to the flip side, and that is how much healing can come from positive emotions and the positive, enhancing, even healing energies they release!

Most of us have heard about broken heart syndrome. There are numerous stories of long term happily married couples dying within days, even hours, of each other with one of them in apparently great health! Physically, it appears that what has happened in these cases is that the wall of coronary arteries experience a sudden intense contraction of the muscles slowing or stopping the blood flow to the heart. This can create a sudden unexpected fatal heart attack in an otherwise healthy heart. Why was there a sudden unexpected contraction of the cardiac muscles? The short answer is emotions! Powerful negative emotions can have a fatal effect on the cells of the heart.

Not only are our cells chemical factories, they are electrical power plants as well! Fear creates a powerful effect on the body. To a degree it is helpful, giving you the rush you need to move fast and get out of the street before the semi flattens you, but unbridled it can kill you as effectively as the semi-truck would have.

Magnified effects due to fear can also cause the voodoo death effect to an otherwise totally healthy body! Walter Cannon wrote about these phenomena almost a hundred years ago. Cannon was a physiologist at Harvard Medical School who investigated peoples' responses to voodoo curses; specifically those filled with such fear, they dropped dead from sudden massive stress response!

Their belief systems killed them as dead as a lethal injection! It appears that our belief systems can be great guides to live by or they can become dysfunctional BS that can elicit powerful emotions that cause damage and even death to our cells. We now know how the heart and nervous system respond to stress and emotions. Negative emotions such as rage, frustration, and hate lead to increased disorder in our autonomic nervous systems and in the heart's rhythm, which in turn adversely affects the entire body. Positive emotions, on the other hand, feelings like appreciation, love, and acceptance, produce heart rhythm coherence, inner harmony, and systemic health. Since the heart is the most powerful electrical source and oscillator in the body, the rhythms set by the cells of the heart are capable of entraining the other organs to oscillate in synchronicity.

Dr. Guarneri has demonstrated this phenomenon to her patients repeatedly with powerful results. She allows them to see the changes in the electrical rhythms and patterns of their hearts as they experience different emotions while connected to monitors in her office. The heart shows the effect first but it doesn't end there. A study comparing the effects of anger versus compassion on the immune system found that a single five-minute session where a subject graphically recalls an angry episode inhibits the production of IgA, suppressing the immune system for more than six hours! On the flip side, even a self-induced state of compassion increased the production of IgA, significantly enhancing the immune system. You are what you eat, yes, and you are what you think, yes; now add to that you are what you feel.

Our conscious cells are clearly influenced by their environment, and in turn they create an environment within our bodies that mirror the external environment. This affects our entire being. Wise doctors are learning how to instruct their patients in the art of directing their thoughts and feelings. They have found that the ability to consciously shift to a positive emotion will reverse the effect of hostility and stress. It could be more important to you and your health than your cholesterol!

In 1983 the heart was reclassified as an endocrine gland when it was discovered that it produced ANF, atrial natriuretic factor. This is another way that the heart communicates with the other organs, through the production of hormones and neurotransmitters such as dopamine and epinephrine which are known to mediate emotions. These discoveries show that even though the brain is still the main decision maker, the "ten ounce" heart is a small brain of sorts, functioning as a sensory organ, a hormone producing factory, an electrical power plant, and it also serves as an information processing center! Wow!

When I was in school we were taught about the mysterious "AV node and SA nodes," like an electrician would speak of electricity. The new science is discovering that cells have "brains" and a form of consciousness, which is taking the science of the heart a few steps further, marrying the physical and electrical and chemical functions with the conscious control of those functions from the cells themselves! So powerful is the evidence today Dr. Guarneri has included a chapter in her book entitled the "Small Brain." Here she details the "new" functions of the "smart heart" that we are just now discovering.

Quantum Theory suggests that there is something nonlocal that connects matter across space and time. It appears that as we gain the ability to look deeper into the cells of our bodies as well as the other living things in the world around us, we find evidence of some level of consciousness. It also appears that as we look deeper into space we see evidence of intent and consciousness there as well. It seems that the larger, gravitational forces, small and large nuclear forces, along with a host of other factors, must perfectly align to provide a hospitable environment for our carbon-based life form. The external universe must meet all these exacting criteria to provide a suitable environment for our internal universe to live and flourish and to even exist. It would appear to me that that there is a consciousness connecting the internal and external universes. It would not surprise me if someday we find a hidden code in the Cosmos that is like the one we found in the software of our cells, the DNA. "God eternal within"! This new one might read "God external without."

Without a doubt, the internal matrix of the human body is an incredibly complex universe of its own, apparently with a consciousness at levels not yet fully understood that defy the theory of evolution. Somewhere it begins to take more "faith" to believe in evolution than it does in an Originator. A random appearance of this complex system appears to be statistically impossible and is an affront to common sense and rational thought. In my estimation, there is a better statistical case to be made for an intelligent designer.

Consider again for a moment the piezoelectric phenomenon in the cells of our body.

We saw that the scientists Penrose and Hameroff studying the myofascial system within our bodies have determined that information "consciousness" is transmitted through the hollow core of the microtubules to all aspects of the mind/body. Knowing this helps to deepen our understanding of the piezoelectric effect when the myofascial system is treated. I can say I am not sure I understand it all yet, but it works!

The fascia is a piezoelectric tissue; therefore when a therapist utilizing the gentle, sustained pressure of myofascial release through compression, stretching, or twisting of the myofascial system generates a flow of bioenergy (information) throughout the mind/body complex by the piezoelectric phenomenon, it facilitates the extracellular matrix to transform as it undergoes its "solid to gel" reorganization during myofascial release. Fascia is behaving as an electrically conductive medium which allows this visco-elastic tissue to rehydrate under the sustained pressure of the therapist's hands.

This rehydration also allows for an elongation of the myofascial system, relieving the pressure on pain sensitive structures for alleviation of the symptoms of pain, headaches, and the restoration of motion.

There is so much yet to learn about cellular consciousness and healing!

So we are connected at every level. From deep within each cell of our being flows information/consciousness via light energy (photons) throughout all aspects of our mind/body, and I dare say, spirit.

The incredible magnification of our new electronic microscopes has allowed scientists to see myofascial structures within the cell. It confirms Dr. Barnes' hypothesis and expands our knowledge while providing us with a more accurate understanding of our myofascial system and its importance to the healthy functioning of our mind/body/spirit/matrix. (MBSM)

If this consciousness is God, it would seem to fly in the face of classical religious explanations. It seems to contradict the god-as-a-man paradigm many religions present. Perhaps our description is off because our science is off or incomplete. Perhaps it is a force throughout the universe and a consciousness that can manifest as a human as well if it intends to. Let's get back to my original question: does God exist and did Einstein believe that or was he just speaking hypothetically when he said he wanted to learn to think like God?

I believe that science may have answered that question back at the beginning of the twentieth century and that Albert Einstein and his mathematics proved, irrefutably, that there is a precisely quantifiable quantity of energy in the universe that is even more vast, powerful, and awesome than any religion's current definition of God. He proved that there was a "Force" or "God Force" or "Energy" that is so mind-blowing it dwarfs even the wildest imaginations of "the power of God."

I believe his scientific work verifies that without dispute.

What Einstein discovered was a force of such magnitude that it should cause thinking persons to fall to their knees, regardless of how they define that force, that power, that God. Yes, it is beyond our ability to define a dimensionless God or Force. After all, if it created and sustains all with this incredible power, how could something it created define it?

Is it defined by a three-letter word such as God, or is it more accurately defined by three letters and a number: $E=mc^2$.

It is appropriate that this formula is known all over the world but understood, truly understood, by only a few. Is it another name for the Creator God?

Perhaps this one describes his power more accurately than any of the other host of names attributed to "Him," as in it lies the truth that every element of creation, of matter itself is but a breath away from complete annihilation at any moment in time. The formula or perhaps all-powerful name holds the secret of the power of the atom from which one of his creations developed the atomic bomb.

Perhaps in this name $E=MC^2$ we find that math and theology are all rolled up into one equation.

Think about this: Add all of the matter on Earth and add that to the rest of God's creation, 100 billion galaxies, each with about 100 billion stars. Then multiply that amount of matter by the speed of light and square that number and then understand that every gram of that incalculable amount of matter has the energy of a Hiroshima nuclear bomb. That's an all-powerful "God" working that equation!

A 100 pound human, for example, contains the force of approximately 45,000 Hiroshimas. A 200 pound person over 90,000 and 6.5 billion humans, with an average of 100 pounds of mass, contain over 292 trillion times the force of an atomic bomb.

Add other animals, mountains, oceans, and the mass of the Earth itself and we have approximately 13 septillion pounds or approximately 6 octillion (6,000,000,000,000,000,000,000,000,000) or 627 atomic bombs worth of force contained in just the Earth itself. Now when you grasp the perspective that Earth is a small part of one solar system, which is a tiny part of one galaxy, which is a tiny part of a universe estimated to have 100 billion galaxies, each with 100 billion such solar systems, you can begin to comprehend that the quantity of Force/Energy/Power/God described by Einstein's tiny formula, $E=MC^2$. Well, maybe YOU can but it is beyond my comprehension.

If Energy is "God", as some believe, or one of many manifestations or reflections of "God" as others may believe, there simply are no words, in any spiritual tradition, that can do "it" ... Him justice!

Despite or perhaps because of his massive intellect, Einstein humbles himself before the unfathomable nature of God. He wrote the following in 1932:

"The most beautiful and deepest experience a man can have is the sense of the mysterious. It is the underlying principle of religion as well as of all serious endeavors in art and science. He who never had this experience seems to me, if not dead, then at least blind. To sense that behind anything that can be experienced there is a something that our minds cannot grasp, whose beauty and sublimity reaches us only indirectly: this is religiousness. In this sense I am religious. To me it suffices to wonder at these secrets and to attempt humbly to grasp with my mind a mere image of the lofty structure of all there is."

Perhaps then, we should not feel inadequate, as we continue on in our search for the quantum God. A relationship with such a being is worth the search!

> *Forget not that the Earth delights to feel your bare feet*
> *and the winds long to play with your hair.*
> *~ Kahlil Gibran*

Chapter 6
Ancient Aliens—our Gods or Parents or ?

"Hello. I'm Leonard Nimoy. The following tale of alien encounters is true. And by true, I mean false. It's all lies. But they're entertaining lies. And in the end, isn't that the real truth? The answer is No!"

~ Star Trek's First Officer, Mr. Spock, from *The Simpsons*

Isn't it interesting that sometimes cartoons contain more truth than network news? I can think of no subject that has more coverups and stigmas attached to it than the subject of aliens. Are they our quantum gods who seeded this earth with us, their children? Or perhaps they are a sinister master race of reptilian creatures that use illusion to look like us, but hide a master plan to consume us for their energy needs. You know it gets that crazy. The truth is buried somewhere out there, just like a dog buries his favorite bone in a secret hiding place, with the dirt of disinformation kicked all around to keep you away.

When I was a young child in the sixties, I was fascinated by the UFO phenomenon sweeping the nation. I wanted to be a pilot when I grew up and UFOs seemed to be the ultimate flying machines around. If they were real, and to a grade-schooler everything can still be real, I wanted a ride on one of those things more than anything!

I was probably the only kid my age who went on a mission mowing lawns to earn enough money to buy a copy of the famous *Blue Book* (official Air Force report on UFOs) when it was released to the public. I even designed my own flying disk, complete with mechanical drawings, including a power plant built around three jet engines that were sold in the ads at the back of *Popular Science* magazine.

My father was a pilot and an inventor, so why couldn't I do the same? He wasn't around to ask, so when my grandfather came to visit, I showed him my drawings and shared with him my plan to build it. My grandfather was a quintessential renaissance man, an award-winning artist, a naturalist, an astronomer who built his own telescopes, and a physician who grew his own penicillin when there were shortages during the Second World War. He designed new and effective surgical instruments and formulated the first commercially available multivitamin supplement. Later I found out he was considered one of the top five eye surgeons in the world.

He was also wise enough not to discourage me or to empower me too much, too soon. I remember him looking at my plans, studying them, and saying, "Hmm, well that could work." I built a wood mockup of my flying saucer, but that's as far as I got. However, my interest in flying machines and the UFO phenomena never died. I eventually learned how to fly, but to this point in time I have not had any contact of the third kind.

But my interest in the possibility of UFOs has inspired me to talk to some who claim they have. One was a retired US Air Force general who claimed not only to have been contacted but to have ridden on a UFO! He described being taken from the Mojave

Desert of California to New York and back in a matter of seconds. Another time he was shown artifacts from Earth's past and was told that UFOs had been involved in our past and would be again at the right time in our future. As the incredible craft landed again, the general said he noticed a name plate on the back of the captain's command chair, and it shook him. The name was Lucifer. It disturbed him so much that when he made it back to his vehicle he decided that was his last trip with them! According to him, it was indeed his last contact with them.

Was he crazy? I don't know! It sure didn't seem like it to me, but I was just a young lad when I heard him speak at our National Guard Armory.

Certainly some UFO groupies are, but many are not! I got to know one fellow doctor who seemed quite sane, and who eventually told me about multiple abductions by aliens when she was young. That blew my mind.

As I searched for meaning in life and a God—if one existed—I was again intrigued by the passion of those who believe that we have and are being visited by extraterrestrials. I also admit quite honestly the stories of the ancient alien theorists did seem to make some sense. Their theories, combined with ancient archeology, joined to make a plausible hypothesis and with the growing acceptance of aliens in our media, TV and movies, etc., the stigma that the doubters and some alleged government agencies fostered was gone.

In the late sixties, even as the governments of the world were engaging in a campaign of denial, a man named Erich von Däniken wrote a book called *Chariot of the Gods* that seemed equally as crazy! If you have watched the series *Ancient Aliens* on the Discovery channel you have seen him along with Giorgio A. Tsoukalos, the Swiss-born Greek author and co-producer of the series. As I watched the evidence they presented I was intrigued. I had always thought that it was quite possible that this world was actually much more sophisticated at one time in the past than we had been taught, and their theories explained how that could have occurred... if it had. These men and other anthropologists and scientists did not seem to be nut cases. They were intelligent—Giorgio is fluent in at least five languages—but these people were not running out to Mount Hermon to wait for the mother ship. They were looking at the facts and coming up with conclusions that others perhaps had not been brave enough to... until now.

History is replete with stories of "ancient gods" that we write off as mythology. I asked myself, what if they were not simply mythology? What if they were supernatural in some form? Were they, or was one of them "The God"... the source of first life? Was it possible that a worldwide deluge—like Noah's flood—wiped out an ancient world that was perhaps even more advanced than we are today? Archeologists have heard stories of and evidence for a universal flood in every corner of the Earth.

And what about the pyramids, not just the ones in Egypt, but the ones that exist all over the world in various forms? How were they built? And how is it possible that pyramids in China and Mexico resemble the three most famous pyramids in Egypt, and that they all align themselves with the stars in the sky above that form the Belt of Orion? What about the "stone star gates" that have been found in Peru and other locales that honestly look like the star gates of the science fiction program's Stargate Atlantis, or Stargate SG1? Were they ever "active" like in the sci-fi dimension or just ancient works of art? How ancient are they?

Just what is the Ancient Alien Theory? Is it real or illusion? According to ancient alien theorists, extraterrestrials with superior knowledge of science and engineering landed on Earth thousands of years ago, sharing their expertise with early civilizations, and forever changed the course of human history. I had to admit I had often wondered how the so-called pre-flood world had become so advanced, like I thought it had. Yes, I believed in a cataclysmic flood, and you will see why shortly. I had found evidence to support that belief, but was there any evidence to support this idea of aliens?

For some the ancient alien theory grew out of the centuries-old idea that life exists on other planets and that humans and extraterrestrials have crossed paths before. The theme of human-alien interaction was thrust into the spotlight in the 1960s, driven by a wave of UFO sightings and television programs like *My*

Favorite Martian and later, popular films like *2001: A Space Odyssey, Star Trek, Star Wars* and more. The space program played no small part in this as well: If mankind could travel to other planets, why couldn't extraterrestrials visit Earth? It made sense to me and apparently to millions of others.

In 1968, the Swiss author Erich von Däniken published *Chariots of the Gods*, which became an immediate bestseller. In it, he put forth his hypothesis that thousands of years ago, space travelers from other planets visited Earth, where they taught humans about technology and influenced ancient religions. He is regarded by many as the father of ancient alien theory, also known as the ancient astronaut theory.

Most ancient alien theorists, including von Däniken, point to two types of evidence to support their ideas. The first is ancient religious texts in which humans witness and interact with gods or other heavenly beings who descend from the sky—sometimes in vehicles resembling spaceships—and possess spectacular powers. The second is physical specimens such as artwork depicting alien-like figures and ancient architectural marvels like Stonehenge and the Pyramids of Egypt.

I wondered, if aliens visited Earth in the past, would they make an appearance again in the future? For ancient alien theorists, the answer is a resounding yes. They believe that by sharing their views with the world, they can help prepare future generations for the inevitable encounter that awaits us.

Now that I have heard their story and done my research I still agree with much of what they say, though I differ on some small points. And as we all know, a small difference in the foundation or theory can make a huge difference in the end result, evidence our DNA as proof.

I found some discrepancies in the body of work presented by the proponents of the Ancient Alien theory. It appears that in several cases von Däniken, Zecharia Sitchin, and others may have actually stretched and or distorted the truth to support some small details where they were lacking in evidence! However, I believe there is incontrovertible evidence that some mythological creatures were much much more than mere mythology. There are spiritual and extra spiritual, historical sources that speak of "the giants," "the fallen ones" that once dominated Earth's environment thousands of years back. These were rebellious shape shifting (able to take human form) supernatural "aliens" if you will, that roamed the Earth mating with earthlings at will, creating an alternative race of half human, half extraterrestrial creatures that threatened to wipe out the human race. Again the Bible, the Quran, and other spiritual and historical writings speak of a more powerful deity that put a stop to all the genetic engineering etc. with a global flood.

This deity, as the accepted story goes, pushed the restart button on the human race with the one family tree that was not yet infected with the alien DNA: Noah and family. I believe the evidence, admittedly and expectedly scarce, favors this explanation over the similar ancient aliens as our "parents" theory... not that they didn't try, it seems.

Clearly most of the evidence has been washed away, but this theory connects all the dots of the other theories and seems to complete them. Keep an open mind and watch and see what we find. Yes, there were those who perhaps flew about in UFOs and some interacted with humans... apparently... and some claimed to be gods and perhaps even demanded worship and odd, twisted and even violent and deadly sacrifices. They were the root of the legends and myths of Greek "gods" and Norse "gods" and Inca "gods" and Mayan "gods" ad infinitum. It seems, though, that when the Supreme Deity spoke and the reset occurred, the others died or left. So the question held in common by all those concerned is: "Will they return?"

Regardless of what theory you eventually subscribe to, my humble opinion is a resounding YES, and I think it is important to explore the subject further.

In the interest of our search for truth, I think we need to expose what seems to be some inconsistencies at best—and lies at worst—in the ancient alien family. As part of that search for truth, I found and viewed a video available online by a group called Debunking Ancient Aliens at ancientaliensdebunked.com.

Let me say that I am not debunking the series myself, but I do feel it is important to stick to the truth no matter how excited we get about our theories. In a search for truth you may find that you have opinions that you have in common with others, but in the end they may take you to different conclusions. With no shortage of good opinions and exciting theories, we have to carefully guard the truth that we do know as a foundation. It becomes an important commodity. Little lies mixed in with big unknowns can take us way off course.

The skeptics point out that in the ancient texts of Sumeria we have descriptions of these beings descending from the sky called the Annunaki. The term Annunaki means 'those who from the heavens came.' They contend that the true meaning of the word is "princely seed" or "princely blood."

A small error, perhaps, and in fact, if these beings had descended from the sky, it is no doubt that some would have worshipped them as "gods," and if they intermarried with humans, they could have created a so-called princely seed in their offspring. Nevertheless, it is an incorrect translation of the Sumerian text. They go on to point out other misinterpretations that the writings of Zecharia Sitchin contain.

Sitchin claimed to be an expert on Sumerian writings, yet they now claim that he didn't seem to even understand the basic grammar and vocabulary rules of the Sumerian language and offer several real scholars who challenge him on his translations, and on his lack of any academic credentials in the field, pointing out that there is no record of Sitchin having anything but a journalism degree. I don't believe one has to have a degree in something to be well-versed on a subject; however, when clear misinterpretations occur, then clearly your credibility is called into question. They also point out that throughout the Ancient Aliens series, pictures of Akkadian winged genies are shown and are referred to as Annunaki. But oddly, enough winged genies aren't Annunaki. In fact, these reliefs are not even Sumerian; they're Akkadian. Ouch... another blow to the credibility zone. Another popular notion that Sitchin promoted was that the aliens had come to our planet from Nibiru, their home planet which was in trouble to mine gold to take back to their planet to be dispersed throughout the atmosphere to shield it from further critical dissipation. A search done today of all the Sumerian writings, now computerized, reveals no such entry at all.

Thanks to meticulous cataloging of the Sumerian texts over the last few decades, and the advent of the internet, we no longer have to take anyone's word for it, and we can see why the academic Sumerian scholars have been so critical of Sitchin. There may be a great deal of truth to what he and other proponents of the Ancient Alien theory profess, but when our beliefs are presented as truth and not simply as our beliefs, then often the baby is thrown out with the bath water... and the truth is also lost.

I do not want to stunt imaginations in the search for truth nor do I want to misrepresent ideas and hunches as facts.

It is very possible that the Annunaki did "come down from the heavens" and that they may have used UFOs, etc., but it is not acceptable to say that an ancient text says something that it does not say to stack the odds behind your theory. I think that they were created by the God of Creation, the one in the "God Code" and I think they are ten-dimensional creatures that rebelled against their creator and fit the descriptions recorded in Gen. 6 of the Bible, and in the Quran, in the book of Enoch, and spoken about by the historian Flavius Josephus. But I am going to do my part to let you decide that for yourself based on the opinions and facts I found without misrepresenting my opinions as facts... even though I am right...

The idea of ancient aliens as astronauts has also spawned a UFO religion named Raëlism. The Raelian Movement teaches that life on Earth was scientifically created by a species of extraterrestrials, which they call the Elohim. Members of the Elohim appeared human and were mistaken for angels, cherubim or gods. The name Elohim is in fact in the text of the Bible, and it is referred to as one of the names used for God.

The Bible is full of accounts of angels, good and evil, and another group called demons. The text mentions millions of angels and their experiences on Earth and in the heavens. In Christian tradition, based on the biblical account, Lucifer was the most elegant created being in the universe second only to God. That fact was not lost on himself and he became conceited and plotted to usurp the control of the universe for himself... the end of unity and the beginning of dualism and the knowledge of good and evil. He enlisted a third of the created angels into his rebellion, and they were all eventually expelled from the heavenly dimension.

The apocryphal Book of Enoch recounts that a group of 200 of these rebellious angels, or Watchers, "left" (were expelled from) heaven, came down to Earth to mate with human women and have children with them.

The Quran depicts a story of angels who are given minds of their own, found in verse [2:34]. One of the angels was Iblis (Satan/Lucifer), who rebelled and was therefore banished on earth to create mischief amongst mankind. According to the Catechism of the Catholic Church, angels were all created as good beings, but some decided to become evil.

Christians understand that God's plan to redeem fallen man required that God himself become a human and come and live on this planet as an example and as a reconciliation for the sin of rebellion of His created beings. Could it have been Lucifer's plan to corrupt the human gene pool so that there was no "pure" human race to become part of... and to save?

Now you know who I think the Ancient Aliens are... ten-dimensional created beings that are yes, alien to this world. Our "war of the worlds" started long ago, and yes, they have been here repeatedly and yes, they have interfered with or manipulated our development and yes, they have an "end game" plan... whatever it is.

Interestingly, an Aztec/Mayan winged serpent-god named Quetzalcoatl, who was part man, part god, is supposed to return "soon" after the end of the Mayan calendar that ended on Dec 21 of 2012. Wouldn't that be interesting! The worship of the feathered serpent deity is first documented in Teotihuacan in the first century AD.

A feathered serpent deity sounds a bit like the Judeo Christian account found in the Bible of the flying, talking serpent possessed by Lucifer in the Garden of Eden that allegedly started the human race on its path of rebellion.

There really are many similar stories shared among the various ancient peoples, but none that is as widely held in common as the story of a universal flood.

Native global flood stories are documented as history or legend in almost every region on earth. Old world Christian missionaries reported their amazement at finding remote tribes already possessing legends with tremendous similarities to the Bible's accounts of the worldwide flood. In the book, *Moons, Myths and Men,* H.S. Bellamy estimates that there are over 500 flood legends worldwide. Ancient civilizations all have their own versions of a giant flood. Let's look at a few of them:

Southwest Tanzania

Once upon a time the rivers began to flood. The god told two people to get into a ship. He told them to take lots of seed and animals. The water of the flood eventually covered the mountains.

Finally the flood stopped. Then one of the men, wanting to know if the water had dried up, let a dove loose. The dove returned. Later he let loose a hawk, which did not return. Then the men left the boat and took the animals and the seeds with them.

China

The Chinese classic called the Hihking tells about "the family of Fuhi." This ancient story tells that the entire land was flooded—the mountains and everything. However, one family—Fuhi, his wife, three sons, and three daughters—escaped the great flood in a boat. It is claimed that he and his family were the only people alive on earth and repopulated the world. The Chinese consider this man the father of their civilization.

Babylon

Gilgamesh met an old man named Utnapishtim, who told him the following story. The gods came to Utnapishtim to warn him about a terrible flood that was coming. They instructed Utnapishtim to destroy his house and build a large ship. The ship was to be ten dozen cubits high, wide, and long. Utnapishtim was to cover the ship with pitch. He was supposed to take male and female animals of all kinds, his wife and family, provisions, etc. into the ship. Once the ship was completed the rain began falling intensely. The rain fell for six days and nights. Finally things calmed and the ship settled on the top of Mount Nisir. After the ship had rested for seven days, Utnapishtim let loose a dove. Since the land had not dried the dove returned. Next he sent a swallow, which also returned. Later he let loose a raven, which never returned since the ground had dried. Utnapishtim then left the ship.

Chaldean

There was a man by the name of Xisuthrus. The god Chronos warned Xisuthrus of a coming flood and told him to build a boat. The boat was to be five stadia by two stadia. In this boat Xisuthrus was to put his family, friends, and two of each animal (male and female). The flood came. When the waters started to recede, he let some birds loose. They came back and he noticed they had mud on their feet. He tried again with the same results. When he tried the third time, the birds did not return. Assuming the water had dried up, the people got out of the boat and offered sacrifices to the gods.

India

A long time ago lived a man named Manu. While washing himself, Manu saved a small fish from the jaws of a large fish. The fish told Manu, "If you care for me until I am full grown I will save you from terrible things to come." Manu asked what kind of terrible things. The fish told Manu that a great flood would soon come and destroy everything on the earth. The fish told Manu to put him in a clay jar for protection. The fish grew and each time he outgrew the clay jar Manu gave him a larger one. Finally the fish became a ghasha, one of the largest fish in the world. The fish instructed Manu to build a large ship since the flood was going to happen very soon. As the rains started Manu tied a rope from the ship to the ghasha. The fish guided the ship as the waters rose. The whole earth was covered by water. When the waters began subsiding the ghasha led Manu's ship to a mountaintop.

Greece

A long time ago, perhaps before the golden age was over, humans became proud. This bothered Zeus as they kept getting worse. Finally Zeus decided that he would destroy all humans. Before he did this Prometheus, the creator of humans, warned his human son, Deucalion, and his wife, Pyrrha. Prometheus then placed this couple in a large wooden chest. The rains started and lasted nine days and nights until the whole world was flooded except for the peaks of Mount Parnassus and Mount Olympus. Mount Olympus is the home of the gods. The wooden chest came to rest on Mount Parnassus. Deucalion and Pyrrha got out and saw that everything was flooded. They lived on provisions from the chest until the waters subsided. At Zeus' instruction they re-populated the earth.

Mexico

The Toltec natives have a legend that the original creation lasted for 1716 years and was destroyed by a flood, and only one family survived.

The Aztecs tell of a man named Tapi who lived a long time ago. He was a very pious man. The creator told Tapi to build a boat that he would live in. He was told that he should take his wife and a pair of every animal that was alive into this boat. Naturally everyone thought he was crazy. Then the rain started and the flood came. The men and animals tried to climb the mountains but the mountains became flooded as well. Finally the rain ended. Tapi decided that the water had dried up when he let a dove loose that did not return.

North America

The Ojibwe natives have lived in an area currently called Minnesota (where I once lived) since approximately 1400 AD and have a flood story that closely parallels the Biblical account. There came a time when the harmonious way of life did not continue. Men and women disrespected each other, families quarreled, and soon villages began arguing back and forth. This saddened Gitchie Manido (the Creator) greatly, but he waited. Finally, when it seemed there was no hope left, Creator decided to purify Mother Earth through the use of water. The water came, flooding the Earth, catching all of creation off guard. All but a few of each living thing died. Only Waynaboozhoo survived by floating on a log in the water with various animals.

The Delaware Indians say that in the pristine age, the world lived at peace; but an evil spirit came and caused a great flood. The earth was submerged. A few persons had taken refuge on the back of a turtle, so old that his shell had collected moss. A loon flew over their heads and was entreated to dive beneath the water and bring up land. It found only a bottomless sea. Then the bird flew far away, came back with a small portion of earth in its bill, and guided the tortoise to a place where there was a spot of dry land.

Inca

During the period of time called the Pachachama people became very evil. They got so busy coming up with and performing evil deeds they neglected the gods. Only those in the high Andes remained uncorrupted. Two brothers who lived in the highlands noticed their llamas acting strangely. They asked the llamas why and were told that the stars had told the llamas that a great flood was coming. This flood would destroy all the life on earth. The brothers took their families and flocks into a cave on the high mountains. It started to rain and continued for four months. As the water rose, the mountain grew, keeping its top above the water. Eventually the rain stopped and the waters receded. The mountain returned to its original height. The shepherds repopulated the earth. The llamas remembered the flood and that is why they prefer to live in the highland areas.

Perhaps the myths of this world have basis in actual events. Perhaps the quantum God's story is intertwined with the story of these mythological "gods."

Perhaps they were also expressions of matter from "His" energy field that is "himself." In other words, created beings perhaps on a higher frequency than human beings, thus with what would appear to be god-like powers to humans.

Perhaps they did follow a Biblical path of separation or rebellion from the "source" and came to this planet to disrupt the plans of the Source to heal the quantum rift in the universe.

Perhaps they did engage in genetic manipulation and engineering to contaminate the human race... and perhaps a universal flood was allowed to disrupt and destroy their work.

Perhaps that's why the world is filled with stories of a worldwide flood.

Perhaps that's why the geology of the Earth reflects the fact that at one time it was completely submerged.

My masked magician friend doesn't just make airplanes and swat team trucks disappear right before your eyes without a flood, but he sometimes shows you how simple sleight-of-hand illusions are done. Let me share the one he calls "the last straw" with you.

He threaded a bright red thread through a black cocktail straw and then showed all who were watching that it went all the way through by pulling it back and forth through the straw from both ends.

Then he folded the straw in half as his beautiful assistant appeared with a dangerous looking exacto knife. (Wow! Beautiful and armed and dangerous!) The masked man carefully accepted the knife; then holding the straw and string up together, he clearly cuts the straw in half for all to see. Instead of the two pieces falling to the ground... surprise, he suddenly produced the red, intact, and uncut thread!

I wanted to see how he did this, getting the feeling that I might be able to do it, too, if he showed me how. Sure enough, this one was much easier than walking on air, three stories up. So what was his secret? Well, it seems that before he came on stage, the masked man got ahold of the exacto knife. He used it to place a hidden slit from end to end in the straw, and when he folded the straw in half to cut it, he allowed the string to slip out of the straw and out of view in his hands. As the two pieces of the straw fell to the ground, he opened his hands with a flair and revealed the uncut red thread, safe and sound.

So what's the moral of our story? Well, even though things may seem cut off from each other, there may still be a thread of evidence connecting them. Perhaps it's like that with the stories of the Global Flood.

These seemingly diverse stories are all related when you break the code and look beneath the surface.

Even if there is no cover-up, the governments of the world do admit that they have no answers for a significant percentage of the UFO sightings, crop circles, and the like. To a reasonable mind, there is enough evidence to believe that not only have they been here but that we are again being visited by beings from another dimension. Why? I don't know but I sense it has something to do with lies, a web of lies. Could it be that the statement by the teacher in the Bible, Jesus, was referring to this condition when he answered his followers' question, "What will it be like when you return as the messiah of Israel?" "As it was in the days of Noah so it will be when I return." The gentile doctor, Luke, recorded that in his book Luke 17:26. Could that mean people living longer, genetic engineering going on, even aliens living on Earth as "gods"? As much as that sounds like science fiction there could be a thread of truth to it that connects it all.

The secret seems to be leaking out all over the world, but for whatever reason the US seems to be dragging its heels in telling the entire story.

On July 8, 1945, the *Roswell Daily Record* captured the world's attention with the headline, "RAAF Captures Flying Saucer on Ranch in Roswell Region." The article began, "The intelligence office of the 509th Bombardment group at Roswell Army Air Field announced at noon today that the field has come into possession of a flying saucer."

This was followed the next day, of course, by an official denial, trying to explain it away as a weather balloon, which started an era of preposterous stories and flawed explanations by the government talking heads blaming everything from mirages to swamp gas for the increasing number of sightings. Which was the truth? The space craft or the weather balloon?

"It was not a damn weather balloon—it was what it was billed when people first reported it," thirty-five-year CIA veteran Chase Brandon told the *Huffington Post*. Mr. Brandon said that in his opinion the craft was extraterrestrial in origin and that he didn't doubt for a minute the original report which included the recovery of alien bodies.

"One day, I was looking around in there and reading some of the titles that were mostly hand-scribbled summations of what was in the boxes. And there was one box that really caught my eye. It had one word on it: Roswell," he told the *Huffington Post*. "I took the box down, lifted the lid up, rummaged around inside it, put the box back on the shelf and said, 'My god, it really happened!'" Brandon was describing the event that changed his mind as he snooped around in a vault in Langley, Virginia. You can't blame him for snooping; after all, he was a spy.

He is not alone. The online version of the UK's Daily Mail has a story authored by Nike Pope last updated on June 30, 2007, where among interviews with other witnesses it releases a final affidavit signed by Walter Haut, the Roswell base Public Information Officer in 1947, not to be opened until his death [2002], he wrote, "Before leaving the base Col. Blanchard took me personally to Building 84, a B-29 hangar located on the east side of the tarmac, upon first approaching the building, I observed that it was under heavy guard both outside and inside. Once inside, I was permitted from a safe distance to first observe the object recovered north of town. It was approximately fifteen feet in length, not quite as wide, about six feet high, and more of an egg shape. Haut's "deathbed" confession goes on to state that the light was poor but that he saw what appeared to be a metallic object, with no windows, portholes, wings, tail section, or landing gear visible. Also from a distance, he was able to see a couple of bodies under a canvas tarpaulin. Only the heads extended from the covering, and he was not able to make out any features. The heads did appear larger than normal and the contour of the canvas over the bodies suggested the size of a ten-year-old child. He was convinced that he had personally observed some type of craft and its crew from outer space, and wanted to release the truth upon his death.

Why didn't he just say so back then? It is said that all military personnel were sworn to secrecy and all civilians were threatened with death and/or imprisonment if they talked about the event. For those who are interested there are many, many more affidavits and death bed confessions. Many of them were able to keep this secret for most of their lives. However, some of the details started leaking out in the 1970s. By the late 1980s the floodgates opened and over the next twenty years WWII vets felt their secrecy, or lack thereof, wouldn't affect their families anymore. Meyers Wahnee, a B-24 crewman in WWII and Roswell witness, said on his deathbed, "Whatever you do, don't believe the government. It really happened."
(http://en.wikipedia.org/wiki/Witness_accounts_of_the_Roswell_UFO_incident#cite_note-48)

It now seems that over 600 witnessed the "event," many who finally talked to researchers and family members on their deathbeds, and just a few years ago, the FBI released their files on the event on the official FBI website.

Moonwalker and Apollo 14 astronaut Edgar Mitchell has made various public statements about the reality of Roswell: "Make no mistake, Roswell happened. I've seen secret files which show the government knew about it—but decided not to tell the public. I wasn't convinced about the existence of aliens until I started talking to the military old-timers who were there at the time of Roswell. The more government documentation on aliens I was told about, the more convinced I became." Mitchell has also spoken about bodies: "A few insiders know the truth [...] and are studying the bodies that have been discovered." Mitchell added a cabal of insiders stopped briefing presidents after Kennedy. (John Earls,10-10-98 Magazine *The People.* "Scientist-astronaut Edgar Mitchell Reaffirms ET Visits to Earth Are Real.") (Waveney Moore, 2-18-04 *Tampa Bay Times,* "Astronaut: We've had Visitors.")

Here is a sampling of what is considered to be true now about the event. The following quotes are from Wikipedia but can be verified many times over from different sources. This is but one of many stories I have researched and believe as credible.

According to four sons of Lt. Col. Marion M. Magruder, their father told them on his deathbed of being shown crash wreckage and a live alien at Wright Field, Ohio, in mid or late July 1947. He had been attending Air War College at Maxwell Field, Montgomery, Alabama, composed solely of the best high-ranking officers in the various services, including generals. They were flown up to Wright Field to get their opinion on a matter of utmost urgency and importance. There the surprised officers were told about the recovery to Wright Field of an extraterrestrial spaceship that had crashed just two weeks previously near Roswell. Wreckage was brought out for them to examine. Then they were taken to another room and shown a surviving alien. According to the description from Mike Magruder, his father said the "creature" was under five feet (1.5m) tall, "human-like" but with longer arms, larger eyes, and an oversized, hairless head. It had a slit for a mouth and two holes but no appendages for a nose and ears. There was no question that it "came from another planet."

But who or what were these alien bodies they recovered, one which was still alive it now seems? Were they aliens, gods, or devils, or none or all of the above? Good question! Let's take a walk on the wild side for a moment and look at some interesting numbers… mathematical codes, you might say, and some interesting possibilities.

When is an Eagle a Phoenix? Would you believe 1947?

I'll explain, but you really need to read Thomas Horn's books to grasp the entire story. One book is called *Apollyon Rising 2012* and another is *Nepilim Stargates*. For now here is something to stimulate thought.

While it is true that the USA was founded as a Christian nation by Christian founding fathers, it is also true, it seems, that a darker element has waged a clandestine war for the heart and soul of this nation since its inception.

An analysis of the American seal shows a number of occult and Masonic symbols in particular, the so-called American eagle. Some consider the American eagle upon the Great Seal as simply a conventionalized phoenix. The word phoenix derives from the Greek name for "Phoenicians," ancient people who inhabited the East coast of the Mediterranean Sea. Although named Phoenicians (meaning redness by the Greeks), the Phoenicians referred to themselves as Sidonians.

Phoenicia was the land of descent of the "Sons of God" described in Genesis 6, according to the history of every ancient culture in the Middle East; Phoenicia was the first place where beings from heaven came to the earth.

Through the influence of these heavenly beings and their offspring, men became gifted with knowledge surpassing any that had yet existed. But then came the flood (in Noah's day) and symbolically the Phoenix perished. The heavenly and supernatural bird, keeper of secrets of the past and future, was consumed in the fire of its own making.

In other words, the knowledge given to man from heaven was lost in a global cataclysm. According to Genesis 6, the destruction of Earth by the flood was in response to the interaction of the Sons of God with the daughters of Adam.

In Spiritual Numerology, '33' symbolizes the highest spiritual conscious attainable by the human being. However 33 and 3 are also featured prominently in occult doctrine. To the ancient cultures the calculation of speed and location under the heavens is considered to be the highest form of sacred knowledge from antiquity. Navigation unites time with space and the heavens with the earth. The number "3" is essential to this process. Without the geometry of the three-sided triangle, establishing location and distance on a map or "triangulation" is impossible.

It is interesting that 33.33 degrees of the great circle of the earth represents 2012 nautical miles from the equator.

The impact area near Roswell lays 33° north latitude, at a distance 2,012 miles from the equator. When the latitude of the impact site 33° north is multiplied by the universal mathematical constant PI, (3.1415926572...) the result is 104°, and that turns out to be the longitude of the impact site. The value of PI is one of the most important numbers of geometry. Without an understanding of this number, the science of building, architecture, and navigation is not possible. So, based on the place of impact and some history the Roswell event and location appear not to be an accident.

The Roswell event appears to be a message left at 33 °. One third of anything is 33 percent. 1/3rd of 100 percent is 33.333333. There is an ancient text that reveals the connection between the messengers and number 33. In this text the number 33 or 1/3rd is explained as the actual percentage of rebellious angels that were "cast" to the Earth. The Bible agrees. Satan is also clearly associated with this same number. According to the illuminated elite, as the first messiah came to establish the Kingdom of

Heaven, the second illuminated messiah will establish a New World Order under his rule. So it is assumed that the chosen location of the first connection of heaven with the Earth on Mt. Hermon at 33.3rd degrees and now the second advent of the phoenix again at 33 degrees and 2012 miles from the equator sets in motion the final phase of a new world order that is to begin to take place behind the scenes in 2012, as this phoenix arises again at 33.3 degrees in Roswell.

To understand it all you need to read some of Thomas Horn's work. They are great, insightful, and accurate! Oh, be sure to have a calculator handy.

Mount Hermon in Phoenicia, the first location of extraterrestrial influence with man, lies precisely at 33.33° north 33.33° east, 2,012 miles from the equator and 2,012 miles from the prime meridian. The sacred number 33 multiplied by Pi just happens to produce the location where a flying saucer crashed landed in 1947.

Yep, there's a code for sure... who or what is it from?

Was it a true code? In the clandestine world there are codes and false codes and dummy codes and a host of counterfeits for every original. It is a nessesecity to know the source of your code to determine its authenticity. Perhaps in time we will know.

I used to think that you must be an atheist to believe in aliens. As I studied and asked questions of more and more people I found that to be totally false!

So what do the religious people think?

Is the Vatican in touch with visitors from other planets? Some sources say they are... some in the church say they are demons and some say they are fellow "children of God."

Thomas Horn and co-author Chris Putnam say in their new book that the Vatican is awaiting an alien savior. The two of them recently appeared on a TV program called *It's Supernatural*, hosted by an American Messianic Jew named Sid Roth. The show explores in a rational manner the supernatural world, or should we call it the extra dimensional world? I find Sid's show interesting and watch it when I can, and I "just happened" to be watching the first week of April 2013 when Mr. Horn and Mr. Putnam were guests.

Complete with videos, Mr. Putman and Mr. Horn recounted their visit to the mountain side in Arizona where LUCIFER resides. This Lucifer is a very powerful telescope, said to be as powerful as the Hubble telescope. It is operated by the Vatican observatory and perched on the mountain top at the Mount Graham International Observatory. I didn't know that so I decided to sit down and listen. I did know through my research that the Vatican observatory in Italy was a reality and that it was (among other things) exploring the possibility of extraterrestrial life and it's contact with Earth, but I didn't know that they had an observatory in the USA on a mountain top in Arizona and that it was tasked to search for extra-terrestrial life. As it turns out it has been looking for them since the late 1980s, along with the observatories in and around Rome. I thought to myself—Lucifer in Arizona! Sounds like a song Charlie Daniels could make into a hit!

Most of us know that the Biblical Satan was once called Lucifer by the God of Creation until his rebellion and eviction from Heaven. What many do not know is that his original name Lucifer means "light bearer," and that he was the highest of the order of extra dimensional beings… the closest being to God that God ever created. So with the benefit of the doubt, perhaps that is what the Vatican astronomers were thinking about when they named it.

What is even more astonishing is that in their book, Tom Horn and Chris Putnam say that the Vatican is awaiting an alien savior.

The claims in the book, called *Exo-Vaticana: Petrus Romanus, Project LUCIFER, and the Vatican's astonishing plan for the arrival of an alien savior* are the result of research the two authors conducted at the Mount Graham International Observatory. Horn and Putnam were granted permission to visit the observatory on Mount Graham, which hosted the Vatican Advanced Technology Telescope (VATT) in September 2012.

"The records in the Vatican go back centuries," said Putnam, who is a theologian. "I read two chapters of history concerning the

Vatican's interest in extra-terrestrials. They have a whole theology developed around what they call the Principle of Plentitude, meaning anything God could do he would do," said Putnam. "So they consider the existence of aliens the inevitable consequence of God's omnipotence." Not only were they able to discuss the study of deep space with the Jesuit astronomers there, but they also gained access to one of the top Vatican astronomers in Rome. Brother Guy Consolmagno, who has also been called the papal astronomer, told the authors some astounding information during five interviews.

"He says without apology that very soon the nations of the world are going to look to the aliens for their salvation," said Horn.

Consomagno also gave the authors private Vatican documents which reveal much of the thinking of high-level theologians and astronomers within the Church. According to Horn, these documents do show that they believe that we are soon to be visited by an alien savior from another world. WOW!

Well, the two authors did predict the resignation of Pope Benedict XVI and the coming of a final pope preceding the second coming of Jesus! So far they are half right. Interesting indeed! The proof was mounting that you didn't have to be an atheist to believe in little green men; if we believe the Bible references to aliens—they weren't little or green—they were powerful fallen angels that gave rise to the giants of old. The "gods" of so-called mythology. Thought provoking, isn't it?

I had already read much about Cardinal Balducci and watched many of his videos as well. Monsignor Corrado Balducci is a theologian member of the Vatican Curia (governing body), and an insider close to the last pope. He has gone on Italian national television several times, including recent months, to proclaim that extraterrestrial contact is a real phenomenon. (You can find his videos on the internet as I did.) Balducci provides an analysis of extraterrestrials that he feels is consistent with the Catholic Church's understanding of theology. All in the church might not agree!

Monsignor Balducci emphasizes that extraterrestrial encounters "are NOT demonic, they are NOT due to psychological impairment, they are NOT a case of entity attachment, but these encounters deserve to be studied carefully." Since Monsignor Balducci is a demonology expert and consultant to the Vatican, and since the Catholic Church has historically demonized many new phenomena that were poorly understood, his stating that the Church does not censure these encounters is all the more remarkable, and frankly a bit confusing when one compares it to the words of Genesis 6, the book of Enoch, and the historical accounts of Josephus!

Did you notice there is no question as to whether they are real or not? Simply who they might be and it appears that Balducci, a prominent religious figure, has exposed a view that is not in harmony with biblical and historical records. These records recount how humanity's first encounter of the third kind was with aliens, yes, but they were expatriates of the place we call Heaven. They were also created beings of the Great Creator God, but their presence here was nefarious and ended with the Creator God wiping out there descendants with a flood and executing an Earth restart with Noah's family that contained no "alien" DNA. So what are we now to believe? That they somehow "repented" and again joined forces with the Creator God and when they appear to us now we are to believe them? Their boss Lucifer is also called the father of lies... so probably not!

So we have seen what some in the largest Christian denomination believe; what about other religions? Do Muslims believe in aliens visiting Earth?

Yes and no. It depends on the spokesperson. It seems the Imams of Islam share one thing with other religions—they disagree with each other on certain points. Some emphatically say there are not aliens while others use common proof texts to support their belief that aliens do exist and were also created by Allah.

Are aliens real? I watched an Imam on YouTube answer this question this way:

Allah knows best... angels, jinn, humans, animals, and aliens are throughout the world. If Allah wills it... all will worship him.

Another believes aliens exist and have their own way of life. He says this is not to be confused with the jinns or angels. The strongest verse in support of his view in the Quran is in Surah 42:9. "And among his signs are the heavens and the earth and the living creatures he has scattered through them and he has the power to gather them together at his will..."

Another points to the Holy Quran 16:8. "And He (Allah) creates things of which (today) you have no knowledge (could things on Earth or Heaven as well)."

"Of course Muslims believe in aliens and beings on other planets.

It is usually not discussed among the majority, but among people of knowledge they do understand. And yes, the whole universe will eventually all believe in Allah."

It's important to understand that Muslims believe that Allah has created other beings, some we know about and some we do not know about. It is also important to understand that when people think of the term "alien" they think of Hollywood's version of aliens.

The following are verses from the Quran supporting this:

Surah 51:47 informs us, "And it is We who have built the universe with (Our creative) power; and, verily, it is We who are steadily expanding it."

Surah 55:33-34, we are addressed, "O ye assembly of Jinn and men! If it be you can pass beyond the regions of the heavens and the earth, pass ye! Not without authority will ye be able to pass! Then which of the favors of your Lord will ye deny?"

Surah 16:8 says, "And (it is He Who creates) horses and mules for you to ride and He will yet create things of which (today) you have no knowledge."

So I wondered what is a jinn? Well, according to the encyclopedia, they are described as spiritual creatures or genies mentioned in the Qur'ān and Islamic mythology who inhabit an unseen world in dimensions beyond the visible universe of humans. The jinn, humans, and angels make up the three sapient creations of God. Like human beings, the jinn can also be good, evil, or neutrally benevolent and hence have free will like humans and unlike angels.

One Imam described the jinn this way: "The root meaning of the word jinn is something hidden or which cannot be seen, meaning we humans cannot see them. Some jinns are Muslim and some aren't. Allah has given jinn the same free will as humans."

I have one note of disagreement with the encyclopedia. We have seen in Genesis that there was free will for the angels and some rebelled and "fell," a story shared in Judaism, Islam, and Christianity. So it would appear angels have free will as well…

What about the elder religion of Judaism? According to a Jewish scientist, who is also an expert in Torah codes, it wouldn't be a tough swap to replace angels (which means messengers) with aliens so long as those messengers were acting in accordance with God's directions.

For Christianity, though, the question arises as to whether aliens need their own Jesus to die on their world for their sins. Father Gabriel Funes, Vatican spokesman and director of the Vatican Observatory near Rome states, "intelligent beings created by God could exist in outer space." A respected scientist who collaborates with universities around the world, he says the search for forms of extraterrestrial life does not contradict belief in God. The official Vatican newspaper headlines his article "Aliens Are My Brother." It goes on to state that just as there are multiple forms of life on earth, so there could exist intelligent beings in outer space created by God. And some aliens could even be free from original sin, he speculates. While this may be true, the financial reality may be that if people think the Bible or our religious history has been impacted by any kind of alien intervention, contributions to the Church may be seriously diminished.

World religions will most likely be faced with this conundrum soon: just who are these aliens and do we believe what they say?

Roswell may have been the kick-off for the end game, but the sightings of UFOs is hardly restricted to that area… what "started again" in New Mexico has spread to all of the countries of the world. Just as the ancient world had its stories of winged serpent gods, etc., in nearly every culture the sightings of modern UFOs is now a worldwide phenomena.

On a Fox news broadcast, Shep Smith can be seen talking with a congressional candidate about a government released video that shows evidence of eleven UFOs over Mexico City. They discuss what perecentage of Americans believe in the UFO phenomena and that world governments are looking to the USA for the time to release the proof of their existence!

Appearing on *Jimmy Kimmel Live*, former President Clinton stated that he "would not be at all surprised if there are aliens."

On CNN Wolf Blitzer discussed the issue at a gathering of solid UFO observers in Washington, DC, with people from the different branches of government—airforce, intelligence community, etc.— with one thing in common: they are retired.

It would seem that the "three great religions" may have something in common. By definition they accept that a Creator designed the Cosmos and that part of His creation, the angels, suffered a rebellion and were evicted from the heavenly dimension. Their leader, Lucifer, enticed the human race to join his rebellion, and with some of his fellow rebellious angels, they interbred and created another race of hybrids. The Creator decided to wipe them out because of their debased and evil behavior and perhaps because the plan was to wipe out the human race with their hybridization program.

There are several other extra-biblical sources that speak about fallen angels procreating with humans. Enoch, Noah's grandfather, and Flavius Josephus a Jewish/ Roman historian, and friend of Caesar, both talk about it in their books. Here is some of what the historian Josephus says, from *Antiquities of the Jews*, Book I:

1. NOW this posterity of Seth continued to esteem God as the Lord of the universe, and to have an entire regard to virtue, for seven generations; but in process of time they were perverted, and forsook the practices of their forefathers; and did neither pay those honors to God which were appointed them, nor had they any concern to do justice towards men. But for what degree of zeal they had formerly shown for virtue, they now showed by their actions a double degree of wickedness, whereby they made God to be their enemy. For many angels (Fallen Angels that accompanied Lucifer) of God accompanied with women, and begat sons that proved unjust, and despisers of all that was good, on account of the confidence they had in their own strength; for the tradition is, that these men did what resembled the acts of those whom the Grecians call giants (gods). There it is, folks. Josephus puts the cross hairs on the original ancient aliens! *But Noah was very uneasy at what they did; and being displeased at their conduct, persuaded them to change their dispositions and their acts for the better: but seeing they did not yield to him, but were slaves to their wicked pleasures, he was afraid they would kill him, together with his wife and children, and those they had married; so he departed out of that land.*

2. Now God loved this man for his righteousness: yet he not only condemned those other men for their wickedness, but determined to destroy the whole race of mankind, and to make another race that should be pure from wickedness; and cutting short their lives, and making their years not so many as they formerly lived, but one hundred and twenty only, he turned the dry land into sea; and thus were all these men destroyed: but Noah alone was saved; And thus was Noah, with his family, preserved. Now he was the tenth from Adam, as being the son of Lamech, whose father was Mathusela; he was the son of Enoch, the son of Jared; and Jared was the son of Malaleel, who, with many of his sisters, were the children of Cainan, the son of Enos. Now Enos was the son of Seth, the son of Adam.

3. This calamity happened in the six hundredth year of Noah's government, [age,] in the second month, called by the Macedonians Dius, but by the Hebrews Marchesuan: for so did they order their year in Egypt. But Moses appointed that · Nisan, which is the same with Xanthicus, should be the first month for their festivals, because he brought them out of Egypt in that month.

4. For indeed Seth was born when Adam was in his two hundred and thirtieth year, who lived nine hundred and thirty years. Seth begat Enos in his two hundred and fifth year; who, when he had lived nine hundred and twelve years, delivered the government to Cainan his son, whom he had in his hundred and ninetieth year. He lived nine hundred and five years. Cainan, when

he had lived nine hundred and ten years, had his son Malaleel, who was born in his hundred and seventieth year. This Malaleel, having lived eight hundred and ninety-five years, died, leaving his son Jared, whom he begat when he was in his hundred and sixty-fifth year. He lived nine hundred and sixty-two years; and then his son Enoch succeeded him, who was born when his father was one hundred and sixty-two-years-old. Now he, when he had lived three hundred and sixty-five years, departed and went to God; whence it is that they have not written down his death. Now Mathusela, the son of Enoch, who was born to him when he was one hundred- and sixty-five-years-old, had Lamech for his son when he was one hundred- and eighty-seven years of age; to whom he delivered the government, when he had retained it nine hundred and sixty-nine years. Now Lamech, when he had governed seven hundred and seventy-seven years, appointed Noah, his son, to be ruler of the people, who was born to Lamech when he was one hundred- and eighty-two-years-old, and retained the government nine hundred and fifty years. These years collected together make up the sum before set down. But let no one inquire into the deaths of these men; for they extended their lives together with their children and grandchildren; but let him have regard to their births only.

5. When God gave the signal, and it began to rain, the water poured down forty entire days, till it became fifteen cubits higher than the earth; which was the reason why there was no greater number preserved, since they had no place to fly to. When the rain ceased, the water did but just begin to abate after one hundred and

fifty days, (that is, on the seventeenth day of the seventh month,) it then ceasing to subside for a little while. After this, the ark rested on the top of a certain mountain in Armenia; which, when Noah understood, he opened it; and seeing a small piece of land about it, he continued quiet, and conceived some cheerful hopes of deliverance. But a few days afterward, when the water was decreased to a greater degree, he sent out a raven, as desirous to learn whether any other part of the earth were left dry by the water, and whether he might go out of the ark with safety; but the raven, finding all the land still overflowed, returned to Noah again. And after seven days he sent out a dove, to know the state of the ground; which came back to him covered with mud, and bringing an olive branch: hereby Noah learned that the earth was become clear of the flood. So after he had staid seven more days, he sent the living creatures out of the ark; and both he and his family went out, when he also sacrificed to God, and feasted with his companions. However, the Armenians call this place, (GREEK) The Place of Descent; for the ark being saved in that place, its remains are shown there by the inhabitants to this day.

Now notice this: Josephus makes mention of the fact that various different cultures all make mention of the Great Flood.

6. Now all the writers of barbarian histories make mention of this flood, and of this ark; among whom is Berosus the Chaldean. For when he is describing the circumstances of the flood, he goes on thus: "It is said there is still some part of this ship in Armenia, (now Turkey) at the mountain of the Cordyaeans; and that some people carry off pieces of the bitumen, which they take away, and use chiefly as amulets for the averting of mischiefs." Hieronymus the Egyptian also, who wrote the Phoenician Antiquities, and Mnaseas, and a great many more, make mention of the same. Nay, Nicolaus of Damascus, in his ninety-sixth book, hath a particular relation about them; where he speaks thus: *"There is a great mountain in Armenia, over Minyas, called Baris, upon which it is reported that many who fled at the time of the Deluge were saved; and that one who was carried in an ark came on shore upon the top of it; and that the remains of the timber were a great while preserved. This might be the man about whom Moses the legislator of the Jews wrote.*

Perhaps we have been too eager to throw out the myths of old.

Perhaps the ancient alien theorists are mostly right.

Perhaps the answers really are right there in the Bible. Research shows that it is the only book of records that has been preserved as accurately and carefully... despite what my friends the atheists and fellow skeptics say.

Perhaps what we found here are not Gods, but counterfeits, demi-gods, imposters! Certainly no quantum all-powerful God among them!

Perhaps we found more codes here, though. We saw the mathematical codes pi, phi, and e in the texts. We also saw that the sacred number of 33 x pi warns us of the touch down spots of the imposters, then and now! We saw the ancient name of God hidden coded in our very DNA; maybe there are more codes to be found? The great scientist, Sir Isaac Newton, thought so. While he was busy discovering the universal law of gravitation, he was also searching out hidden meanings in the Bible and pursuing a hidden code within its texts.

Born on Christmas day in 1642, the same year that Galileo died, Newton discovered the binomial theorem, the method of fluxions (calculus), the law of gravitation and the composite nature of light—all before age thirty. The foundations of modern astronomy and physics are still largely based on theories Newton presented more than 300 years ago, and guess what? Members of a society named after him have discovered the code he never found.

Is there any compatibility between Josephus, the historian, and Caesar's friend, the Bible, and modern genetics? Is it "out of Africa" or "Out of the Planes of Shinar" in modern Iraq?

In every outthrust headland, in every curving beach,
in every grain of sand there is the story of the Earth.
  ~ Rachel Carson

Chapter 7
Flood Gates, Star Gates, and Genetics

Why waste your money looking up your family tree?
Just go into politics and your opponents will do it for you.

~ Mark Twain

Modern geneticists say that about 4000 years ago there was an event that created a chokepoint in our human genetic history. Let's go back in time and see if Josephus says anything about an event like that. [*Antiquities of the Jews* by Jospehus]

1. Now the sons of Noah were three—Shem, Japhet, and Ham—born one hundred years before the Deluge. These first of all descended from the mountains into the plains, and fixed their habitation there; and persuaded others who were greatly afraid of the lower grounds on account of the flood, and so were very loath to come down from the higher places, to venture to follow their examples. Now the plain in which they first dwelt was called Shinar. God also commanded them to send colonies abroad, for the thorough peopling of the earth, that they might not raise seditions among themselves, but might cultivate a great part of the earth, and enjoy its fruits after a plentiful manner. But they were so ill instructed that they did not obey God; for which reason they fell into calamities, and were made sensible, by experience, of what sin they had been guilty: for when they flourished with a numerous youth, God admonished them again to send out colonies; but they, imagining the prosperity they enjoyed was not derived from the favor of God, but supposing that their own power was the proper cause of the plentiful condition they were in, did not obey him. Nay, they added to this their disobedience to the Divine will, the suspicion that they were therefore ordered to send out separate colonies, that, being divided asunder, they might the more easily be Oppressed.

2. Now it was Nimrod who excited them to such an affront and contempt of God. He was the grandson of Ham, the son of Noah, a bold man, and of great strength of hand. He persuaded them not to ascribe it to God, as if it was through his means they were happy, but to believe that it was their own courage which procured that happiness. He also gradually changed the government into tyranny, seeing no other way of turning men from the fear of God, but to bring them into a constant dependence on his power. He also said he would be revenged on God, if he should have a mind to drown the world again; for that he would build a tower too high for the waters to be able to reach and that he would avenge himself on God for destroying their forefathers! (Nephilim?)

3. Now the multitude were very ready to follow the determination of Nimrod, and to esteem it a piece of cowardice to submit to God; and they built a tower, (perhaps a pyramid with a Stargate on top) neither sparing any pains, nor being in any degree negligent about the work: and, by reason of the multitude of hands employed in it, it grew very high, sooner than any one could expect; but the thickness of it was so great, and it was so strongly built, that thereby its great height seemed, upon the view, to be less than it really was. It was built of burnt brick, cemented together with mortar, made of bitumen, that it might not be liable to admit water.

When God saw that they acted so madly, he did not resolve to destroy them utterly, since they were not grown wiser by the destruction of the former sinners; but he caused a tumult among them, by producing in them divers languages, and causing that, through the multitude of those languages, they should not be able to understand one another. The place wherein they built the tower is now called Babylon, because of the confusion of that language which they readily understood before; for the Hebrews mean by the word Babel, confusion. The Sibyl also makes mention of this tower, and of the confusion of the language, when she says thus: "When all men were of one language, some of them built a high tower, (stargate?) as if they would thereby ascend up to heaven, but the gods sent storms of wind and overthrew the tower, and gave every one his peculiar language; and for this reason it was that the city was called Babylon." But as to the plan of Shinar, in the country of Babylonia, Hestiaeus mentions it, when he says thus: "Such of the priests as were saved, took the sacred vessels of Jupiter Enyalius, and came to Shinar of Babylonia."

This is the area of modern Iraq. It is also the area where ancient Sumaria sprung up and the "gods from above came down." Where the Annunaki held court. Clearly the ancient aliens didn't give up even with the flood that wiped out most of their descendants. Is it possible that the fallen angels returned to the grandsons of Noah and incited another rebellion? You would think hearing from their parents what the "false gods" had caused would have been enough to send them packing, but time dulls the memory and as it says in Josephus' writing "they were poorly instructed." Unfortunately, it seems that due to their lack of good instruction, it was back to the future, and into the same mess that had so recently caused the destruction of the world. Are those who do not remember history doomed to repeat it?

I propose that if we are to ever move into a higher place of enlightenment and spirituality as a human race we must learn to learn... from both science and history. We must watch what comes from science as we move into the future and we must keep looking back to make sure we are on course, not circling around to repeat our past.

With that in mind, let's look into what our modern science has discovered in light of history. What can we learn about a quantum God from looking at our modern genome project through Josephus' view of history?

Noah and the Old World in Light of Modern Genetics

The first thing that jumped out at me was that the evolutionary map of world migrations is startlingly close to ancient historical writings of Josephus and biblical accounts of a single dispersal of people from the "plains of Shinar" and the Tower of Babel. The evolutionary "Out of Africa" theory tells us there was a single dispersal of people, centered near and travelling through the Middle East, with three main mitochondrial lineages. What is a mitochondrial lineage?

Although most DNA is packaged in chromosomes within the nucleus, mitochondria also have a small amount of their own DNA. This genetic material is known as mitochondrial DNA or mtDNA. The mitochondria are the power plants of the cells. After the digestive system converts the food into a form that can be distributed by the blood, they take it and further transform it to a form that the cell can use. The mitochondria play a part in numerous other cellular functions including the production of substances such as cholesterol and heme, a component of hemoglobin, that incredibly complex molecule we looked at earlier that carries oxygen in the blood. Mitochondrial DNA contains 37 genes, all of which are essential for normal mitochondrial function. Thirteen of these genes provide instructions for making enzymes. The remaining genes provide instructions for making molecules called transfer RNAs (tRNAs) and ribosomal RNAs (rRNAs), which are chemical cousins of DNA. These types of RNA help assemble protein building blocks (amino acids) into functioning proteins.

But what does mitochondrial DNA have to do with family tree genetics?

Well, mitochondrial DNA is passed down from the mother to the children, because a father's mitochondrial DNA (mtDNA) is destroyed at fertilization, so a child inherits only the mother's mitochondrial DNA, thus preserving the maternal link to the ancient past. How about that for women's rights!

Noah had three sons who each had one wife; three sources of mitochondrial DNA at a "single dispersal" point in time, just like the "Out of Africa" evolutionary theory says. But what about Noah's wife? According to the Biblical record, Noah and his wife didn't have any more children after the flood. So could it be that the "Out of Africa" folks are part right and part wrong? Probably, aren't we all? How about the same theory, with a slight change? A chokepoint in the mountains of Turkey, where the Ark landed, and the dispersal point down the hill on the plains of Shinar in what we now call Iraq?

Three main mitochondrial lineages, perhaps the families of the three sons AND wives of Noah? That slight modification gives us a check list that matches in every detail the historical account of the Tower of Babel! Every item on that list is something directly predicted by the Tower of Babel account in the Bible as well.

It may come as a surprise to hear that there is abundant evidence that the entire human race may have come from two people just a few thousand years ago (Adam and Eve perhaps?), that there was a serious population crash (chokepoint) in the recent past (like at the time of the Flood), and that there was a single dispersal of people across the world after that! (The Tower of Babel story fits!) It surprises me even more to learn that much of this evidence comes from evolutionary scientists. In fact, an abundant testimony to biblical history has been uncovered by modern geneticists. It is there for anyone to see, if they know where to look!

Permit me to take you onto a road less traveled as we look at the science of genetics through the lenses of history as recorded by Flaviaus Josephus and others and yes... the Bible. It is often the 700 pound gorilla in the room that is ignored. I suggest that you don't have to take it as gospel or get religious, but have an open mind and look for reasonable facts and information... that's what I did. Clearly there is some evidence that we must consider, or at least respect.

When looking for the genetics of the ancients, the most important places to look are in the Y chromosome (which is only found in males and which is passed on directly from father to son) and in the mitochondrial DNA, that small loop of DNA that we inherit from our mothers. Remember males do not pass it on to their children. Together, these two pieces of DNA record some startling facts about our past. There it is—the balance that nature always has. The yin and the yang, "The rest of the story" as Paul Harvey used to sign off with! Looking at the record of our mitochondrial DNA from Mom and our Y chromosomes from Dad, we can get a pretty good idea of our ancient family tree.

Over the last decade, a vast amount of information has been collected that allows us to answer questions we could not even consider a few decades ago. The tools of modern genetics allow us to specifically ask questions about history, for our genes carry a record that reflects where we came from and how we got where we are. The tools at our disposal are more powerful than at any other time in history, post flood anyway.

Creation and Genetics

There are two short passages in the Creation account we can use to draw some conclusions about human genetic history.

"And the Lord God formed man out of the dust of the ground, and breathed into his nostrils the breath of life; and the man became a living being." Gen 2:7

"And the Lord God caused a deep sleep to fall on Adam, and he slept; and he took one of his ribs, and closed up the flesh in its place. Then the rib which the Lord God had taken from the man he made into a woman, and He brought her to the man." Gen 2:21–22

These simple statements have profound implications. If true, they would seem to put a limit on the amount of diversity we should find in people living today. The Bible clearly says the human race started out with two people only. But here is an important question for you to consider! How different were these two people? There is an intriguing possibility that Eve was a clone of Adam. The science of cloning involves taking DNA from an organism and using it to manufacture an almost perfect copy of the original. In the Creation story, God is taking a piece of flesh, with cells, organelles, and, importantly, Adam's DNA, and using it to manufacture a woman. Of course, she could not be an exact clone, because she was a lady! But consider this hypothetical... what if God had taken Adam's genome and used it to manufacture Eve? All he would have had to do was to leave out Adam's Y chromosome and double his X chromosome and, there you go—Adam's perfect mate.

Of course, I do not know if Eve was genetically identical to Adam. The only reason I bring this up is because we have two possibilities in the biblical model of human genetic history. Some variables to consider in the theory: one original genome or two. Either result is still vastly different from the most popular evolutionary models. In the interest of scientific truth, though, it makes sense to give the historians and the Bible account equal time and consideration. If it can't stand then throw it out, but it appears that not only can it stand the test of science, it takes less "faith" to "believe" it in the end.

Your genome is like a biological equivalent of Wikipedia in your cells! Like the former printed hard copy encyclopedias, the genome is broken down into volumes—volume A through Z—called chromosomes, but you have two copies of each volume (with the exception of the X and Y chromosomes; women have two Xs and men have one X and one Y). Imagine comparing two duplicate volumes side by side and finding that one word in a particular sentence is spelled differently in each volume. Those with the secret science glasses on will be able to see that if Eve was a clone of Adam, there would have been, at most, two possible variants at any point in the genome. If Eve was not a clone, however, there would have been, at most, four possible variants at any point in the genome (because each of the original chromosomes came in four copies). The Y and the X from Dad, and two more Xs from Mom. This still allows for a lot of diversity overall, but it restricts the variation at any one spot to 2, 3, or 4 original readings.

The scientific method always demands that we periodically stop and ask this question: Does this fit the evidence? In this case, yes... absolutely! Most variable places in the genome come in two versions and these versions are spread out across the world. There are some highly variable places that seem to contradict this, but most of these could be due to mutations that occurred in the different subpopulations after the Babel event.

I remember a genome study in New York City. It was astounding to watch as participants were matched to others who were most closely related genetically. One "genome family" started with an African American, an Irish immigrant, and a Filipino American all with nearly identical genomes. Watching this on television was truly a myth buster moment!

This should come as no surprise to us now though, not after Chapter Four. "God Eternal within" imprinted on every strand of

DNA in the world! That was a powerful moment in time for me when I realized that perhaps there was indeed a designer, an artist, and that He had sculpted us out of clay and then signed His work of art on our DNA!

When I let that sink in along with the visual diversity yet extreme genetic similarity that I saw on the "Genome Special," I experienced another "aha" moment: essentially all of the genetic variation among people today could have been carried within two people, even if you discount mutations that occurred after our dispersion across the globe. We are all more alike than we are diverse, inside at least.

Historical Flood and Genetics

In the Biblical Creation story, there are only a few verses in the account of the Flood to draw from. As usual it is short and sweet. But these verses are profound.

There were ten generations from Adam to Noah. Ten generations into current human history a bottleneck occurred, a chokepoint. From untold numbers of people, the entire world population was reduced to eight souls with only three reproducing couples. From "Creation" until the flood was a span of approximately 2500 years.

"Noah, with his family, preserved. Now he was the tenth from Adam, as being the son of Lamech, whose father was Mathusela; he was the son of Enoch, the son of Jared; and Jared was the son of Malaleel, who, with many of his sisters, were the children of

Cainan, the son of Enos. Now Enos was the son of Seth, the son of Adam."… Flavius Josephus

"So Noah, with his sons, his wife, and his sons' wives, went into the ark because of the waters of the flood." Gen 7:7

"Now the sons of Noah who went out of the ark were Shem, Ham, and Japheth… These three were the sons of Noah, and from these the whole earth was populated." Gen 9:18–19

We can draw many important deductions from these statements. For instance, based on Genesis 7 and 9, how many Y chromosomes were on the Ark? The answer: one. Yes, there were four men, but Noah gave his Y chromosome to each of his sons. Unless there was a mutation (entirely possible), each of the sons carried the exact same Y chromosome. We do not know how much mutation occurred prior to the flood. With the long life spans of the antediluvian humans, it may be reasonable to assume little mutation had taken place, but all of Creation, including the human genome, had been "cursed," so it may not be wise to conclude that there was no mutation prior to the Flood. The amount of mutation may be a moot point, however, for if it occurred, the Flood should have wiped out most traces of it (all of it in the case of the Y chromosome).

How many mitochondrial DNA lineages were on the Ark? The answer: three. Well, four really, but according to historical and Biblical records Noah's wife didn't have any more children after the Flood (in this case specifically, girl children). And notice the claim in Gen 9:19, "These three were the sons of Noah, and from these the whole earth was populated." This is a strong indication that Noah's wife did not contribute anything else to the world's population. At first glance, we expect a maximum of three mitochondrial lineages in the current world population. Scientists looking at the Creation Theory say there is a chance that there could be less, if there was very little mutation before the Flood or if several of the daughters-in-law were closely related. At most, we do not expect more than four.

My belief that interspecies and interdimensional genetic engineering was a reason for the abrupt end to the pre-deluvian world could be a wildcard. However the reason given in the Bible for saving Noah and his family appears to be the purity and wholeness of his human DNA.

"These are the generations of Noah: Noah was a just man and perfect in his generations, and Noah walked with God. And Noah begat three sons, Shem, Ham, and Japheth. The earth also was corrupt before God," KJVGen. 6:9

"Perfect" in the sense that his DNA was not mutated or contaminated with "ancient alien" DNA like the rest of the population may have been.

"Now God loved this man for his righteousness: yet he not only condemned those other men for their wickedness, but determined to destroy the whole race of mankind, and to make another race that should be pure from wickedness; and cutting

short their lives, and making their years not so many as they formerly lived, but one hundred and twenty only, he turned the dry land into sea; and thus were all these men destroyed: but Noah alone was saved; And thus was Noah, with his family, preserved."
… Flavius Josephus

So let's now figure, hypothetically, how many X chromosome lineages would have been on the Ark? That depends. If you count it all up, you get eight. If, by chance, Noah's wife passed on the same X chromosome to each of her three sons (25 percent probability), then there were seven. If Noah had a daughter after the Flood (not recorded, but possible), there could be as many as nine X chromosome lineages. Either way, this is a considerable amount of genetic material. And since X chromosomes recombine (in females), we are potentially looking at a huge amount of genetic diversity within the X chromosomes of the world.

Does this fit the evidence? Yes, again, it absolutely does! It also turns out that Y chromosomes are similar worldwide. According to the evolutionists, no "ancient" or highly mutated or highly divergent Y chromosomes have been found. This serves as a bit of a puzzle to the evolutionists, who have had to resort to calling for a higher "reproductive variance" among men than women, high rates of "gene conversion" in the Y chromosome, or perhaps a "selective sweep" that wiped out the other male lines. For the biblical model, it is a consistent correlation and you can simply take it as is.

The evidence from mitochondrial DNA fits the biblical /historical flood model just as neatly as the Y chromosome data. As we saw before, there are three main mitochondrial DNA lineages found across the world. The evolutionists have labeled these lines M, N, and R, so we'll refer to them by the same names. The Flood model says these came off the Ark. The evolution-based model claims the "Out of Africa" story.

It also turns out that M, N, and R differ by only a few mutations.

We can safely assume from Josephus' writings and the biblical account that there were ten (male and female) generations from Eve to the ladies on the Ark. M and N are separated by about eight mutations (a small fraction of the 16,500 letters in the mitochondrial genome). R is only one mutation away from N. This could be an indication of the mutational load that occurred before the Flood. Given the assumption that mutations occur at equal rates in all lines, about four mutations separate M and N each from Eve (maybe four mutations in each line in ten generations). But what about R? It is very similar to N. Were N and R sisters, or perhaps more closely related to each other than they were to M? We'll never know, but it sure is fascinating to think about.

In my search I found that the amount of genetic diversity that has been found in people worldwide to be one more argument for the Historical Creation/flood account. We find there is less than most evolutionists predicted. The general lack of diversity among people is the reason the Out of Africa model has humanity going through a disastrous, near-extinction bottleneck with only about 10,000 (and perhaps as few as 1,000) or perhaps eight people surviving.

However, is it possible that the reason for this lack of diversity is due to something else? What if the human race started out with only two people?

What if the human race as we know it is not that old and has not accumulated a lot of mutations, despite the high mutation rate?

What if they were right and there actually was a bottleneck event in the form of a worldwide flood?

The Tower of Babel and Genetics

The Tower of Babel has been a favorite bedtime story for generations. But is it more than a fairy tale? Could it be possible that there is evidence to back up this tale of rebellion and judgment? Like the Creation and Flood accounts, there are only a couple of Bible verses from the events at the Tower of Babel that apply to the Historical Biblical model of genetics. But, like the others, these verses are as profound as they are simple.

"Now the whole earth had one language and one speech." Gen 11:1

"And they said, 'Come, let us build ourselves a city, and a tower whose top is in the heavens; let us make a name for ourselves, lest we be scattered abroad over the face of the whole earth.'" Gen 11:4

Josephus says:

2. Now it was Nimrod who excited them to such an affront and contempt of God. He was the grandson of Ham, the son of Noah, a bold man, and of great strength of hand. He persuaded them not to ascribe it to God, as if it was through his means they were happy, but to believe that it was their own courage which procured that happiness. He also gradually changed the government into tyranny, seeing no other way of turning men from the fear of God, but to bring them into a constant dependence on his power.

He also said he would be revenged on God, if he should have a mind to drown the world again; for that he would build a tower too high for the waters to be able to reach and that he would avenge himself on God for destroying their forefathers (Nephilim?)

3. Now the multitude were very ready to follow the determination of Nimrod, and to esteem it a piece of cowardice to submit to God; and they built a tower, (perhaps a pyramid with a Stargate on top) neither sparing any pains, nor being in any degree negligent about the work: and, by reason of the multitude of hands employed in it, it grew very "high," sooner than any one could expect.

It sounds like they were in a homogenous culture, with no desire to fan out and repopulate the Earth. Would you expect them to mix freely thereby mingling their DNA? Yes, most likely. They didn't go far from each other. It seems they were definitely under the rule of one man gone bad: Nimrod.

Were languages or cultural barriers present that would have prevented the sons of Shem from marrying the daughters of Japheth? The answer to that appears to be no! Would the daughters of Ham be expected to marry freely with the sons of any of the three men? It would seem the answer is yes! In Genesis 11 the Bible tells the story of the post flood world and how they were of one language and in one accord and stuck close together in the then-fertile land of Shinar. They knew God, the true one, who had allowed the flood, wanted them to move on, spread out and repopulate the Earth. He had His reasons, it appears, but they were happy where they were so why move on? They were prospering, things were great, no discontent. But slowly one man named Nimrod took more and more control of their lives. In fact, they were "of one mind" so it was easy to plant the "Nimrod" virus and affect everyone. They all just went along to get along. "Nimrod stood before God"; in other words, he took the place of God! Short memories, great land, great crops, and super grapes and out of this world wine; it was all good. God had His reasons for wanting them spread out to prevent such a tyrannical leader from ascending to power over them all! At least that's how it would seem from reading the story.

Is it possible that under the tyranny of Nimrod they were forced back into a worship of false gods—ancient aliens—giving rise to the same evils that existed before the Flood? Whatever the state of affairs, history records a form of Pagan sun worship began under the rule of Nimrod... as the Bible says, the Creator came down and divided the people, perhaps to stop the growing false religion. Perhaps there was again contact between the Fallen Angels, i.e. ancient aliens, and the women of Earth and it gave rise not only to pagan religions but to the stories of what would become the Greek, Norse, and Mayan gods, etc. Perhaps this time "He" chose to nip it in the bud before it got too far out of hand. At this time the life span of mankind began to decrease dramatically as well.

"Come, let Us go down and confuse their language, that they may not understand one another's speech.' So the Lord scattered them abroad from there over the face of all the earth, and they ceased building the city." Gen 11:7–8

There are tremendous implications that come from the Babel account. First, it explains the amazing cultural connectivity of ancient peoples—like pyramid building, common flood legends, and ancient, non-Christian genealogies that link people back to biblical figures (e.g., many of the royal houses of pagan northern Europe go back to Japheth, the son of Noah). Also the prevalence of supernatural creatures in the mythology of peoples worldwide!

Let's keep exploring the possible connection between history and genetics and what they might say about who we are and where we come from.

The dramatic rise in world population over the past several decades is a well-known fact. From a biblical perspective, the current human population easily fits into the standard model of population growth using very conservative parameters. In fact, starting with six people and doubling the population every 150 years more than accounts for the current human population (a growth rate of less than 0.5 percent per year!) Population size would have increased quickly given the rate at which the post-Flood population reestablished agriculture, animal husbandry, industry, and civilization.

So we must ask the question, "Why are there so few people in the world today?" Could it be that the world at least in its present populated state is "young" and we have not been here many tens of thousands of years? In other words: Life, at least life as we know it in its current state on this planet could be more in line with the Biblical time frames and those recorded by the historian Flavius Josephus. Is it possible that the Earth is older than we as a human race are? I think yes. There are an infinite number of possibilities and one is that the Bible is also a book of records for our civilization and the human dispensation on Earth.

When did this dispersion occur? Josephus says it was during the time of Nimrod, the great great grandson of Noah, fourth generation post flood. It is possible that the fifth and sixth or more generations from Noah were alive and following him in his rebellion as the lifespan was decreasing dramatically.

The best clue from the Bible about the timing of the event known as Babel comes from Genesis 10:25. In referencing the fifth generation descendent of Shem, a man named Peleg, it says, "in his days the earth was divided." To what is this referring? Many people believe this is referring to a division of the land masses (plate tectonics). This may be true, but it would require a huge amount of geologic activity after the Flood, and this would have occurred in historical times with no record of the events, in nonpopulated areas, so who knows? The interpretation I now favor is that this passage is referring to the division of people at Babel. Just a few verses after the Peleg reference, the section is summed up with another reference to the division at Babel. This fits both the context and the science. In context, Peleg was closely associated with Babel. Certainly it could have taken generations for the division and dispersement to occur.

How large was the population at the time? We would expect rapid population growth, but we cannot know exactly. There are sixteen named sons born to the three brothers, Shem, Ham, and Japheth. If we assume about the same number of daughters, Noah had on the order of thirty grandchildren. At that rate of growth, there would have been about 150 children in Salah's generation, about 750 in Eber's generation, and about 3,750 in Peleg's generation. Of course, these generations overlap, so let's say there were at least between 1,000 and 10,000 people alive at the time of Babel. This fits nicely with the available data. It is a high rate of growth, but wars and disease had yet to start taking their toll.

There is one more verse in this section that we need to discuss:

"These were the families of the sons of Noah, according to their generations, in their nations; and from these the nations were divided on the earth after the flood." Gen 10:32

It is possible that at Babel, God did not separate the nations according to language. He used language to separate them according to paternal (male) ancestry! This could have monumental significance and be the key to understanding human genetic history.

Do you see the implication in this simple verse? Paternal sorting would lead to specific Y chromosome lineages in different geographical locations. Since males and females from the three main families should have been freely intermixing prior to this, it also leads to a mixing of the mitochondrial lines. It is as if God decided to sort the nations out according to their fathers, giving each its own language, then sending them off to populate different parts of the Earth. Since they could no longer communicate with each other, off they went with those who spoke their language. The division of the human race may have occurred along family lines to prevent another disaster. Someday, one would hope that the divisions will be dissolved and the entire family reunited!

We already saw that Y chromosomes have little variation among them. We now add the fact that this little bit of variation is almost always geographically specific. That is, after the nations were separated according to Y chromosome, mutations occurred in the various lines. Since the lines were sent to specific geographical areas, the mutations are geographically specific. The current distribution of Y chromosome lines is a tremendous confirmation of the biblical model, and the historical records of Flavius Josephus.

Mitochondrial DNA (mtDNA) adds another confirmation. We have already learned that there are three main lineages of mtDNA that go back to a chokepoint in human history. We now add the fact that these three lineages are more or less randomly distributed across the world. Also, the various mutations within each of the three main families of mtDNA are geographically specific as well. In other words, the three mixed mitochondrial lines were carried along with the Y chromosome dispersal, each line in each area began to pick up new mutations, just like we would predict. In other words, it fits the biblical and historical account of Babel as the chokepoint and dispersal of the sons following the Y chromosomal fathers with their mitochondrial brides across the world. Different Y chromosomal groups in different places with cute little mitochondrial DNA brides evenly dispersed right beside them all over the globe.

After the Flood, and after the dispersion at the tower of Babel, where did everybody go? If the Bible account is true, there should be some record, right? Genesis chapters 9-12 mentions what Bible scholars call the "Table of the Nations," where the survivors of the Flood and Nimrod's rebellion at Babel went when they were dispersed from the Valley of Shinar in what is now called Iraq.

It appears that we have a match in genetics in the "Out of Africa" model for what the Bible and ancient historian's record as happening just a few hundred years after the Flood! At the very least, it is a possibility we must consider with an open mind! Another code, another small evidence of a quantum God perhaps?

So who was this Josephus I keep referring to? Fair question. Let's go back a few thousand years and I'll introduce you to part of the family tree:

Josephus was born to a royal family in Jerusalem, but through war and politics of the time became friends with Flavius Vespasian, the Caesar who replaced Nero, when he was but a mere general.

Perhaps Josephus shrewdly reinterpreted the Messianic prophecies, and perhaps he got a "download"; either way, he predicted that Vespasian would become the ruler of the 'entire world.' Josephus acted as consultant to the Romans and a go-between with the revolutionaries. Unable to convince the rebels to surrender, Josephus ended up watching the second destruction of the Temple in 70 AD and the defeat of the Jewish nation.

His prophecy became true in 68 C.E. when Nero committed suicide and Vespasian became Caesar. As a result, Josephus was freed; he moved to Rome and became a Roman citizen, taking the Vespasian family name Flavius. Vespasian commissioned Josephus to write a history of the war, which he finished in 78 C.E., the Jewish War. His second major work, the *Antiquities of the Jews,* was completed in 93 C.E. He wrote *Against Apion* in about 96-100 C.E. and *The Life of Josephus,* his autobiography, about 100. He died shortly after.

Despite his ambivalent role, Josephus was an eyewitness to history, and his writings are considered authoritative. Now you have "met" the man whose eyes and ears recorded the oral traditions and history of his time as well as the history that unfolded in front of him at a critical time in earth's history.

Chapter 5. After What Manner the Posterity of Noah Sent Out Colonies, and Inhabited the Whole Earth.

1. AFTER this they were dispersed abroad, on account of their languages, and went out by colonies every where; and each colony took possession of that land which they light upon, and unto which God led them; so that the whole continent was filled with them, both the inland and the maritime countries. There were some also who passed over the sea in ships, and inhabited the islands: and some of those nations do still retain the denominations which were given them by their first founders; but some have lost them also, and some have only admitted certain changes in them, that they

might be the more intelligible to the inhabitants. And they were the Greeks who became the authors of such mutations. For when in after-ages they grew potent, they claimed to themselves the glory of antiquity; giving names to the nations that sounded well (in Greek) that they might be better understood among themselves; and setting agreeable forms of government over them, as if they were a people derived from themselves.

Chapter 6. How Every Nation Was Denominated From Their First Inhabitants.

1. Now they were the grandchildren of Noah, in honor of whom names were imposed on the nations by those that first seized upon them. Japhet, the son of Noah, had seven sons: they inhabited so, that, beginning at the mountains Taurus and Amanus, they proceeded along Asia, as far as the river Tansis, and along Europe to Cadiz; and settling themselves on the lands which they light upon, which none had inhabited before, they called the nations by their own names. For Gomer founded those whom the Greeks now call Galatians, (Galls), but were then called Gomerites.

Magog founded those that from him were named Magogites, but who are by the Greeks called Scythians. Now as to Javan and Madai, the sons of Japhet; from Madai came the Madeans, who are called Medes, by the Greeks; but from Javan, Ionia, and all the Grecians, are derived. Thobel founded the Thobelites, who are now called Iberes; and the Mosocheni were founded by Mosoch; now they are Cappadocians. There is also a mark of their ancient denomination still to be shown; for there is even now among them a city called Mazaca, which may inform those that are able to understand, that so was the entire nation once called.

Thiras also called those whom he ruled over Thirasians; but the Greeks changed the name into Thracians. And so many were the countries that had the children of Japhet for their inhabitants. Of the three sons of Gomer, Aschanax founded the Aschanaxians, who are now called by the Greeks Rheginians. So did Riphath found the Ripheans, now called Paphlagonians; and Thrugramma the Thrugrammeans, who, as the Greeks resolved, were named Phrygians. Of the three sons of Javan also, the son of Japhet, Elisa gave name to the Eliseans, who were his subjects; they are now the Aeolians. Tharsus to the Tharsians, for so was Cilicia of old called; the sign of which is this, that the noblest city they have, and a metropolis also, is Tarsus, the tau being by change put for the theta.

Cethimus possessed the island Cethima: it is now called Cyprus; and from that it is that all islands, and the greatest part of the seacoasts, are named Cethim by the Hebrews: and one city there is in Cyprus that has been able to preserve its denomination; it has been called Citius by those who use the language of the Greeks, and has not, by the use of that dialect, escaped the name of Cethim. And so many nations have the children and grandchildren of Japhet possessed. Now when I have premised somewhat, which perhaps the Greeks do not know, I will return and explain what I have omitted; for such names are pronounced here after the manner of the Greeks, to please my readers; for our own country language does not so pronounce them: but the names in all cases are of one and the same ending; for the name we here pronounce Noeas, is there Noah, and in every case retains the same termination.

2. The children of Ham possessed the land from Syria and Amanus, and the mountains of Libanus; seizing upon all that was on its seacoasts, and as far as the ocean, and keeping it as their own. Some indeed of its names are utterly vanished away; others of them being changed, and another sound given them, are hardly to be discovered; yet a few there are which have kept their denominations entire. For of the four sons of Ham, time has not at all hurt the name of Chus; for the Ethiopians, over whom he reigned, are even at this day, both by themselves and by all men in Asia, called Chusites. The memory also of the Mesraites is preserved in their name; for all we who inhabit this country (of Judea) called Egypt Mestre, and the Egyptians Mestreans. Phut also was the founder of Libya, and called the inhabitants Phutites, from himself: there is also a river in the country of Moors which bears that name; whence it is that we may see the greatest part of the Grecian historiographers mention that river and the adjoining country by the apellation of Phut: but the name it has now has been by change given it from one of the sons of Mesraim, who was called Lybyos. We will inform you presently what has been the occasion why it has been called Africa also. Canaan, the fourth son of Ham, inhabited the country now called Judea, and called it from

his own name Canaan. The children of these (four) were these: Sabas, who founded the Sabeans; Evilas, who founded the Evileans, who are called Getuli; Sabathes founded the Sabathens, they are now called by the Greeks Astaborans; Sabactas settled the Sabactens; and Ragmus the Ragmeans; and he had two sons, the one of whom, Judadas, settled the Judadeans, a nation of the western Ethiopians, and left them his name; as did Sabas to the Sabeans: but Nimrod, the son of Chus, staid and tyrannized at Babylon, as we have already informed you.

Now all the children of Mesraim, being eight in number, possessed the country from Gaza to Egypt, though it retained the name of one only, the Philistim; for the Greeks call part of that country Palestine. As for the rest, Ludieim, and Enemim, and Labim, who alone inhabited in Libya, and called the country from himself, Nedim, and Phethrosim, and Chesloim, and Cephthorim, we know nothing of them besides their names; for the Ethiopic war, which we shall describe hereafter, was the cause that those cities were overthrown.

The sons of Canaan were these: Sidonius, who also built a city of the same name; it is called by the Greeks Sidon Amathus inhabited in Amathine, which is even now called Amathe by the inhabitants, although the Macedonians named it Epiphania, from one of his posterity: Arudeus possessed the island Aradus: Arucas possessed Arce, which is in Libanus. But for the seven others, [Eueus] Chetteus, Jebuseus, Amorreus, Gergesus, Eudeus, Sineus,

Samareus, we have nothing in the sacred books but their names, for the Hebrews overthrew their cities; and their calamities came upon them on the occasion following.

3. Noah, when, after the deluge, the earth was resettled in its former condition, set about its cultivation; and when he had planted it with vines, and when the fruit was ripe, and he had gathered the grapes in their season, and the wine was ready for use, he offered sacrifice, and feasted, and, being drunk, he fell asleep, and lay naked in an unseemly manner. When his youngest son saw this, he came laughing, and showed him to his brethren; but they covered their father's nakedness. And when Noah was made sensible of what had been done, he prayed for prosperity to his other sons; but for Ham, he did not curse him, by reason of his nearness in blood, but cursed his prosperity: and when the rest of them escaped that curse, God inflicted it on the children of Canaan. But as to these matters, we shall speak more hereafter.

4. Shem, the third son of Noah, had five sons, who inhabited the land that began at Euphrates, and reached to the Indian Ocean. For Elam left behind him the Elamites, the ancestors of the Persians. Ashur lived at the city Nineve; and named his subjects Assyrians, who became the most fortunate nation, beyond others. Arphaxad named the Arphaxadites, who are now called Chaldeans. Aram had the Aramites, which the Greeks called Syrians; as Laud founded the Laudites, which are now called Lydians. Of the four sons of Aram, Uz founded Trachonitis and Damascus: this country

lies between Palestine and Celesyria. Ul founded Armenia; and Gather the Bactrians; and Mesa the Mesaneans; it is now called Charax Spasini. Sala was the son of Arphaxad; and his son was Heber, from whom they originally called the Jews Hebrews.

Heber begat Joetan and Phaleg: he was called Phaleg, because he was born at the dispersion of the nations to their several countries; for Phaleg among the Hebrews signifies division. Now Joctan, one of the sons of Heber, had these sons, Elmodad, Saleph, Asermoth, Jera, Adoram, Aizel, Decla, Ebal, Abimael, Sabeus, Ophir, Euilat, and Jobab. These inhabited from Cophen, an Indian river, and in part of Asia adjoining to it. And this shall suffice concerning the sons of Shem.

It is important to keep several things in mind. First, the account was written by a person in the Middle East and from a Middle Eastern perspective. It is incomplete in that there are huge sections of the world that are not discussed (sub-Saharan Africa, Northern Europe, most of Asia, Australia, the Americas, and Oceania). It also reflects a snapshot in time, and expansion comes in waves over time, and it was written after the dispersion began, but not necessarily before the dispersion was complete. Indeed, much has changed in the intervening years. Population groups have migrated, cultures have gone extinct, languages have changed, separate cultures have merged, etc. The history of man since Babel is very complicated. Modern genetics can answer some of the big questions, but answers to many of the smaller details may elude us forever.

I discovered a newly published study suggesting that Europeans are closely related, finding on a genealogical level that everyone in Europe traces back to nearly the same set of ancestors only a thousand years ago! Yeah, the rest of us came to the "New World."

Could this also be pointing to a chokepoint in genealogical history? From Ireland to the Balkans, Europeans are basically one big family.

The study, "The Geography of Recent Genetic Ancestry across Europe," is authored by professors Peter Ralph and Graham Coop in the May 2013 issue of *Journal of Plos Biology*. Both authors were on staff at Department of Evolution and Ecology and Center for Population Biology, University of California, Davis. Few of us know our family histories more than a few generations back. It is, therefore, easy to overlook the fact that we are all distant cousins, related to one another via a vast network of relationships. They use genome-wide data from European's to investigate these relationships over the past 3,000 years, by looking for long stretches of genome that are shared between pairs of individuals through their inheritance from common genetic ancestors. They quantify this ubiquitous recent common ancestry, showing for instance that even pairs of individuals from opposite ends of Europe share hundreds of genetic common ancestors over this time period. Despite this degree of commonality, there are also striking regional differences. Southeastern Europeans, for example, share large numbers of common ancestors that date roughly to the era of the Slavic and Hunnic expansions around 1,500 years ago, while most common ancestors that Italians share with other populations lived longer than 2,500 years ago. The study of long stretches of shared genetic material promises to uncover rich information about many aspects of recent population history.

"What's remarkable about this is how closely everyone is related to each other. On a genealogical level, everyone in Europe traces back to nearly the same set of ancestors only a thousand years ago," Coop said. "This was predicted in theory over a decade ago, and we now have concrete evidence from DNA data," he said, adding that such close kinship likely exists in other parts of the world as well.

Coop and co-author Peter Ralph, now a professor at the University of Southern California, set out to study relatedness among Europeans in recent history, up to about 3,000 years ago. Drawing on the Population Reference Sample (POPRES) database, a resource for population and genetics research, they compared genetic sequences from more than 2,000 individuals.

Just as they expected, Coop and Ralph found that the degree of genetic relatedness between two people tends to be smaller the farther apart they live. But even a pair of individuals who live as far apart as the United Kingdom and Turkey—a distance of some

2,000 miles—likely are related to all of one another's ancestors from a thousand years ago! Really?

"Subtle local differences, which likely mark demographic shifts and historic migrations, exist on top of this underlying kinship," Ralph said. Barriers like mountain ranges and linguistic differences have also slightly reduced relatedness among regions.

Coop noted, however, that these are all relatively small differences.

"The overall picture is that everybody is related, and we are looking at only subtle differences between regions," he said.

Findings like these can be spun in a multitude of directions (like the political hacks of the world do every day). Clearly this new data could support the historical/biblical account of a "chokepoint" event in human history… about 4000 years or so ago. Where the gene pool was very, very small and closely related; a chokepoint that flowed through Shem, Ham or Japheth.

The biblical record states that it was ten generations from Adam to Noah—2656 years. It was then another ten generations from Noah to Abraham. From flood to birth of Abraham was 292 years. Noah was 600 when the flood is recorded and he lived 350 years after the flood. Baby Abraham was fifty-eight-years-old when Noah died. Abraham's family had migrated to the area called Ur of Caladees. There is no record of where Noah was, or if they ever met.

When did Tower of Babel occur? Nimrod, who was four generations from Noah, was the instigator. It seems that Noah's great, great grandson was longing for the good old days, when the giants "of old" roamed the earth, did "superhuman" things, had the wildest parties, and maybe even took you on off world excursions through their stargates. He was all for bringing back the perversion that the giant flood had just wiped out!

It would appear that this new rebellion occurred just six dramatically shortened generations before Abraham was born. Enough time, it seems, for corruption and false gods to be reestablished. How do I know? Well the biblical record says that when God called Abraham to follow Him, he was asked to leave his father's house and land and the false gods he worshipped and head out on a journey to an unknown land, to God's secret location.

It would seem that the chokepoint and the dispersion all occurred within a three hundred year period of time. In fact, it appears that the dispersion that is said to have occurred on the plains of Shinar at Babel may have occurred a mere 150 years after the flood. According to my calculations of the dates recorded in the Bible and echoed in the writings of Josephus, the chokepoint was about 4,300 years ago. Just about the right amount of time to match the findings of the human genome project and its unexplained chokepoint in the human experience!

How accurate is this human genome project information? Well, for me, it was dead on when compared to the genealogical research my maternal grandfather had done over many years. It was one of his many hobbies. As a prominent physician, he traveled and taught and learned in many locations around the world and always took time to visit the library, where he would always do some genealogical research on the branches of the family. He traced us to the voyage of the Mayflower, back to Scotland and one branch of the family to Maria Theresa, the first woman to rule the fabled Hapsburg Empire that included Austria. When I had my maternal DNA done by the HG Project it came back with a confirmation: my mother's side migrated north through Europe, west through Belgium across the channel into Scotland! The other part of the Haplagroup turned south and headed right into Austria as his research from many years ago had revealed. It was a big confirmation of his hard work. I found it fascinating and it started me on my quest to find out more about the human genome for myself!

It is true that some do not look at the history in the Bible in a favorable light. In fact, some disparage it, sometimes with open hostility. Attacks are often centered on the claim that the Bible is not reliable on historical grounds, and if the history of the Bible is inaccurate, what about the theology? However, as time goes by more and more archeological finds support the history as recorded in the Bible and by Flavius Josephus and others, as they are quite similar. In Israel alone there are incredible discoveries every year authenticating the stories in the Bible. I have seen some of them myself, standing on the excavated ruins of an ancient city ruled by virtually every world empire back to Assyria, even before Egypt took its turn. Talk about a split level city; this one had layer upon layer of history to be seen!

Perhaps those who have a less than honest scientific approach and agenda tend to attack the Bible fearing that its claim to be the message from an all-powerful God might affect their lifestyle; if they accept the history, then they might also have to accept the theology it contains. Well, they may be right!

Think about what Jesus told Nicodemus in John 3:12: "If I have told you earthly things and you do not believe, how will you believe if I tell you heavenly things?" Many of us today have been taught to disbelieve the history in the Bible, and therefore, the spiritual implications as well. Why? What is the agenda? If it is fiction, well, we read fiction and enjoy it! If it is history, well, we should be free to compare it to other historical sources and learn from it, because those who do not learn from history are doomed to repeat it! If it is more than that, if it is a message from an extraterrestrial source, don't we deserve to know? There must be something there... we have seen the mathematical codes in significant texts. If that is true, who is that extraterrestrial source? Is it our "big brothers," the ancient aliens, or are they simply another race of disgraced rebellious creatures created by the "One." If so, who is the "One?"

He signed His name to our DNA. Is there a chance He has another code in the Bible? As I mentioned, the scientist Sir Isaac Newton believed there was. Many rabbis throughout the ages have believed so as well. Is there a story within a story, within a story, in the Great Book of records? Maybe.

There is no king who has not had a slave among his ancestors, and no slave who has not had a king among his.
~ Helen Keller

Chapter 8
Sir Isaac Newton's Secret Code Found?

On his communication with friends coming to America before him, Russian Comedian Yaakov Smirnoff said,

"Before they left, we worked out a code that they would say the opposite of what they meant in their letters. When they wrote that 'the streets are filthy and the people are rude,' we thought that they meant the people were friendly and the streets were clean. Since they live in Cleveland, we later learned they had forgotten the code."

Sir Isaac Newton, one of the fathers of physics, believed there was a secret code contained in the Bible. When he wasn't busy discovering gravity and laying a foundation for the study of physics, he searched its pages for this code he believed it contained. Perhaps it was left there by the Creator himself as Newton believed, but try as he might he was unable to find it. With the advent of computers the search became much easier; well, perhaps less difficult would be a better way to put it. But even before computers, some Jewish sages also shared Newton's belief and some found evidence to back it up!

The Vilna Gaon, an eighteenth-century rabbi in Luthuania, was considered a child prodigy and one of the most brilliant men of Jewish history. He wrote, "all that was, is, and will be unto the end of time is included in the torah...not merely in a general sense, but including every species and of each person individually, and the most minute details of everything that happened to him from his day of birth until his death."

After decades of research, I agree. But it raises a litany of ethical questions about the search for and use of the code, and if we are meant to have free unfettered access to it. If so, how much of it? Where does the search and research of the code become fortune telling and not just science? Is there a built-in safeguard against that? We are able to confirm that an extra-terrestial intelligence recorded history while it was still future to us within the code, but what if we are able to sort out future events from it… would we then be able to alter them? Does that mean we are to have free access to it? Is there a master code to access all of its information? If there is a code hidden here perhaps the question then would be: what are the rules, how do we use it? Perhaps some wise guidelines are contained in the written and readily available text of the book itself, say for instance:

Isa 48:16 "Come near to Me, hear this: I have not spoken in secret from the beginning; from the time that it was, I was there. And now the Lord GOD and His Spirit have sent Me."

In Deuteronomy, God warns Israel about the occult so certainly He is not offering His own version of it in His own book, is He?

Deut 18:9-12

9 When you enter the land the LORD your God is giving you, do not learn to imitate the detestable ways of the nations there.

10 Let no one be found among you who sacrifices his son or daughter in the fire, who practices divination (fortune telling) or sorcery, interprets omens, engages in witchcraft.

11 Or casts spells, or who is a medium or spiritist or who consults the dead.

12 Anyone who does these things is detestable to the LORD...

NIV

It would appear then that using the code to access the hidden information contained in the Torah and the rest of the Old Testament for predicting the future could be dangerous at best. But is there even a code? The short answer is... yes! Why is it there? Perhaps for the same reason the God code is in our DNA! Perhaps it is just another means of authenticating His creation and demonstrating that there is an all-knowing designer behind it all, a way of letting us know that He lives outside time and space and therefore knows the ends from the beginnings!

The Bible talks about a book of records where every deed of all of mankind is recorded. What if this Highly superior entity, God, is using this same book of stories and rules and guidance through the use of an access code to do just that. We have seen His mathematical clues left for us in Gen 1:1 and John 1:1 and other place's that we have discovered so far. Can it be so hard for a God that builds universes with mathematics in a manner that we still have yet to fully comprehend to build another back door to His creation?

Like a jigsaw puzzle, facts and information and history are recorded ahead of time in His personal Divine jigsaw puzzle; actually, it is more like a hologram, I suspect. The Hebrew language is certainly perfectly designed for that purpose. No vowels to confuse the issue, reading from the right to the left without spaces.

Close your eyes for a moment and picture the past... then visualize the future. Now point to the past and point to the future.

Most of you will have pointed to the left as the past and the right as the future. God says He declares the ends (future) from the beginning. Hebrew reads from right to left. His language starts in the future! Time is just a dimension that cannot contain Him! Could it be that Hebrew is a language of extraterrestrial origin? Perhaps the content that the code unlocks is what Daniel saw when God told him to "shut up the book until the time of the end." Well, now in the "end times" (not the end of time) we have computers that are unlocking some of the secrets contained in the book. How to interpret them... well... that is an entirely different matter. The words from the Plain text warn against Divination, or fortune telling, so it is wise to tread very carefully here ... I would guess! It would seem to be somewhat crazy to use the book in a way that the book itself warns you not to do. Check out the story of King Saul as a reference.

He often ignored the prophet Samuel and did his own thing until it didn't work so well. Then he consulted the prophet and asked him for an insight from God. Well, this stubborn king got himself into another battle after the Prophet died and wanted help, so what did he do? He went to the witch of Endor to conjure up the "spirit" of the dead prophet for an answer on how to fight his battle.

He was aware of the law of the land, God's law, that he was charged with enforcing! It said not to imitate the detestable ways of the surrounding nations (Endor). But off he went to seek out a witch, (spiritism) in Endor, and asked to talk to the dead prophet. (Avoid those who consult the dead.) Anyone who does these things is detestable to the LORD. Not likely that this was going to turn out well for him!

That should be a good enough reason for anyone to avoid those practices, especially when that person, the King, in this case, had seen the power of this God before. Based on reading the written text, my feeling is that by doing so he did not speak with the dead prophet, because the same written text of the Bible says, "the dead, they know nothing." Duh! They are dead, so if you are speaking to the dead, to whom are you really speaking? Well, it's a counterfeit, and the master counterfeiter is the rebel—Lucifer—and that's exactly what he was doing, going to a witch (spiritism) to connect him with a seducing spirit that left heaven with the great liar, Lucifer, in the great rebellion. At least that's what the Bible says, and we will let it interpret itself. According to its record, the judgment was swift; he was killed the next day in battle!

Even before computers got involved, Sir Isaac Newton's belief that there was a hidden code to unlock the secrets of the Bible was partially born out. Bible scholars have always known that the number 7 is special in biblical numerology. It is a sign of His Creative power. He rested on the seventh day because all Creation was spread out before him as he spoke it into existence with frequencies that called energy into different forms of matter. I am sure on a cosmic basis it sounded like a Big Bang! But perhaps what we read in the Biblical creation account was more specific for Earth and its surrounding solar system. It seems to say that it existed but was in a state of disorder... God came on the scene and reversed the entropy and brought order out of disorder. To that disorder He spoke, applied frequencies, and brought order! Seven, then is the Number of God and His seal of order and completion. The Israelites were given a day to pause and reflect every seven days, every seven years, and every 7x7=49 years in the Jubilee year they had a year-long party! Let's start there. Lets look for an ELS code every 49 letters!

But first here's a quick explanation of the art of code-making and breaking. If you count every—in this case—49 letters and take that letter and combine it with next letter 49 letters away and on and on, and if you happen to be a computer or a code specialist you can conceal a message.

Starting in Genesis, the first book of the Torah, every 49 letters the code's system spells out the word Torah! Over and over again.

The next book of the Torah is Exodus, and sure enough every 49 letters spells out T-o-r-a-h and starts again every 49 letters, all the way through! Wow we are on to something here! The next book of the Torah is Leviticus... but the code doesn't work. Some "die hard" code breaker went on to the next book, Numbers (interesting name) of the Torah and searched for it there anyway, but it wasn't there either. But wait a minute; something is here, it's Torah spelled backward! Yes, every 49 letters. Well, let's check the next book as well. Surprise! Deuteronomy shares the same pattern! Every 49 letters spells the word Torah—backwards.

What's up with the book in the middle, Leviticus? I have an idea... the Torah was supposed to be written with God's hand; it's God's book, so let's try an ELS of "His" number... seven... Wow! Something is here but it's not Torah! What is it? It turns out that the rabbi had found the sacred name of God there... the Tetragrammaton—yes, every seven letters over and over throughout the book! So what do we see? From whatever direction you come from in the Torah, it points to God... His name, His presence, is in the center of it... coming or going! The first two point forward to His name, in the third and the next two point back again to His name! There's a code for you, and that's how an ELS works on a large and simple scale!

A few decades ago Doron Witztum, whose area of study is in modem physics and general relativity, got the bug to find a key to the code and began looking for hidden word patterns in the Torah.

He enlisted the cooperation of world renowned mathematician, Dr. Eliyahu Rips, Associate Professor of Mathematics at the Hebrew University of Jerusalem. Rips developed the mathematical system for measuring the statistical significance of the results. (Both men are Orthodox Jews and believe the Bible is of divine origin.)

By mathematical formulas, Rips can determine the probability of whether the ELS words extracted from the Bible by computer are only random coincidences or can be statistically proven to be deliberately encoded by a Higher Power or an intelligent designer. He found that mathematically the odds are too large for it to have "just happened." He states theoretically there is no limit to the amount of information that could be encoded. At least ten or twenty billion combinations and permutations are possible. If you start from 1 and never stop day and night, it will take you 100 years to count up to three billion. And he claims that is only the first and crudest level; and that we don't have a powerful enough mathematical model to reach it. He believes it is probably less of a crossword puzzle and more like a "hologram." I told you so.

Witztum and Rips enlisted the help of Yoav Rosenberg who created the computer program that could search the letters of the Torah for hidden codes. Together they began to make what seemed to be astonishing discoveries of hidden information which could never have been extracted until this generation... with the aid of a computer. In their now famous experiment, they took a sample of thirty-four renowned rabbis and wrote out their names, dates of birth or death, taking the information from the *Encyclopedia of Great Men in Israel*, for the sake of uniformity and objectivity. (I have successfully used a newer version of their software proving to myself beyond a shadow of a doubt that it is real and it works!)

What their computer returned to them, well, it stunned them! It found the names of all thirty-four rabbis plus their dates of birth and/or death encoded in the letters of the Torah. They took a second list of thirty-two rabbis and performed the test again. Similar results. They used a copy of *War and Peace*, which is of similar length as a control text and attempted to find the same rabbis encoded there. This time with negative results.

According to Mr. Drosnin, the author who made this code famous, in the Rips-Witztum experiment the odds for finding the information on the rabbis by random chance was one in 1,000,000. Some say Drosnin steps over the red line of divination with some of his code claims. He is an avowed atheist, so that might not bother him much. Now that he has researched and written about this code he is a confused atheist, the last I heard; from my perspective, that's progress.

So many codes have been found over the last few years with the help of the programs to search for them that they will certainly soon catch up with the volume of the written text. As a book of records, it is quite complete containing crossword puzzle-like codes, sometimes with as little as two words that connect to historical events like "Wright Brothers/airplane," "Marconi/

radio," "Edison/electricity/light bulb," "Newton/Gravity," "Rembrandt/Dutch Painter," "Einstein/scientist, he overturned present reality." Also more morbid records, such as the assignation of President Kennedy where along with his name "To die" and "Dallas" can be found. The volumes of information that have been decoded expands daily with serious scientists now involved in the search.

There is always that tension between finding current and historical events and the temptation to make it like a crystal ball and indulge in fortune telling. Even if one does venture off into the unknown of the future and finds what would seem to be something significant... it is statistically possible that the story will change after the event with the discovery of another word or word series that dramatically changes the ultimate message to match the current historical event. Attempting to look into the future with the code is a gamble at best and perhaps divination at worst!

Howard Gans, a senior cryptological mathematician (codebreaker) at the Pentagon with twenty-eight years of experience from the NSA, heard about the Bible code and decided to investigate. He is an Orthodox Jew. Skeptical, he figured he would prove it a hoax. He wrote his own computer program and checked out one list of the rabbis and then the other. His computer program found the same information that Witztum, Rips, and Rosenberg found, but he could not believe it. The data was correctly matched, which seemed to rule out random chance.

He decided to look for entirely new information. He figured if this phenomena was real then the cities where these men were born and died ought to be encoded as well. In his 440-hour experiment, Gans checked not only the names of the thirty-two sages Rips used, but also thirty-four others from an earlier list, checking all sixty-six against the names of the cities. The results made him a believer. "It sent a chill up my spine," recalled the Pentagon code-breaker. The cities also matched the names of the sages in the Bible code.

As the code research has evolved more complex compound messages have appeared, and the serious investigators such as Eliyahu Rips, Alexander Rotenberg, Doron Witztum, Harold Gans, Barry Roffman, Moshe Aharon Shak, Ed Sherman, Nathan Jacobi, and more have developed sets of rules and guidelines that statistically rule out "false" codes and increase the chances that the code is used in an accurate fashion.

It is all too easy to cherry-pick the words that appear and make it say different things but with the guidelines established and followed it promotes the statistically most likely words and even the order they may fit into the message. One way they do that is by judging the proximity of the different words found to each other on the matrix. If they are close together or even touching each other then there is a high probability that they are related and will fit together in a sentence that contains a valid message. Another way to zero in on an important message is to compare the surface text with the code when it is found. If they share the same subject material, then you not only have a valid code but just hit the jackpot as those are considered to be the Rolls Royse of codes. I'll show you some examples of some of those below and guess what? The code involves aliens!

I used the code one 4th of July weekend to watch an event unfold. As the day went on I watched CNN report on the shooting of a famous college athletic coach. In between barbequing and playing with my kids and grandkids in my safe backyard, I did a search on my computer with the software. I started with the coach's name and sure enough it showed up along with a number of other words. I set the search parameters so that any legitimate words would show up in the matrix within a reasonable distance, etc. Along with his name appeared the code, but I didn't know it until it played out on TV in front of me throughout the day. The coach's name showed up with the suspects, "will shoot" "from" "White Taurus," "Will shoot at Shabbat Remnant," and more details, including a tattoo the suspect had that was disclosed when he was captured. Each time another detail was announced on CNN I spotted it on my matrix. The suspect was spotted driving a White Ford Taurus; while on the run in another town he shot at some Orthodox Jews walking home from temple. Many other details appeared in my matrix and the code suddenly stood out! When they captured him the news even mentioned his Nazi theme tattoo that the Bible code had also revealed earlier that day. It was a spooky moment!

At that moment my life paradigm was obliterated. I didn't really believe in all this supernatural stuff... yet I watched it play out right before my eyes, on my computer and on my television! That day turned out to be a quantum leap forward in my life's search for a quantum God that until then I really wasn't sure I believed in. But at the moment this code came together I felt how small I was and how inadequate my belief system was. So I disposed of it and opened my mind at another level. After all, that's the scientific approach! If proven wrong admit it and start again in your search for truth. New information demands new paradigms! As the day developed I began to share it with my oldest son, David, who also purchased the software and began studying the codes for the next several years in his spare time.

So are you ready for a shocking code about aliens? Did you think we were done with those "little green men?" Not yet!

Here is the English translation: Notice how the relevant words can be coming or going climbing or descending in a three-dimensional manner.

Remember what I shared with you about the word proximity and how the closer they are the more valid the code is considered.

Well, consider this code: "Roswell alien crash" is all connected. The S in Roswell is shared with the S in crash. The first L in Roswell is shared with the L in aliens. It's a tight fit! There are many other codes and one that also intersects the word, Roswell, says "Part terrestrial bodies", "Part celestial bodies" "Aliens." They all intersect Roswell in some fashion. Interesting, huh?

One of the more respected researchers of the Torah or Bible Code is Barry Roffman. I have had the honor of communicating with him in late 2012 about another Bible code before starting this project. I found him to be an intelligent and honest researcher, even though some of his subjects are controversial, which is good because it means he is outside the box of stale convention. Look at this code he found and has posted on his website:

AND THE SONS OF GOD SAW THE DAUGHTERS OF MAN THAT THEY WERE FAIR AND THEY TOOK THEM FOR WIVES (Genesis 6:2).

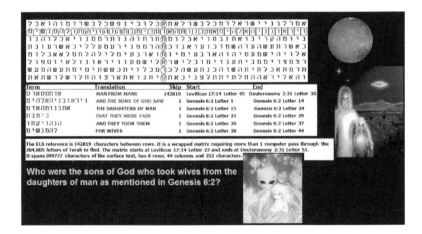

Please notice how the last five sentences of this code begin and end in Genesis 6:2. In the code they are back-to-back! Care to guess what the surface text is there? You can look back a couple of chapters and find out. It is the chapter and verse that describes the fallen angels mating with humans and creating a giant race of Nephilim... in fact, it is a direct quote of those verses found in the code in the same place that the surface text says the same thing...Wow! The finger is pointing at the fallen angels as the source of aliens in both the surface text and in the Bible code AND in the very same place!

Half terrestrial and half celestial, you say? You cannot get a more statistically significant code than that... in my humble opinion. Did you also notice the general shape of this bible code? Look at the text again and see if it reminds you of any famous shape. Keep that in mind, but let's not get sidetracked for now. Not only is this source one of extraterrestrial origin with a knowledge of future and past events, it seems to be clarifying things. In a manner of speaking it is "telling" on or exposing another extraterrestrial source that came to Earth, whose actions we have already seen led to a global cataclysmic flood and a restart of the human race at the chokepoint of human history reportedly about 4000 years ago!

This text in Gen 6:2 and then this incredible Bible code in the same place exposes the same source of alien life on Earth... the Nephillim and their parents, the fallen angels! If this code is from the quantum God, and it would seem it is, He just uncovered the plans of some of his rebellious Creation. It seems they would like for history to repeat itself, but with them writing a new ending!

I am sure some of you are having your life long paradigms rocked, too. Rest assured, I am trying and if I have not offended you yet, please be patient; I will get to you directly.

Right now I am about to do just that to some of my dearest friends. I just go where the facts take me and I must do so to be true to my search for the source! This text from the Old Testament Prophet Isaiah has yielded numerous ELS codes:

Isaiah 53

Who has believed our message and to whom has the arm of the LORD been revealed?

2 He grew up before him like a tender shoot, and like a root out of dry ground. He had no beauty or majesty to attract us to him, nothing in his appearance that we should desire him.

3 He was despised and rejected by men, a man of sorrows, and familiar with suffering. Like one from whom men hide their faces he was despised, and we esteemed him not.

4 Surely he took up our infirmities and carried our sorrows, yet we considered him stricken by God, smitten by him, and afflicted.

5 But he was pierced for our transgressions, he was crushed for our iniquities; the punishment that brought us peace, was upon him, and by his wounds we are healed.

6 We all, like sheep, have gone astray, each of us has turned to his own way; and the LORD has laid on him the iniquity of us all.

7 He was oppressed and afflicted, yet he did not open his mouth; he was led like a lamb to the slaughter, and as a sheep before her shearers is silent, so he did not open his mouth.

8 By oppression and judgment he was taken away. And who can speak of his descendants? For he was cut off from the land of the living; for the transgression of my people he was stricken.

9 He was assigned a grave with the wicked, and with the rich in his death, though he had done no violence, nor was any deceit in his mouth.

10 Yet it was the LORD's will to crush him and cause him to suffer, and though the LORD makes his life a guilt offering, he will see his offspring and prolong his days, and the will of the LORD will prosper in his hand.

11 After the suffering of his soul, he will see the light [of life] and be satisfied; by his knowledge my righteous servant will justify many, and he will bear their iniquities.

12 Therefore I will give him a portion among the great, and he will divide the spoils with the strong, because he poured out his life unto death, and was numbered with the transgressors. For he bore the sin of many, and made intercession for the transgressors.

Christians have claimed that Isa. 53 is one of the many Old Testament texts describing the first appearing of the Messiah, Jesus, or Yeshua.

Interestingly, over the last fifteen-plus years it seems more codes have been found in this chapter than anywhere else in the Bible. The first to do so was Yacov Rambsel, Jewish by birth but Christian by faith. With his intimate knowledge of Hebrew, he did it all by hand, without the aid of the computer. In Isa. 53 he found the coded phrase "Yeshua (Jesus) is my name." He also found over forty names of individuals and places associated with the crucifixion of Jesus were encoded as well within this "suffering servant" messianic passage. If that was not enough to make your head spin, consider this: it was all dictated to the prophet and recorded by him centuries before the birth of (Jesus) Yeshua of Nazareth.

One of the more recent codes discovered in Isaiah 53 seems to many to describe the healing and subsequent resurrection of Yeshua (Jesus) by the Father God. It reads: "But the Lord is for us the miracle of his death, (his resurrection) and the Father has dressed Yeshua's (Jesus') wound."

There is much yet to be found here.

Have you ever wondered why in Genesis and in the beginning of the New Testament there exists this somewhat... well... totally boring list of names: so-in-so begat so-in-so, ad infinitum. A giant Banyan-like family tree thing that I quite frankly couldn't get through when I tried to read it. Then one day I heard my friend Dr. Missler talking about it. I figured I would listen because if anyone could decode what that was all about, it would be him. Sure enough, there was a code in it! Beyond the surface purpose of detailing the life and longevity of the early humans in the Old Testament and continuous lineage from Adam to Jesus in the New Testament, there was a code, a secret message for someone with discernment to uncover!

Here is how it works. It's really a simple one. You know that every name has a meaning, that history and our specific cultures and languages attach to it. Well, if we simply go back and see what those names are in the Biblical family tree, and what they mean, we find that it contains a relevant message! Hiding in plain sight right there in the human family tree is a message of hope for all of humanity. From Adam to Noah there were ten generations, and their names carry a message for all of humanity? Yes! If you have the time, you don't have to stop at Noah. Some folks with a quantum level of curiosity have found that the genealogy of Jesus from Adam to Jesus gives us another even more complex message! For now let's keep it simple and see what the message carried by the first ten generations was.

Here are the names and what they mean, along with the hidden message they conceal.

There was God, then Adam, then Seth, and Enosh, Cainan, Mahalalel, Jared, Enoch, Methuselah, Lamech, and Noah. Now let's consider the meanings of those names:

The first one is easy: God equals God, Adam means man, Seth "is appointed," Enosh "a mortal a man of," Cainan means "sorrow is born," Mahalalel means "the glory of God." Next comes Jared, which means "shall come down," Enoch, whose name means "instructing or teaching," (He did a lot of that as he 'walked with God'), then his son Methuselah (the man who lived the longest in human history) which means "his death shall bring," his son Lamech's name means "those sinking down in despair," and finally, Noah the tenth generation, and his name means "comfort or rest."

Do you see the code contained in the names of the first ten generations of man as recorded in the Bible? No rush, it took them a few thousand years to live it out. God man is appointed, a mortal man of sorrow is born, the glory of God shall come down, instructing or teaching. His death shall bring those sinking down in despair comfort and rest. Really?

Wow, that sounds like a relatively intelligent sentence, doesn't it? In fact, it is a code that conveys a serious yet joyful message that many call the gospel. It is a promise that God would become man and through sorrow and his death he would teach them and bring comfort and rest-toration to the human family tree. Clever and hidden in plain sight! If you follow that family tree and decode the meaning of the names found in Matthew on down to Jesus of Nazareth, you find it also contains an encouraging message. Now you know why so and so begat so and so was recorded for your reading boredom. Not so boring now, right? That took some planning on someone's part! Nothing random style about it!

I was finding that this unique book was not an irrelevant boring old piece of literature like so many believe! It had codes and layers upon layers of deeper meanings in its written words. It had my attention!

Okay, there is a message here, but how do we know who sent it? How does God authenticate? How do we know the Bible is really from Him, not just a collection of stories or even myths or fables knitted together simply by man? One of the authors says He declares the ends from the beginnings, and from ancient times things not yet done; in other words, from His perspective, time is relative. He lets us know the message is from Him by predicting what is yet to come in our time-space dimension. How does he do that? One way is through the many written prophecies in the text of the Bible. There He demonstrates His ability to be outside of space and time and accurately predict the future even centuries in advance. The more one sees this phenomena repeated it is easier to believe that it is coming from an extraterrestrial source outside of time, etc. Besides the future events that have been recorded and fulfilled as predicted in the written text, you now know that there are also hidden codes in the matrix that are formed by the Hebrew language, another source of authentication and verification of an extraterrestrial source. This source dictated to many different humans (forty authors) many different stories, admonitions, history, family trees, and future events in a contiguous fashion throughout sixty-six books.

Recorded in the Old Testament in the extraterrestrial language of Hebrew, the text contains hidden messages in a equal distance sequencing code throughout. Many say it is the book of records where everyone who has ever lived or will live on earth and all their deeds are recorded ahead of time, and yet in a fashion that largely prevents its unauthorized use for fortune telling. It appears clear to me that Hebrew is indeed a language of extraterrestrial origin with multiple facets to it, the plain written text which reads from right to left or from the future to the past. It is also one of the few languages that is designed so that each letter has a numerical value so as to be able to communicate with the universal language of mathematics, and now this hidden ELS code. One has to wonder what else is still to be discovered?

We were taught that time was linear, but that is not what physics says. Eternity is not having all the time in the world; it is being outside of the time space dimension. Is there a God, a Designer, an Originator out there in eternity outside the time-space dimension ready and willing to communicate with us?

Have you ever watched a holiday parade in person? What you see from your vantage point—your perspective—is limited to what you can see from where you sit, so to speak. Your reality is what is in front of you, like the linear time graph we were all taught in grade school from left to right or right to left, depending on your culture. History is off in one direction and the future is coming from the other and the present is right before you. But what if... what if you were in a helicopter above the parade? Perhaps 1000 feet right above it; would your perspective change? Is it possible that you could now see not only your present but also your recent past and approaching future as far as the parade is concerned? Is it possible that the space-time dimension is as simple as that for a designer who designed it that way? Perhaps we are all spectators AND participants in the progression of time, the parade of the ages, but He is not. He is "above" it all in "eternity," outside his creation of the time/space dimension.

People like us who believe in physics know that the distinction between the past, the present, and the future is only a stubbornly persistent illusion.
~ Albert Einstein

Chapter 9
The Shroud of Turin… a Quantum Event?

Seen on the manufacturer's warning label reported to be on the Shroud:

HANDLE WITH CARE: This product contains countless, minute, electrically charged particles moving at extremely high speeds.

WARNING: Due to its heavy mass, this product warps the space surrounding it. No health hazards are yet known to be associated with effect.

NOTE: This product may actually be nine- or ten-dimensional but, if this is the case, functionality is not affected by the extra six dimensions.

HEALTH WARNING: This product (and every product of the Manufacturer) emits low-level nuclear radiation.

DISAPPEARANCE EXCLUSION: Due to quantum tunneling, there is an extremely tiny chance that this product may suddenly disappear at any time (and reappear elsewhere). The Manufacturer will not be responsible for such mysterious disappearances.

Is the famous Shroud of Turin a result of a quantum event that involves the "missing" other six dimensions quantum physicists say exist?

I had never really thought much about the Shroud until I watched the special that December night in 2012. I had seen strange pictures of it and had heard people speak of it in passing before, but I simply didn't have much interest in religious relics. As I unpacked my things in the hotel room, I half-watched the television and gathered that a team of scientists had examined the Shroud. Several of them had previously held the opinion that it was a fake and now they felt that new facts had come to light which had caused them to change their minds. Still only mildly interested, I gave it polite attention as I settled in; then they flashed up one of those photos of the Shroud that perhaps I had seen before but couldn't figure out. This time I could make out the face of a bearded man and the arms folded across the front of a body. Suddenly the thought flashed through my mind! What if that was the result of a quantum event? What if the story of the resurrection is true and this is tangible proof?

Ideas and thoughts began arranging themselves in my mind. My study of quantum physics has me believing that humans were once ten-dimensional beings; maybe they still are, but those other six dimensions are dormant, and maybe that happened when the human race decided to rebel and go their own way. Maybe it was a part of the "consequences" of leaving the connection with God as described in the Biblical Eden story. Perhaps a fully functional ten-dimensional human was what the Bible was describing when it said that God and Adam would commune continually and "walk and talk together," etc. Maybe then when Jesus came and reconnected humanity to divinity something was restored in those dimensions, too. Perhaps when he was resurrected the additional dimensions were reestablished at that moment, and then that supernatural quantum event was captured and recorded on the burial cloth as he simply transcended it and moved right through it into life again with all dimensions restored.

So in case you have not paid the Shroud much attention like I hadn't, let me share with you what I have discovered since that night! It won't be boring, I promise you that.

You've heard of the mysterious Knights Templar? Well, I found that their secret order was involved with the Shroud as well!

Science alone doesn't have an explanation for the Shroud, although quantum physics might hold the key to its understanding. Religion alone doesn't hold the answer either although the faithful may believe it does.

The Shroud of Turin Research Project (STURP) scientific team's initial examination and subsequent investigations are important in understanding the Shroud and how it became what it still is today... an enigma. It is fairly safe to say it is not a fake since no one has been able to duplicate it or even propose a method to do so. Science has proven that it is not paint and that male human AB positive blood stains are on both the Shroud and the sudarium (more about that in a minute), and that the stains match exactly... to each other! Therefore, it is reasonable to believe that they once covered the same face. They both contain pollen from the geographical area surrounding Jerusalem, and the sudarium has been dated—without dissent—to the time of Christ!

Simple logic would ask how and why the C-14 dating of the Shroud samples revealed a twelfth century dating? That's a good question, and there are reasonable answers that satisfy both scientific and religious experts. Could the Shroud of Turin do what nothing else has been able to do in the western world... that is, reunite the disciplines of spirituality and science?

The Shroud is a fourteen-foot long by 3.5 feet wide cloth. It is made of "flax"... with a very distinctive three-to-one herringbone weave; similar, I am told, to the weave in a pair of blue jeans. In 1532 a fire severely damage the Shroud, which now bears the marks of the fire in several burn points and three small holes. In fact, they are more prominent than the figure of the man... a Man who has been tortured and crucified, a man whose wounds are forensically a perfect match to the Biblical account of the torture and death of Jesus of Nazareth. There is male human blood—type AB—over the face and in his hair, on his beard, etc. There are puncture wounds through the top of the wrist as they would have been, not through the palm as many pictures show. The Shroud contains a dorsal and ventral print of the full length of the body. It is a coded imprint of information that can reveal much. A team of forensic experts have matched the information with the account and determined that there is an accurate match. Another team of computer 3D experts who work in the movie industry have reproduced the face from the information encoded as well. They have done this with many historical figures, but were never as touched as they were on this project. They considered it a sacred search for what no one has seen in 2000 years the face of Jesus Christ.

The image they found on the cloth was very subtle and is actually a negative—a photographic negative record. They confirmed what the first photographers of the Shroud found, that the first photo negatives actually contained positive imprints! This astounded and confused the first photographers long ago... that what shows up on photo negatives is a positive image.

Experts say that even if we accepted what we now "know" as false C-14 dating and accepted the Shroud as only 750 years old, a counterfeiter would have to have had technology not yet invented for another 500 years to record it in the negative state! The negative and positive images of photography were unknown at the time. From a scientific perspective, there is no plausible explanation for how that image came to be on the Shroud.

Dr. John Jackson, who now heads the Shroud Center in Colorado Springs, Colorado, led a team of investigators to Turin in 1978. The team included Jews, Christians, and atheists, etc. Barrie Schwortz, the official photographer and Jew by faith, said he thought it was courageous of the Catholic Church to allow the STURP team (of which he was part) to examine and photograph the Shroud for five days. They had their detractors and many in the church at Turin did not want the "sacred cloth touched," even though records now indicate that for centuries it was common for pilgrims to handle and kiss the cloth, as it was for the monks when the Knights Templar had possession of it.

In that five-day period, as the scientists slept on coats in the room with the Shroud, they worked around the clock, conducting over a thousand different tests, taking over 30,000 photos. You can bet the official photographer, Barrie, went through some serious rolls of film that week! Remember they didn't have digital back then.

The most significant result of the tests were that ALL the tests of the cloth proved that there were no signs of paint pigmentation or other materials that would have indicated a possibility that a human made the image.

One thing that separates the Shroud of Turin from every other artifact of history is the codifying of information that the two-dimensional image carries that allows the reconstruction of a three-dimensional reality. I feel vindicated! There exists within it the presence of information that allows the reconstruction of missing dimensions. Like a hologram... like the word I heard. What if it is the result of a quantum event where missing dimensions were restored?

The painted forgery allegation was debunked. After years of studying the 1000 tests performed, photographers, physicists, chemists, agnostics, and believers can tell you what it is not... but they cannot tell you what it is, or how it was formed.

The trail of the Shroud's historical journey north begins in the city state of Edessa, in what is now Turkey, where a king dying of leprosy was presented with the Shroud by a Christian disciple. History records that King Abgar was healed after coming into contact with the Shroud. A number of years later a pagan king came to power and the Shroud was hidden away for safe keeping. It reappeared or was rediscovered 300 years later in 525 AD as the linen cloth with the mysterious image of Christ on it.

It is believed to have been moved to Constantinople in 944. A burial cloth, which some historians maintain was the Shroud, was owned by the Byzantine emperors but disappeared during the Sack of Constantinople in 1204.

As that city was under seige by Crusaders, the Shroud was secured by them and taken to Athens where it showed up in the hands of the French Duke of Athens. From there it made the journey home with him to his estate in France. It next surfaced in 1356 in Lirey, France. Remember that name—Lirey—you will see it in a code shortly!

In 2009 a Vatican researcher unearthed a document that stated the mysterious and secretive group of French Monks known as the Knights Templar were reported as having possession of the Shroud for some time and paid homage to the cloth with the image of Jesus on it throughout the thirteenth century. In fact, their initiation rights were reported to include grasping the cloth by the edges and honoring it with a ceremonial kiss.

In 1453 Margaret de Charny deeded the Shroud to the House of Savoy. Since the seventeenth century, the Shroud has been displayed in the chapel built for that purpose by Guarino Guarini in Turin. It was first photographed in the nineteenth century (after photography had been invented) during a public exhibition.

From 1450 to 1983 it was the possession of the Savoy family. When the exiled king of Italy, a member of the Savoy family died, it was discovered that he had willed it to the Vatican and that is how they became the uncontested owners of the cloth.

The history of the Shroud from the fifteenth century is well recorded. In 1532, the Shroud suffered damage from a fire in the chapel where it was stored. A drop of molten silver from the reliquary produced a symmetrically placed mark through the layers of the folded cloth. After that, nuns of the order Poor Clare Nuns attempted to repair this damage with patches. In 1578 the House of Savoy moved the Shroud to Turin and it has remained at Turin Cathedral ever since.

In 1694, repairs were again made to the Shroud by Sebastian Valfrè to improve the repairs of the Poor Clare nuns. Records indicate that again in 1868 further repairs were made by Clotilde of Savoy.

On April 11th, 1997, there was a fire of very suspicious origin; many suspect arson, which again threatened the Shroud. In 2002, the Vatican had the Shroud restored. The cloth backing and thirty patches were removed, making it possible to photograph and scan the reverse side of the cloth, which had been hidden from view. A ghostly part-image of the body was found on the back of the Shroud in 2004. The last time the Shroud was on public exhibition was in 2010.

The image on the cloth or Shroud of Turin confirms the gospel account of torture and crucifixion of the Biblical Jesus! The figure's wounds are marked and recorded on the image that appear on the Shroud: the crown of thorns, the spear wound in the side, the wounds from the scourging etc. It is very interesting that when tested these very stains revealed male human type AB blood—a type of blood common in the middle east, but not in Europe. As one of the recent Shroud investigators, Ray Downing said: "They beat this man to hell."

Ray Downing worked with the renowned Shroud expert and part of the original STRUP team, Dr. John Jackson, to produce a three-dimensional version of the face on the Shroud, which reveals a badly beaten and disfigured face. The scientists were shocked to find that the information stored in the Shroud contains not only the second image seen as a negative on the Shroud, but actually has information recorded that can produce a 3D image like that of a hologram—meant perhaps to be viewed in 3D once man gained the technology to do so. Sounds a bit like the Bible code here, doesn't it? Once the technology appeared, so did the hidden information stored within the second images of the Hebrew text. Now we see there is another dimension—a third dimension that contains the ELS Bible codes. Are the Bible and the Shroud ancient artifacts with hidden technology just now being revealed?

Is there a connection here with the famous text from Daniel where God instructs him to shut up or code the words of the book until the time of the end? As God then says: knowledge would be increased. It fits both of these phenomena; I wonder if one speaks of the other. Do you think the Shroud is mentioned in the Torah (Bible) code?

Ray Downing says that "the image of the face on the Shroud is not a simple picture but a database of information in 3D like a hologram." Like the result of a quantum event? It's starting to sound that way!

Could this Shroud actually have covered the body of Jesus 2000 years ago? Could a quantum event have occurred restoring and activating the dormant extra… say… six dimensions… to the battered body of Jesus as it lay in the tomb wrapped in the Shroud? If so, did that bring about a restoration and resurrection of life to the lifeless body? Did this event occur with the explosive energy of a reaction on the atomic and subatomic level extending through into the "extra dimensional" dimensions? We could be looking at the evidence of a quantum event of extra dimensional nature!

In 1988 the Catholic Church allowed the C-14 dating of the Shroud and it came in about 700 years old! What? Only as old as the 1300s? In an attempt to understand the seemingly contradictory C-14 results and history of the Shroud, scientists have reexamined their work every step of the way.

There now exists clear evidence that the small sample removed from the corner of the Shroud for C-14 dating was from areas of reinforcing cloth added to the Shroud during the middle ages to support and protect it from wear and tear of the hands of the curious and the faithful!

There are numerous paintings and then pictures, as photography came of age, of exhibitions of the Shroud where the people are holding the Shroud by those exact corners. The outside edge is where it was handled for centuries by everyone who could get close enough to touch or kiss it. Others point out the fact that handling and subsequent deposits of more recent material alone could distort a C-14 test; along with the more recent carefully reinforced cloth around the edges… the same edges where the C-14 sample was taken from… are enough to explain the one anomaly in an otherwise airtight case! Actually, if the case of the Shroud of Turin were to be heard in court with the historical, scientific, and religious sides all told, it would surely pass the legal test for validity. Granted, the scientific requirements are more stringent. With that in mind, though, more recent tests have placed it at a date consistent with the life of Jesus matching the

Sundarium, not only in stains and blood typing, but in age as well. It would be nice if the church would allow another sample from another location or three on the Shroud for more C-14 dating, but that is unlikely as the custodians of the Shroud in Turin felt the first examination was sacrilegious. There is always that tension between religion and science, though when they are in balance it is a good thing!

Besides the religious and the scientific schools of thought, there is another somewhere between… the mystics. It is an area of discomfort for many. There is a dimension of mysticism that leads to union with the dark side such as the Nephilum, the fallen angels, and Lucifer, but I suggest we don't throw the baby out with the bath water. God is a mystic to us in our current state of understanding and until we advance a lot further in our understanding of science, much of it will remain mystical to us.

Most advances are instigated by people willing to think outside the box. Not everything outside the box is good or correct or functional, but it is wise to take some journeys outside the box now and then to compare what we find there with the known facts and thus advance our body of knowledge.

With that in mind and at the risk of being called a heretic by some, applauded by others, and simply laughed at by even others, I suggest we keep an open mind about some of the theories the ancient Gnostics proposed.

The Gnostics were called heretics for saying that most of the universe is invisible, but science has proven that to be true today… one branch of religion rejecting another that had the science right! Maybe they both had their theology wrong.

Additional testimony found in France suggests the cloth we know as the Shroud of Turin was well known and that as part of their training and initiation, the "Holy Crusaders" (the Knights Templar) handled and kissed the cloth and had possession of the Shroud in 1287.

In addition, the Vatican archives have now revealed the memoirs of a Knights Templar who described this same training.

Before the Shroud entered into the mysterious protectorate of the Knights Templar, it was recorded in the so-called Hungarian prayer manuscript. Illustrations showed Jesus laid out on the Shroud and a "close up" of the very distinctive weave of the Shroud as if under a magnifying glass, and then a painting of the empty Shroud in the empty tomb; the burn holes on the magnified illustration are the L-shaped burn holes that predate the fire in 1532. It is displayed in the Budapest National Library, the oldest surviving text of the Hungarian language, written between 1192 and 1195 AD (sixty-five years before the earliest Carbon-14 date in the 1988 tests).

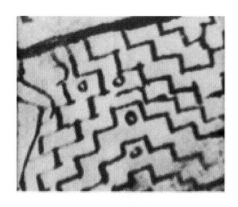

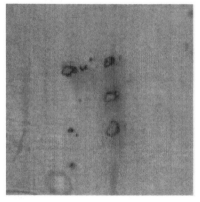

These burn holes from the illustration of the 1100s are an accurate representation of what we see today, shooting the 1300 century fake hypothesis out of the water...

There is also the fact that the blood stains on the face of the image contained on the Shroud of Turin match exactly the blood stains on the Sudarium documented to the year 616 in Oviedo, Spain. Both have been matched using modern forensics and both contain the same human AB blood type, typed by Dr. Baima Ballone in Turin and confirmed in the U.S. This blood type is rare (about 3 percent of the world population), with the frequency varying from one region to another. Blood chemist Dr. Alan Adler

(University of Western Connecticut) and the late Dr. John Heller (New England Institute of Medicine) found a high concentration of the pigment bilirubin, consistent with someone dying under great stress or trauma and making the color more red than normal ancient blood. Drs. Victor and Nancy Tryon of the University of Texas Health Science Center found X and Y chromosomes representing male blood and "degraded DNA" (approximately 700 base pairs) "consistent with the supposition of ancient blood."

That's enough to convict or exonerate in a court of law! Science rightly demands a higher level of evidence, but this is not all the evidence in this case! There is plenty more. The image on the Shroud is only two microfibers thick, making it impossible that some great artist painted a fake. (There are several other reasons that could not be as well.)

Let's talk about the trail of evidence from its supposed starting point in Jerusalem. Is there any evidence that either of these cloths were ever in Jerusalem? Forensic studies of the pollen on both the Shroud and the Sudarium indicate that both started in Jerusalem, but took different routes into different locations in Europe. The pollen they contain tells a story.

Researchers at The Hebrew University have said that pollen and plant images on the Shroud put its origins in Jerusalem sometime before the eighth century. "Shroud of Turin could date to time of Jesus, examiner says," *USA Today*, January 29, 2005.

Even before, in 1995, Israeli botanist and expert on the plant life of Israel, Dr. Avinoam Danin, a Professor at Hebrew University in Jerusalem, confirmed findings by Dr. Alan Whanger, Professor Emeritus at Duke University in North Carolina, of floral images on enhanced Shroud photographs. They were joined by Dr. Uri Baruch of the Israel Antiquities Authority, a palynologist and expert on Israel's pollen. Danin studied the plant images and Baruch analyzed the pollen grains found by the late Swiss criminologist and botanist Dr. Max Frei via the sticky tape collection of materials that Frei had taken from the Shroud in 1973 and 1978.

The team identified the "inflorescence of the crown chrysanthemum (Chrysanthemum coronarium)"; the Rock Rose (Cistus creticus) lateral to the left cheek of the figure on the Shroud; a bouquet of bean caper plants (Zygophyllum dumosum); and a thorn tumbleweed (Gundelia tournefortii), which Whanger speculates comprised the Crown of Thorns.

So clearly these forensic experts place the Shroud in Jerusalem and not only that but at least 1300 years ago!

Let's investigate the Sudarium of Oviedo, since we already know the blood stains match perfectly. Just what is the Sudarium? I am glad you asked…

The Sudarium Christi-The Face Cloth Of Christ

In the Cathedral of Oviedo in northern Spain is a linen cloth called the Sudarium Christi, or the Face Cloth of Christ. It is often referred to as the Cloth of Oviedo. Using infrared and ultraviolet photography and electron microscopy, modern studies at the Spanish Centre for Sindonology by Drs. Jose Villalain, Jaime Izquierdo, and Guillermo Heras of the University of Valencia, as noted by Oviedo scholar Mark Guscin, have demonstrated that this Cloth, along with the Shroud of Turin, both touched the same face! Tradition and historical information (now supported by contemporary scientific research) support the belief of millions of people that the face touched by both cloths was that of the historical Jesus of Nazareth. The two cloths are believed to have touched the same face at different points in the burial process. The Oviedo Cloth was placed around the head from the time death occurred on the Cross till the body was covered by the Shroud in the Garden Tomb. Then it was removed and placed to one side [John 20:7]. Mark Guscin notes that the practice of covering the face is referenced in the Talmud [Moed Katan 27a]. He adds that Rabbi Alfred Kolatch in New York talks of the Kevod Ha-Met or "respect for the dead" as the reason for covering the head. Rabbi Michael Tuktzinsky of Jerusalem in his Sefer Gesher Cha'yim [Volume 1, Chapter 3, 1911] offers as a reason that it is a hardship for onlookers to gaze on the face of a dead person.

The Sudarium Christi is a poor quality linen cloth, like a handkerchief, measuring 84 x 53 centimeters. Unlike the Shroud of Turin, it does not have an image. However, it does have bloodstains and serum stains from pulmonary edema, fluids which match the blood and serum patterns and blood type (AB) of the

Shroud of Turin. The length of the nose on both cloths is eight centimeters (3 inches).

Pollen grains found on the Cloth of Oviedo by Dr. Max Frei in 1973 and 1978 and studied also by Monsignor Giulio Ricci match pollen grains found on the Shroud of Turin. Dr. Uri Baruch, our expert palynologist from the Israel Antiquities Authority has indicated that again one of these pollen matches is Gundelia tournefortii - a thorn/thistle bush that is indigenous to the Holy Land. Dr. Avinoam reports that Gundelia tournefortii serves as a "geographic and calendar indicator" that the origin of the cloths is the Holy Land.

The Sudarium Christi has a well-documented history. One source traces the cloth back as far as 570 AD. Pelayo, Bishop of Oviedo in the 1100s, noted in his Chronicles that the Oviedo Cloth left Jerusalem in 614 AD in the face of the Persian attack led by King Chosroes II, and made its way across North Africa to Spain. It was transported to Oviedo in a silver ark (large box) along with many other sacred relics. The fact that both cloths touched the same face, and that the Oviedo Cloth can be traced historically to a date as early as 570 AD are further proof that the Carbon-14 dating of the Shroud to between 1260 -1390 AD cannot be accurate. Those wishing to learn more can read the work of Oviedo scholar Mark Guscin, *The Oviedo Cloth* [The Luttenworth Press 1998, Cambridge, CT.]

It appears that many bouquets of flowers were once placed on the Shroud, leaving pollen grains and imprints of plants and flowers on the linen cloth. It provides important evidence regarding the origin of this cloth in the Holy Land, and indicates that the man of the Shroud was entombed with flowers from his waist to his head.

There are many historical references to the Shroud. Among them are the ancient Abgar Legends, which place the cloth in the City of Edessa (Turkey), 400 miles north of Jerusalem somewhere between 30-40 AD during the reign of King Abgar V. He was the one reportedly healed of leprosy by the Shroud.

Pollen finds confirm the presence in Edessa (Anatolian Steppe). Ancient historians Eusebius and Evagrius speak of the Cloth moving with disciple Thaddeus to Edessa. The Acts of Holy Apostle Thaddeus (6th Century) speaks of the tetradiplon (cloth doubled-in-four). Dr. John Jackson's raking light test of 1978 confirms fold marks matching tetradiplon. The Byzantine Greeks speak of the Acheiropoietas—image not made with human hands.

All of that sounds pretty impressive, but when Dr. Ray Rogers joined the STURP team back in the 70s he was an agnostic and publically stated he believed it was indeed created with human hands! "Give me twenty minutes and I'll tear it all to shreds," he said in reference to people's belief in the Shroud. He was convinced it was a painted fake.

Dr. Rogers was a respected chemist with Los Alamos National Scientific Laboratories, who examined the Shroud in July 1978. Rogers's task was to collect particles from the Shroud by pressing sticky tape on its surface and then later help analyze them. He authored a number of important scientific papers on the Shroud. Schwalbe, L.A. & Rogers, R.N., "Physics and Chemistry of the Shroud of Turin," Analytica Chimica Acta, 135, 1982, pp.3-49, reported STURP's finding that the Shroud's image was not a painting and the bloodstains really were blood! But Rogers found that the sample radiocarbon-dated in 1988 was not part of the original Shroud, and therefore could not validly be used for determining its true age. Over the years of analyzing the data he changed the direction of his thoughts 180 degrees.

Pyrolysis-mass-spectrometry results from the sample area coupled with microscopic and micro chemical observations prove that the radiocarbon sample was not part of the original cloth of the Shroud of Turin. The radiocarbon date was thus not valid for determining the true age of the Shroud.

The combined evidence from chemical kinetics, analytical chemistry, cotton content, and pyrolysis-mass-spectrometry proves that the material from the radiocarbon area of the Shroud is significantly different from that of the main cloth. The radiocarbon sample was thus not part of the original cloth and is invalid for determining the age of the Shroud.

It took him a bit longer than fifteen minutes but Dr. Rogers determined that not only was it not a fake but it really was old enough to be what it claimed to be: "Because the Shroud and other very old linens do not give the vanillin test [i.e. test negative], the cloth must be quite old... A determination of the kinetics of vanillin loss suggests that the Shroud is between 1300 and 3000 years old."

Good science is science without an agenda; a working hypothesis yes, but an open mind like Dr. Ray Rogers modeled for us all. He has my respect. It may very well be that the radiocarbon datings were relatively accurate, but because the samples were from cloth that was not part of the original Shroud, they are irrelevant regarding the age of the image area.

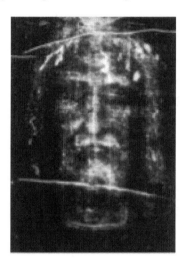

Pope Francis has made comments on the Shroud of Turin, though he stopped short of declaring the piece an official relic. "This image, impressed upon the cloth, speaks to our heart," the

Roman Catholic Church leader said in an Italian TV Easter Saturday special.

"This disfigured face resembles all those faces of men and women marred by a life which does not respect their dignity, by war and violence which afflict the weakest. And yet, at the same time, the face in the Shroud conveys a great peace; this tortured body expresses a sovereign majesty," he added.

The Shroud made news again when a research team from Padua University used carbon dating and concluded that the artifact is not a medieval fake, as some had previously suspected, but dates back to somewhere between 280 B.C. and A.D. 220.

Giulio Fanti, an associate professor of mechanical and thermal measurement at Padua University, analyzed fibers from the Shroud with infrared lights, which allowed him to measure radiation intensity through wavelengths.

"We carried out three alternative dating tests on the Shroud, two chemical and one mechanical, and they all gave the same result. They all traced back to the date of Jesus, with a possible margin of error of 250 years," Fanti told CNN.

The latest carbon dating findings might be the strongest evidence that the Shroud was indeed used in the time period of Jesus' death, but whether the imprints truly belong to Christ will be harder to prove.

Pope Francis' remarks are in line with the Roman Catholic Church's general position on the Shroud. Catholics have remained neutral on the subject of the Shroud's authenticity, leaving it up to scientific research, but he insists that the cloth still serves as an important symbol of Christians' faith.

So, does the Bible code say anything about the Shroud of Turin? Yes, as a matter of fact it does! Here are a couple of codes I found. Don't forget look for relevant terms and enjoy. Again I urge its use for confirmation, not divination.

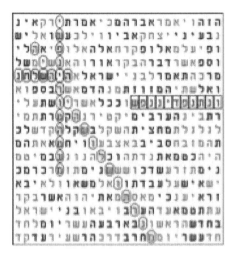

The Matrix starts at Genesis 20:10.37 and ends at Deuteronomy 1:2.6

The ELS is 14066

The vertical red code says: Shroud of Turin is spiritual

The horizontal green says: He gave for the redemption of the soul

The horizontal blue says: Resting for the Lamb of God

The diagonal pink says: From the light mark of three points to God

Another researcher discovered this matrix:

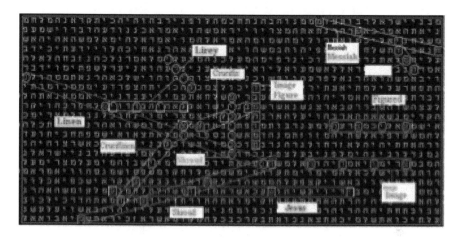

The Matrix starts at Genesis 44:28 and ends at Exodus 29:77

The ELS is 1412

The central search term was "shroud"

Additional terms found in close proximity: Jesus, Messiah, Crucifixion, Textile, Linen, Image, Figure, Figured, Photo, Face, Body, True, Edessa, Tirey, Chambéry, Turin, Weep

Fascinating, is it not?

Poets say science takes away from the beauty of the stars- It does not do harm to the mystery to know a little about it. For far more marvelous is the truth than any artists of the past imagined it.
~ Richard Feynman

Chapter 10
Astrology of Origin...
A Code in the Stars, and More?

Gen 1:14-15 Then God said, "Let there be lights in the firmament of the heavens to divide the day from the night; and let them be for *signs and seasons*, and for days and years; and let them be for lights in the firmament of the heavens to give light on the earth"; and it was so.

Are we, the so-called sophisticated and scientifically advanced residents of Earth in the twenty-first century, missing something that the very first dwellers of this Earth saw each night and accepted as common knowledge? Is there a macro code played out in the skies above us every night of every month of every year, known from eternity past that we have missed?

Yes, there could be! It is said by many that true astrology is the story in the stars that God arranged and placed there as an eternal message. He instructed Adam in the details of the symbolism of the positions of the stars and the message that was contained in their path through the heavens during the passage of the seasons. God showed him how it contained His promise to undo the duality that Adam had unleashed on the Earth and throughout the universe. The story of how he would do it and the battles that would be fought and won against the Rebel and his fallen Angels, the sacrifices that God would make, and His ultimate victory was told chapter by chapter, month by month, over and over, year by year. Every new season brought with it a new and unique chapter of the road back to unity with the quantum God! But like many ancient truths, time and the studied efforts of those who desire to hide the truth have hidden His story in the skies. They have buried the true symbolism hidden in the stars and perverted its messages so that the original good news of the reconciliation of the Creator and His creation that it contained was all but lost. Except for a few who have carefully passed the truth from generation to generation. Look at the night sky the next chance you get and you will see, it is still there to remind us of the immenseness and power of the God of Creation and of His promise to reunite and restore us to a complete unbroken relationship with Him again.

What I am about to share with you is the story within the story in the skies, the universe as we see it from Earth and the lost promise that yet remains in the progression of the Zodiac!

This is more than a fascinating theory. It fits! There is also a historical precedent for it as well. Before there were written records and scriptures, God seems to have used the clustering of stars that we call constellations as object lessons about His future plans for reunification and other prophetic subjects. Another code? I think so!

There is a great book written by Joseph A Seiss called, *The Gospel In The Stars*. Originally published in 1882, it might be a bit hard to find, but well worth it if you have an interest in this field and can find a copy.

The theory is that (and there is evidence to support it) the original study of astrology was actually a story given by God to man that would display nightly on the original Big Screen in the sky, the greatest story ever told and the original Star Wars saga rolled into one big production. It was an action story as well with battles between good and evil played out across the universe. With each station of the Zodiac or mazzaroth, there were new chapters to the story. Together they tell a story of a kingdom of light and peace that fell into rebellion. A kingdom where the dashing handsome rebel led an army into the depths of evil and perversion and that the only one who could save the kingdom was the king himself. To do that He would have to step down and secretly become one of the common men and pay the ultimate price of rebellion—death. He would substitute himself for the rebels and die a repulsive death, treated as a common criminal, but then he would have the right to resurrect himself and reestablish himself on his throne and bring unity and peace and harmony back to his kingdom.

It's a story that has everything: a kind king; an evil but handsome rebel whom the King had trusted and done everything for; a betrayal, a rebellion, a war, a romance, a tragedy, a surprise no one would expect; and a happy ending that Hollywood could not improve on… all for us to watch and learn from.

So God in the stars, huh? I can hear some out there sounding a bit skeptical, maybe even a bit rude like Bruce Nolan in *Bruce Almighty*. He is suddenly faced with a non-assuming man who claims to be God and he has his doubts:

> *Bruce: (shocked) "Are you spying on me? Who are you?"*
> *God: "I'm the one. Creator of the heavens and earth, Alpha and Omega. Bruce, I'm God."*
> *Bruce: "Bingo! Yahtzee! Is that your final answer? Our survey says, 'God'! Bing, bing, bing, bing, bing, bing, bing! Well, it was very nice to meet you, God. Thank you for the Grand Canyon, and good luck with the Apocalypse. Oh, and by the way, you suck!"*

Honestly, many of us would react the same way under similar circumstances. Most of us disbelieve in, or at least distrust, God to some degree. The Rebel has had thousands of years to disseminate his propaganda. If there is a God, we don't like him anymore than Bruce Almighty did.

The Bible does say that the lights in the heavens were to be used for signs and seasons [Genesis 1:14], and it indicates that God, who created them, calls the stars by name [Isaiah 40:26; Psalm 147:4].

Psalm 19:1-6 says that the heavens are telling of the glory of God.

According to John 1:14, Jesus revealed the glory of God. This could mean that the heavens foretell the coming of the Christ (Messiah). Verse 6 of this passage in Psalm 19 also speaks of the apparent circuit of the Sun, which is known to us as the ecliptic and the Constellations that surround it are also mentioned in the oldest book in the Bible [Job 9:9; 38:31-33].

Perhaps the sign in the heavens most of us are familiar with is the Star of Bethlehem, that history tells us was used to lead the wise men to the baby Christ after He was born [Matthew 2:1-2, 9-10]. But I sense most of us have missed the big picture.

The Zodiac is a band of constellations in the sky within eight degrees on either side of the ecliptic, the passage of the Sun. The word actually means "The Way," which is very interesting since that was the first name given to Christianity [Acts 9:2; 19:9, 23; 24:14, 22].

The Hebrew word "mazzaroth" has the same meaning and is translated "constellations" in Job 38:32. "Mazzaroth therefore... clearly signifies the twelve constellations of the zodiac through which the sun appears to pass in the course of the year, poetically likened to the 'inns,' in which the sun successively rests during the several monthly stages of its annual journey." [*The International Standard Bible Encyclopedia*, Vol. I, p. 312]

Luke 1:69-70 and Acts 3:21 imply the possibility of ancient or prehistoric prophets. According to history, the Bible was not written until long after the Creation and the flood, but the oral traditions were carefully passed down until Moses could record them under what is called "the inspiration of the Holy Spirit"... which is accepted as another name for the Creator God. He does have many! Hebrew traditions say that Adam, Seth, and Enoch could have been among these early prophets. Since people lived for nearly a thousand years before the Flood, and of course, their evenings were not spent watching television, but often, sleeping under the stars, it is certainly possible—in fact highly possible—that the average person was thoroughly familiar with the star patterns and that God might have revealed a system of identifying the constellations which foretold the story of reunification or salvation as the theologians like to call it.

They say that Genesis 3:15 is a clear prophecy of the future conflict between the seed of the woman and the seed of the serpent (the ancient alien rebel, Lucifer), which would ultimately be fulfilled in Christ's death and resurrection for us. He, Lucifer, "would bruise the heel" but would end up with his rebellion and his "head" crushed.

Read the following scenario and decide for yourself whether these constellations make more sense in a Biblical framework or in a mythological one. The dominant sign of each season consisted of a main constellation and a support group of three others, which are called Decans, from the Semitic word "dek," which means "part." Together, these twelve signs and their Decans appear to tell the amazing story of the Gospel! The Gospel is the name that some have given to the story of God's plan to defeat the Rebel and reunite the Universe in a state of peace and harmony.

The first four signs represent the opening chapter in the saga of God implementing His plan to reunite himself with humanity again. The story begins with His plan to enter into the Earthly dimension as one of us coming through a miraculous birth to a virgin symbolized by the constellation Virgo. This was also foretelling the season in which the God of Creation would be born in His Human form.

Virgo, the Virgin, is the first sign, the beginning of the story of reconciliation. She has an ear of wheat in one hand and a branch in the other. The wheat is actually seed, and symbolizes the "seed of the woman." The branch is a familiar Old Testament name for the Messiah. The same woman is seen in the first Decan of this sign, Coma, holding a baby, the Branch, or the Desire of Nations. The next Decan in this group is Centaurus, a half-horse, half-man. This could represent the child who is born, having two natures: being both God and man. The last constellation in this sign is Bootes, or Arcturus, who is the Great Shepherd and Harvester.

Together these images seem to portray a virgin birth of a child who has two natures, and the role of that child when he is grown as The Great Shepherd, leading His flock or followers.

Next stop is Libra, the Scales. It is a pair of balances, the universal symbol of trade or commerce. It depicts a purchase, or in this case, a redemption. It stands for the price to be paid by God to win Humanity back from the Rebel. The three Decans of this sign are the Cross (or the Southern Cross), the Victim, and the Crown. Clearly, these symbolize that he would become a victim; His death, and the method on a cross, and the promise that he would put his crown back on when it was over.

Next comes Scorpio, the Scorpion, a giant deadly insect with its tail and sting ready to strike. It obviously portrays the Rebel Angel and mortal enemy of the Deliverer. The three Decans of this sign all seem to depict the dreadful struggle between the rebel angel as the Scorpion King and the Creator God as the Savior of Humanity. The Decans are The Serpent, Ophiuchus, and Hercules. The first two of these are engaged in a fight. The serpent is coiled around Ophiuchus. At the same time the scorpion stings the man in one heel, but the man crushes the head of the scorpion with his other foot. Hercules, our Hero (God), the strong man, is wounded in his heel, but places his other foot over the head of the dragon.

Hercules also has a club in his right hand poised to crush the three-headed Dog of Hell held in his other hand.

Together, these images appear to point to the triumph of the Redeemer of Humanity over the Devil who is portrayed in all of the negative symbols of the scorpion, serpent, dragon, and three-headed Dog of Hell... The Unholy Trinity etc.

The next season brings Sagittarius, the Bowman, the figure of a horse with the body, arms, and head of a man. This is the centaur, a creature that never existed as a mere animal, but would be an interesting depiction of the God-man with two natures. His bow is drawn, and the arrow is pointed at the scorpion. These images continue the theme of the struggle between good and evil from the former sign, and seem to assure us of the certain triumph of the Savior of Humanity, the Messiah. The three Decans of this sign are Lyra, Ara, and Draco. Lyra, the heaven-bound eagle holds a lyre, symbolic of the song of victory. Ara, the Altar, faces downward, presumably burning with the fires of punishment. Draco, the Dragon, symbolizes Satan in the throes of defeat, winding himself about the North Pole.

The next four signs depict our Hero's future work as a mediator. This section foretells the formation and work of the body of believers.

Capricornus, the Goat, is another figure of an unlikely animal, partly a goat, sinking down, as if dying, and partly a fish with a strong tail. This could symbolize the death and new life of the

Savior. The Decans that accompany this sign are Sagitta, the arrow of God, bringing death, Aquila, the pierced and falling eagle, and Delphinius, the Dolphin, springing up out of the sea, apparently with new life.

Aquarius, the Waterman, is a man with a large vase of water that he is pouring out from the sky. This could be an accurate picture of Jesus back in Heaven now pouring out His spirit on the Earth which he said was like streams of living water [John 7:37-39]. One of the Decans of this sign is The Southern Fish, drinking in the heavenly waters. As we all know, the early Church chose the sign of the fish to symbolize their faith. It is also interesting that the Greek word for fish, ichthus, forms an acrostic meaning, "Jesus Christ, Son of God, our Savior." The other two Decans are Pegasus, the winged white horse, presumably carrying the Good News with all speed, and Cygnus, the Swan, flying with the Cross over all the earth.

Pisces, the Fishes, portray two large fishes. This, again, would be a valid representation of the Church, as seen in the former sign. The vernal (spring) equinox, the point where the sun passes from the south to north of the celestial equator. It moves very slowly from one of the twelve sections of the Zodiac to another. During the so-called church age that point has been in the area of Pisces. The point is now between Pisces and Aquarius, giving rise to the so-called New Age teaching that we are entering the Age of Aquarius. Some believe this happened in 1982 while others believe it will happen about the year 2200. Whenever this occurs, it could symbolize the passing of the age of the Church that will give way to the age of the Kingdom, an even more glorious age of The Holy Spirit, The Millennium and New Beginnings complete with Unity of the Human and Divine.

The Decans of the sign of Pisces are The Band, Cepheus, and Andromeda. The Band attached to the fishes is held by the Lamb (Aries, the Ram). This could symbolize Christ's (the male lamb) hold on His church. Cepheus is a crowned king holding a band and scepter, with his foot planted on the pole-star as the great victor. Andromeda is a woman in chains, threatened by the serpents of Medusa's head. She could be a picture of the church as Christ's bride, bound and exposed on earth for the moment.

Aries, The Ram, is a strong lamb with powerful curved horns, lying down in peace and conscious strength over the field around it. This would be a fitting picture of Christ in Heaven, ascended and victorious. The Decans for this sign are Cassiopeia, Cetus, and Perseus. These all symbolize victory and dominion. Cassiopeia is a woman enthroned. This might be the bride, now released from bondage, and perhaps caught to the heavens with her Hero. Cetus, the Sea-Monster, a symbol of the evil Rebel, is firmly held down, still alive, but subdued by Aries. Perseus, the armed warrior who has winged feet, would be another reference to the victorious Savior. He is carrying away the cut-off head of a monster full of writhing serpents.

The last four signs stand for the final consummation of all things. This section foretells the coming judgments on the earth and the glorious outcome of the Christ's reign.

Taurus, the Bull, is an angry, rushing animal, which would be a meaningful symbol of God delivering His wrath during the period on Earth called the Tribulation. The Decans are Orion, Eridanus, and Auriga. Orion is the warrior-prince with a sword on his side and his foot on the hare or serpent. Eridanus, the torturous River, is the River of Judgment belonging to Orion. Auriga, the Shepherd, is a picture of a powerful shepherd-king who tenderly holds a she-goat and two little goats in his left arm.

Ancient manuscripts say this could be a picture of God's comfort of the persecuted believers of this coming period of judgment.

Gemini, The Twins, are two human figures seated together in loving closeness. This could portray the Marriage of the Lamb. Which is the term used for the return of Jesus for his bride, the church. Also the dual nature of the God/man, Yeshua. The Decans are Lepus, Canis Major, and Canis Minor. Lepus is the mad hare, also called a serpent, the enemy under Orion's feet. Canis Major, Sirius, the Great Dog, could prefigure the Prince coming in His glory. Then Canis Minor, Procyon, The Second Dog, would be his princely following.

Cancer the Crab is the figure of a crab, in the act of taking and holding on with its pincers. This could be a picture of the victorious King of Kings when He returns, and the Decans, Ursa Minor, the Lesser Bear, Ursa Major the Greater Bear, and Argo, could picture His privileged followers. Ursa Minor could also mean the lesser sheepfold, and stand for the first-born who will be rulers, and Ursa Major could be the greater sheepfold, the ones born later. Argo, the Ship, brings the weary travelers home from their toils and travels.

The final chapter in this cosmic story has Leo, the Lion King as Jesus Christ in His final victory over the Devil. All three of the Decans point to the destruction of the enemy, pictured as a serpent. Hydra, the fleeing Serpent, is about to be pounced upon by the lion. Crater, the Bowl of Wrath, is placed on the serpent. And Corvus, the Raven, the bird of doom, is also on the serpent, devouring his carcass. If not a peaceful scene, it is the promise of a happy ending in the war between good and evil.

Put them all together and read the coded message that the heavens have displayed for all to see, and decide for yourself. Yes, it foretold the future, and apparently still does. The prophetic future redemption of the human race according to the ancients. A code in the skies every night of the year, every year, for one generation to pass on to another so that every inhabitant of this fallen rebel planet would always know the secret "hidden in plain sight" right in front of them.

There is another carrier of secrets that the God of Creation gave to his people to preserve His story. It fits hand-in-glove with the yearly cycles in the sky. It is the yearly cycle of holidays. Just like the twelve signs of the Zodiac, these seven holidays, or feasts as they were also called, contained a code hidden in plain sight! This code also contained the Creator God's plan to heal and reunite His creation, to abolish duality and reestablish unity in the Cosmos... the real "Age of Aquarius!"

I am ready to unwrap another code; are you?

In Lev. 23:1, The LORD said to Moses, 2 "Speak to the Israelites and say to them: 'These are My appointed feasts, the appointed feasts of the LORD, which you are to proclaim as sacred assemblies.'"

He gave them holidays and he called them His Holy-days—His moeds— (appointments or rehearsals), specific times of the year when Humanity had an appointment with their God for a rehearsal. A rehearsal of what? Each of these holidays would represent another phase of the plan to save humanity. Just as He had done with the masseroth, the great love story in the stars. Now He brought it down to Earth. Each holiday would illustrate another aspect of His plan to rescue Humanity and each holiday would also represent an actual event in their national history!

Tucked away within the seven annual holidays, God hid the story of His plan to eventually deal with the rebellion, once and for all and reunite man with God in a happily ever after!

Dual meanings with deeper hidden meanings; should that surprise us? This God loves codes and hidden meanings and minds that are willing to search them out! He would keep His plan before them and they would pass it on from generation to generation and at least some would not miss the big picture. Even though to many it would remain a simple tradition and they would miss the beauty of His promised code, there would always be some enlightened souls who would look deeper and see the secrets of the codes. They would understand that they revealed His love and His plan to reunite Humanity with Himself.

Let's look at these holidays and explore their significance. What did they mean? What did they celebrate? What did they prophetically point to in the future? The Ancient World ran on a lunar calendar so let's start in the fall with Virgo, where we did with the stars... I always did dream of starting at the top... and yes, I am a Virgo.

God commanded his tribe to observe seven yearly holidays, not surprisingly since seven is one of the numbers that refer to His creation. It is recorded as the day He celebrated His Big Bang... the creation of matter from His energy that formed our Cosmos, or at least the remodeling of our corner of it.

Two more feasts were added later to commemorate God's supernatural intervention in the affairs of his tribe to save them from extinction, for a total of nine. In biblical numerology, nine is the number of the supernatural, naturally.

The New Year starts with a feast, or holiday, called Yom Teruah or Feast of Trumpets. It occurs when Virgo is prominent in the heavens, just like the beginning of the "star story." It is recorded through tradition as the day Adam was created. It also has a third name—Rosh Hashanah—which means the head of the year. Yom Teruah, means "the day of the awakening blast." It is observed on the first day, the new moon, of the seventh month (Tishrei). Tradition states it will be the day the Messiah is crowned King and the day of the resurrection of the dead. This day is both the Jewish New Year and the beginning of a period of soul-searching known as the High Holy Days, or the Days of Awe, culminating on Yom Kippur.

As just mentioned, Yom Kippur is the next holiday and it comes ten days later (the days of awe). It is also called the Day of Atonement. It was the one day that the High Priest of Israel was allowed to enter the Most Holy place of the temple and meet God "face to face." Atonement and At One Ment, get it? The High Priest would enter and sprinkle the blood of the sin offering on the Mercy seat of the Ark of the Covenant, which among other things contained the Law, the Ten Commandments written by God's hand. I find it interesting that even back then, the law was covered by the Blood, and under the Mercy seat of God! Many Christians today would call that Great Grace even in the age of the Law!

It is followed by Sukkot or the Feast of Tabernacles, a week-long feast celebrating the entrance into the Promised Land.

These all occur in the fall. In the spring were four more holidays, starting with Passover.

Passover comes in the early spring and once was considered the head of the year. It is also called Pesach and celebrates the deliverance from slavery when God brought Israel out of Egypt. It was celebrated with the sacrifice of a lamb for the remission of sins of the people. The blood of the lamb was painted on the doorposts in Egypt and those under the blood, Egyptian or Israeli, had their sins forgiven and the angel of death passed over them. Those who were not under the blood lost the the first born of their family and flocks to this "Angel of Death."

After Passover came The Feast of Unleavened Bread, also called the Hag HaMatzah. It was a time when the house was swept clean and any leavening (which makes bread rise or puff up), was treated as a type of sin. It is a time of ceremonial washing and cleansing, symbolic of sanctification (mikvah). It is also said to have been the day Israel left Egypt.

Feast of first fruits—also known as Bikkurim—was the first fruits of the Barley Harvest. It was symbolic of a new beginning, overcoming the results of sin and receiving a fresh start. It was also the day the Israelites crossed the Red Sea untouched. When they were safely on the other side, the sea crashed back together and destroyed Pharaoh and his armies.

Pentecost or Shavuot comes fifty days after The Feast of First Fruits. It is also called the Feast of Weeks.

From the Exodus story, we can see that the lamb was slain on the fourteenth of the lunar month of Nisan, the day of Passover. On the fifteenth of Nisan, the day of Unleavened Bread, the people left Egypt; on the seventeenth of Nisan the children of Israel crossed the Red Sea; and fifty days later on Pentecost, God gave them the Torah on Mount Sinai.

In the Book of Leviticus Chapter 23, God tells Moses what He expects: "These are My feasts, My holy days; instruct My people to keep these from year to year, generation to generation." In other words, these are not your holidays like Mother's or Father's day, Thanksgiving, etc. These are "MY" days set aside as a sign to all generations.

We don't want to forget the other two sacred holidays that have been grandfathered into the Jewish calendar. Neither are called His days as the previous seven, but both commemorate His power in moving in a supernatural way to bless his people.

Purim is the story of Esther and how God lifted her up to a position of favor at a time when her people were about to be exterminated, and how she used that favor to influence the King of Persia to do the right thing. The Israelites were saved from a death sentence. The movie *One Night with a King* with the Egyptian actor Omar Sharif tells the story quite dramatically.

Hanukkah, also called the Festival of Lights, celebrates the Maccabees, a group who rose up to cleanse the temple that was being disrespected and trampled on by the Syrian–Greek occupying forces. After they regained control of the temple they only had a very small amount of the sacred oil hidden away that fueled the menorah in the Holy Place of the temple. They needed the oil to symbolically cleanse the temple and give it a fresh start. It might have burned for a few hours, perhaps a day, but through an "act of God" it lasted for eight days, the number that symbolizes "New Beginnings"! In Hebrew, the word "Hanukkah" means "dedication." The name reminds believers that this holiday is a fresh start and a new beginning commemorating the re-dedication of the Holy Temple in Jerusalem following the Jewish victory over the Syrian-Greeks in 165 B.C.E.

The New Testament refers to these holidays and in several places infers that Jesus celebrated them as well, which any rabbi of his time would have done.

John 10:22-24:

22: Then came the Feast of Dedication at Jerusalem. It was winter...

23: and Jesus was in the temple area walking in Solomon's Colonnade.

24: The Jews gathered around him, saying, "How long will you keep us in suspense? If you are the Christ, tell us plainly."

But there is another connection between the Festival of Lights and Yeshua (Jesus). Are you ready to see the hidden prophetic code that is contained in the Holidays that God claims are His days, and rehearsals of things to come?

The Bible tells the story of the angel Gabriel (good one), not a fallen one, who appeared to Mary and told her that she had been chosen to be the Earth Mother to the God Man who would be the Messiah not only for Israel but for all of the descendants of Noah and before him, Adam. In other words, the entire world. I have visited the very spot in Nazareth where it is said that this conversation occurred.

While researching these feasts in the mid-nineties, I found out about an astronomical event that was to occur on 9-11-99, and that it was a replay of the same alignment in the heavens that had occurred on this same holiday, Feast of Trumpets, 2000 years ago! It was also a celestial fulfillment of the story described in Revelation Chapter Twelve. I discovered that many rabbis have acknowledged that the event on 9-11-3 BC 2000 years ago was a well-kept secret.

It appeared that Yeshua, Jesus of Nazareth was born that day, which just so happened to be the day of the Feast of Trumpets that year, just as it was in 1999. It also "just so happened" to be the only other day in history that I could find that the stars aligned in such a fashion as to play out the Revelation 12 story overhead. The NASA software confirmed it! Two thousand years apart, same date in the Hebrew and Gentile calendar, the Lunar and Solar calendar and on a feast day, called Trumpets. Wow. What was going on?

Something had to be! I had also discovered a favorite saying of the rabbis: "There is no such thing as a coincidence." So I ruled that out. Revelation 12 describes a birth in the heavens by Virgo the Virgin constellation. I did some math and discovered that if you counted back nine months from 9-11-3 BC, you came to the holiday of Hanukkah! There is reason to believe that this event—Gabriel speaking with Mary—occurred on Dec. 13 4 BC! He appeared to Mary on Hanukkah and nine months later on 9-11-3 BC, the baby Jesus was born... on the Feast of Trumpets (not Christmas)!

Really? Yes, a reasonable search of history will reveal that the Christmas holiday is a result of the mingling of Christianity with Paganism, sun worship etc., but that's another book and another time.

What were the odds? So what was this astronomical event? Take out your Bible if you have one and read Revelation 12... it describes it to a tee. If you don't have one, here it is:

Revelation 12

12:1 And a great sign appeared in heaven: a woman clothed with the sun, and the moon under her feet, and on her head a crown of twelve stars;

12:2 And she was with child; and she cried out, being in labor and in pain to give birth.

12:3 And another sign appeared in heaven: and behold, a great red dragon having seven heads and ten horns, and on his heads were seven diadems.

12:4 And his tail swept away a third of the stars of heaven, and threw them to the earth. And the dragon stood before the woman who was about to give birth, so that when she gave birth he might devour her child.

12:5 And she gave birth to a son, a male child, who is to rule all the nations with a rod of iron; and her child was caught up to God and to His throne.

12:6 And the woman fled into the wilderness where she had a place prepared by God, so that there she might be nourished for one thousand two hundred and sixty days.

12:7 And there was war in heaven, Michael and his angels waging war with the dragon. And the dragon and his angel's waged war.

12:8 And they were not strong enough, and there was no longer a place found for them in heaven.

12:9 And the great dragon was thrown down, the serpent of old who is called the devil and Satan, who deceives the whole world; he was thrown down to the earth, and his angels were thrown down with him.

12:10 And I heard a loud voice in heaven, saying, "Now the salvation, and the power, and the kingdom of our God and the authority of His Christ have come, for the accuser of our brethren has been thrown down, who accuses them before our God day and night.

12:11 And they overcame him because of the blood of the Lamb and because of the word of their testimony, and they did not love their life even to death.

12:12 For this reason, rejoice, O heavens and you who dwell in them. Woe to the earth and the sea, because the devil has come down to you, having great wrath, knowing that he has only a short time.

12:13 And when the dragon saw that he was thrown down to the earth, he persecuted the woman who gave birth to the male child.

12:14 And the two wings of the great eagle were given to the woman, in order that she might fly into the wilderness to her place, where she was nourished for a time and times and half a time, from the presence of the serpent.

12:15 And the serpent poured water like a river out of his mouth after the woman, so that he might cause her to be swept away with the flood.

12:16 And the earth helped the woman, and the earth opened its mouth and drank up the river which the dragon poured out of his mouth.

12:17 And the dragon was enraged with the woman, and went off to make war with the rest of her offspring, who keep the commandments of God and hold to the testimony of Jesus.

As we saw above in the fall, Virgo is the sign of the zodiac that rules the sky. According to the original "astrology," the quantum God arranged it that way to begin His story recorded in the stars. His plan is to bring God and man back together again by bridging the gap in the estranged relationship. What caused the estranged relationship? Well, we saw historical and biblical accounts of how the rebel alien angels visited Earth and stole the hearts and minds and bodies of many of the humans at that time and genetically modified the human race to create one of their own, the Nephilum of Gen 6 that Enoch and Josephus and others spoke about. Humanity was in the arms of another lover and being replaced by mutants. The Flood put a stop to that as the chokepoint of human genetic history, when Noah's pure family human DNA restarted the population.

So on 9-11-3 BC we find Virgo dominant in the night sky and on this night a strange thing occurs. The Moon, along with Jupiter considered by many to represent the Messiah, travels through the birth canal of Virgo the Virgin. Just below her feet the constellation Draco the dragon or serpent was poised to devour the newly birthed child, but just before dawn it is caught up away from the threatening serpent. It appears that what we have here is a combination of, and an intersection of two code systems left by the quantum God that essentially tell the same story.

This is where the story in the sky, the original zodiac, and the holidays claimed by the quantum God of creation meet. A Virgin birth indeed. Let's look deeper at the story hidden in the holidays or feasts as they have played out so far.

Gabriel appears to Mary during Hanukkah 4 BC and tells her that she will be the Earth Mother to the God of Creation. He will cause His energy to become matter within her and that He himself would become human and do what only He could do: reunite God and man. This all occurs on the Festival of Lights! It makes sense; God is called the Father of Lights (another of His many names).

It would be appropriate then, if His plan were to "father" a messiah (himself in human form) through supernatural means, that He would do it on the Festival of Lights. The light of the world enters the world in the form of an embryo of energy on the Festival of Lights that celebrates a victory of good over evil and a new start with a supernatural light. Indeed! Nine months later on the Feast of Trumpets 9-11-3 BC, the God of Creation is "born" on the day that history and Jewish tradition says Adam was "born" (created). Many scholars call Jesus the second Adam. It appears that they even share the same birthday. A lot of study of rabbinical records and some instant inspiration, and yes, even a hidden Torah code have shown me it is very possible that Yeshua was indeed supernaturally conceived on the Feast of Hanukah 24-25 Kislev, 3758, which was Dec.13th, 4 BC.

Yeshua was pure energy wrapped in humanity within the sealed womb of a human being. Better than science fiction... it was the quantum God at work. How appropriate that the Father of lights chose the Festival of Lights to introduce Himself. His son as an embryo into the Earth that He had created. Nine months later, the ideal gestation time, Yeshua is born on the Feast of Trumpets 9-11-3 BC. The sign of Revelation 12 appeared in the sky that night as it did again on 9-11-99 also the Feast of Trumpets, the day that, is set aside for repentance. This is the primary theme, although the rabbis also teach that:

* This is the day that Israel will be gathered.

* This is the coronation day of the King of kings. On His "birthday?"

* This is the resurrection day.

* This is a day for judgment. Psalm 81:4

* This is a day to remember the fathers.

* This is a day to blow the shofar.

* This is the day that the world was created... sixth day and Adam's birthday

Again, you can check the NASA software regarding the sign in the heavens that day.

Before NASA existed, astrologers from the eastern kingdoms of Babylon and Medo Persia (Iran and Iraq area) who were trained in the school of Zoroaster by Daniel, recognized the sign in the Zodiac that night. Daniel had taught them of the ancient meaning of the Zodiac and the timing of the Messiah's birth.

But before the 9-11 sign they observed some other alignments that Daniel told them to watch for! On what would have been August 12 3 BC the Magi from Medo–Persia, from a school of stargazers formed and trained originally by Daniel, would have seen the two planets Jupiter and Venus rise in conjunction. (A conjunction is when celestial bodies line up so closely that they appear to the naked eye as a single super bright light.) Jupiter signified kingship or Messiah and Venus meant birth and motherhood. This occurred in the constellation of Leo, which is the symbol of the Hebrew tribe Judah. The Magi were studied in the Hebrew scriptures and probably knew from Genesis 49:10 that the Messiah would come from the tribe of Judah!

Then a month later they saw the next sign! On September 3, they saw Jupiter rise in conjunction with Regulus. Regulus is the brightest star in the constellation of Leo—a symbol of rulership. Then came the night of 9-11-3 BC. They knew the Messiah was being born as they watched this sign play out in the skies as Daniel had said it would many years before. They may have had their camels saddled already!

Matthew 2:1 "After Jesus was born in Bethlehem of Judea in the days of Herod the king, behold, wise men (magi) from the East came to Jerusalem, saying, "Where is He who has been born King of the Jews? For we have seen His star in the East and have come to worship Him."

Many have missed this and think that they showed up the same night as the shepherds. It does not sound that way to me. They saw the series of signs and then saddled up for Jerusalem on 9-12-3 BC, if you ask me. But how cool is that? They were guarding a word passed on from the great prophet Daniel, a member of the Creator's chosen tribe, a slave, prime minister, friend to rulers of the known world and someone who could play with lions all night without being injured.

They held on to his word, which shows the credibility he held with those who came even generations after his death. They believed his word about the future and watched for generations for it to occur, and when it did play out in the skies as He predicted they acted on it! Not even from the same tribe, but they realized that we are all from the same family!

They not only came to honor the King but to provide the finances for his youth, much of it spent on the run in Egypt from a misguided Edomite king ruling in the land of His birth.

"The people that do know their God shall be strong." Daniel 11:32

It appears that they believed Daniel's word and when they saw the Rev. 12 sign on 9-11-3 BC that the Messiah was born, they knew that if they took the first step, a supernatural star would guide them to the King. It did.

Let's see how Jesus was related to the other feasts. The night before His sacrifice he celebrated the Passover Seder, the "last supper." He broke the bread into the customary three pieces, wrapped one in clean linen, which was hidden away until later when it was found and reassembled with the other two parts symbolizing His death, burial, and resurrection, and the rejoining of the triune Godhead, three parts of one whole... back into one.

Crucified at the proper hour on the Passover, he was the fulfillment of the Passover lamb for all of humanity. Then resting on the Feast of Unleavened Bread, He was the bread of life without sin or corruption, without leaven. He was then raised on the Feast of First Fruits, the "first fruits" to gain victory over death. The proper number of days later on Pentecost, His spirit flowed throughout the Earth, making its symbolic mark in the symbolic city of Jerusalem.

What is next? What feasts has He yet to touch and fulfill? It appears that they are the Feasts of Atonement, (at-one-ment) and Tabernacles. I suggest we should study those for their timing, sequence, and prophetic meanings. Atonement, among many other things, acts out the "next step" in the trail of atoning blood. In the old days it was the only time blood was placed on the mercy seat that has always covered the law. It was the only time man saw God face to face. Could we expect the symbolic and literal fulfillment of the feast or holy days by Jesus to continue? Following the Day of Atonement is the Feast of Tabernacles. What could be its ultimate fulfillment?

Rev 21:2-7

21:2 And I saw the holy city, new Jerusalem, coming down out of heaven from God, made ready as a bride adorned for her husband.

21:3 And I heard a loud voice from the throne, saying, "Behold, the tabernacle of God is among men, and He shall dwell among them, and they shall be His people, and God Himself shall be among them,

21:4 and He shall wipe away every tear from their eyes; and there shall no longer be (any) death; there shall no longer be (any) mourning, or crying, or pain; the first things have passed away."

21:5 And He who sits on the throne said, "Behold, I am making all things new." And He said, "Write, for these words are faithful and true."

21:6 And He said to me, "It is done. I am the Alpha and the Omega, the beginning and the end. I will give to the one who thirsts from the spring of the water of life without cost.

21:7 "He who overcomes shall inherit these things, and I will be his God and he will be My son.

Rebellion resolved. Duality banished! Unity established forever!

It's where Hollywood got the happy in its happy endings. It's the greatest love story, the greatest war story, the great spy flick, the most real sci-fi alien film ever produced! It could be that Shakespeare was right: all the world is a stage and we are just actors in the play! I would add co-producers.

In summary, let's consider the life and times and historical facts of Yeshua and how he energizes and gives meaning to the feasts or dress rehearsals. How he decodes the code in the holidays. He was:

Conceived during Hanukkah. Probably Dec. 13th 4 BC

Born on the Feast of Trumpets 9-11-3 BC, 1 Tishri

Died on Passover Friday

He rested wrapped in linen like the affikomen on the Feast of Unleavened Bread, a double Shabbat

He rose from the dead on the Feast of First Fruits Sunday morning

Sent His Spirit to cover the Earth on Pentecost

I am unaware of a connection on Purim... yet

Yet to come:

At one ment... coming together as one with Him

Tabernacles... dwelling together with Him

Coincidence? The rabbis say there is no such thing!

So what happens when the astrology of origin overlaps with the feasts of the Bible? Usually some interesting things. Take, for instance, the much-talked about four blood red moons that are facing us now. Starting in the spring of 2014, on Passover begins an interesting astronomical phenomena called a tetrad, four complete lunar eclipses in a row with no partials in between. Astrology of Origin says that this could be a sign and signal a change of conditions here on this little rebel planet. What events or seasons could they be signaling? Remember that the key to the codes said:

Gen 1:14 Then God said, "Let there be lights in the firmament of the heavens to divide the day from the night; and let them be for signs and seasons, and for days and years;

Gen 1:15 And let them be for lights in the firmament of the heavens to give light on the earth"; and it was so.

Lev. 23:1 The LORD said to Moses, 2 "Speak to the Israelites and say to them: 'These are My appointed feasts, the appointed feasts of the LORD, which you are to proclaim as sacred assemblies.

Luke 21:25 And there shall be signs in the sun, and in the moon, and in the stars; and upon the earth distress of nations, with perplexity; the sea and the waves roaring;

It was becoming clear to me that before man existed, the Creative Force we call God designed a system in space to communicate "His" times and seasons.

Then, at a time when the earthlings had been infested with a Rebel and his lies, and he had done his worst to obliterate the truth contained in the astrology of origin, the Creator God introduced another system, the biblical feasts that again contained His plan to reunite Divinity with Humanity. At that point in time the branch of the family tree he entrusted it to was no longer blessed, but found it to be in a primitive state, beaten down with a slave mentality, working for a nation that lorded over them their connection to the Rebel. It was into this state that the Creator God introduced "His" holidays, Holy – days, appointments with the Source, where God and Man would meet for dress rehearsals of what was to come. They were designed to point to "His" coming attraction, His plan to reunite God with man as man matured.

You just saw that this tetrad of 2014 and 2015, the blood red moons as NASA calls them, begins on one of the days this Creator God calls His Holy days, Passover. Now if more than one of these blood red moons were to fall on God's moeds (holidays), well, we are told by God back in Genesis that it would be for a sign... to mark a season. But guess what—all four are! The first one is on Passover in 2014 and the second on Tabernacles 2014, the third on Passover 2015, and the fourth on Tabernacles 2015!

You think that might have some significance? But that's still not all! There is a sign in the sun during this time period as well. Right in the middle of these four unique total lunar eclipses come a couple of signs in the Sun... yep, you guessed it—on a holiday, too!

Are you ready for some more interesting data? On Nissan 1 (the day Moses set up the Tabernacle) the head of the "Jewish" spiritual new year 2015—approximately April 1st—there will be a solar eclipse followed two weeks later by the lunar eclipse on Passover (third of four)... followed by another solar eclipse on The Feast of Trumpets, followed a few days later by a lunar eclipse (fourth of four) on The feast of Tabernacles. Really? Yes! What does it mean? I don't know, but perhaps it bears some time in study...

If the source of Creation, that energy field, that spirit that maintains this Cosmos said these were appointments with "Him" and that the "signs in the heavens"—the sun, moon, and stars—were markers of special events and doubly when they coincide with His Holidays or moeds, then one would reasonably expect something profound from the spring of 2014 to the fall of 2015, or close to it.

I decided to look back and see if and when this had ever happened before.

Guess what? In 1967-68 it happened just as it will in 2014 and 2015! What significant event occurred that year involving "His

Tribe"? The six-day war—the Yom Kippur (a moed) war—where the Islamic nations that surround Israel attacked her! On Israel's most holy day the Islamic nations surrounding her executed a vicious surprise attack, and miraculously Israel not only survived, but soundly defeated the attackers and regained more of its Biblical birthright land, including the temple mount in Jerusalem. Did it happen any other time in recent history? Well, surprise, it did! Right after Israel became a modern nation in 1948 this same sign occurred in '49 and '50 on these same holidays, or moed, set times of the Creator. Some skeptics may say that probably happens all the time, but if you check the NASA site, you will see that it has not occurred in previous four or five hundred years anyway. But go back to 1492, when Columbus sailed the ocean blue, when all the Jews were expelled from Spain, and you will see that this same sign occurred as well in 1493 and 1494. Some historians have said they believe that some of the Jews expelled from Spain came to the new world at this time. In 32 and 33 AD this sign occurred as well. History records the Crucifixion of Jesus on Passover 33 AD in conjunction with the 3rd eclipse of that Tetrad. Coincidence? Probably not!

It is illogical to believe that this is simply coincidence. It takes less faith to believe that a higher power, the source of Creation, the Torah code, and the Cosmos itself, is indeed doing what it said in Genesis, that is, using the Sun, the Moon, and the stars as signs to His people. All the inhabitants of the Earth, His Earth, were free to see these signs marking major events occurring on His appointed days, the moeds.

As you saw above in the Torah, Leviticus 23, the Hebrew term moed was used for appointments and convocations. The meaning? Appointments between God and man, His dress rehearsals of coming attractions. He wanted to communicate with us what was coming next! And He designed a system that even primitive man could understand and observe.

Perhaps it would be wise to consider the author of Genesis and "His" claim to be the source of all things and then consider His communication and timekeeping system. After all, it was designed so that even primitive man could understand.

You might come to the realization that the feasts/holy days appointments have all been prophetically fulfilled with the exception of the feasts of Yom Kipper and Tabernacles. One explanation could be for those remaining fulfillments to occur when the God-man, Jesus, who fulfilled all the others, will have His feet touch down on the Mount of Olives, as Zechariah 14 says, on Yom Kipper the one day when man saw God face-to-face, and then begin His millennial reign on the Feast of Tabernacles… Tabernacling, living together with us!

"The people that do know their God shall be strong."

Ezek 37:11-23

37:11 Then he said to me: "Son of man, these bones are the whole house of Israel. They say, 'Our bones are dried up and our hope is gone; we are cut off.'

37:12 Therefore prophesy and say to them: 'This is what the Sovereign LORD says: O my people, I am going to open your graves and bring you up from them; I will bring you back to the land of Israel.

37:13 Then you, my people, will know that I am the LORD, when I open your graves and bring you up from them.

37:14 I will put my Spirit in you and you will live, and I will settle you in your own land. Then you will know that I the LORD have spoken, and I have done it, declares the LORD.

37:15 The word of the LORD came to me:

37:16 Son of man, take a stick of wood and write on it, 'Belonging to Judah and the Israelites associated with him.' Then take another stick of wood, and write on it, 'Ephraim's stick, belonging to Joseph and all the house of Israel associated with him.'

37:17 Join them together into one stick so that they will become one in your hand.

37:18 When your countrymen ask you, 'Won't you tell us what you mean by this?'

37:19 Say to them, 'This is what the Sovereign LORD says: I am going to take the stick of Joseph—which is in Ephraim's hand—and of the Israelite tribes associated with him, and join it to Judah's stick, making them a single stick of wood, and they will become one in my hand.'

37:20 Hold before their eyes the sticks you have written on.

37:21 And say to them, 'This is what the Sovereign LORD says: I will take the Israelites out of the nations where they have gone. I will gather them from all around and bring them back into their own land.'

37:22 I will make them one nation in the land, on the mountains of Israel. There will be one king over all of them and they will never again be two nations or be divided into two kingdoms.

37:23 They will no longer defile themselves with their idols and vile images or with any of their offenses, for I will save them from all their sinful backsliding, and I will cleanse them. They will be my people, and I will be their God.

NIV

Now that's unity… that's a heavenly happy ending that even a skeptic hopes is true. This former skeptic does. This brief study of the Zodiac and the holidays as they appear arranged by the Creator still acts as an eternal witness to His plan to reunite humanity and divinity. If true, He became one of us 2000 years ago, the night of the Rev 12 sign in the sky on 9-11-3 BC on the Feast of Trumpets. That should get our attention. Many believe that on 9-11-99 "The time of the Gentiles was fulfilled" as refered to in the Bible. What does that mean? Many theories abound but one thing is for certain, we are in a transition time between epics as we enter the seventh millennium, since this part of Earth's history began with the "birth" of Adam. We are entering the seventh day in "God's" timetable. It has also been referred to as the third day... being the seventh day since the first Adam, and the third day from the second Adam... Jesus the Messiah. If this is true, then the seventh day since "Creation" is the same as the third day, since the Creator became one of us in the form of the Messiah, and He has promised in the New Testament that a "wedding will take place "on the "third day." He says He is returning for His bride, those who believe in Him. He also said He would be rejected and go back to His place for two days, then return and "rejuvenate his people" in Hosea 5 and 6 of the Old Testament.

David said in Psalms that "A day is as a thousand years to you," so 2000 years later to us and two days later to Him, perhaps He is preparing to make a return engagement sometime in the not-too-distant future? Time is relative, as we know, so if true, only He would know for sure when! Please may I caution you not to fall into a luanitic fringe and run out in to the desert and wait to be beamed up. Even if you believe everything I have just shared, I think that would be stupid. I present this material for further exploration and because it was part of my own personal search.

As I mentioned, the Torah code also speaks about this Revelation 12 sign in the sky on the night of 9-11-3 BC. It "confirms" that it was the night of the birth of Jesus. I found this "Bible Code" myself the night of 9-10-99.

This is part of the information in the Bible code I found:

1. Announcement to Mary took place on 22 Kislev 3758, (December 10/11, 4 BC.)

2. Mary conceived the Child by the Holy Spirit took place on the end of 24 Kislev, beginning of 25 Kislev in the evening, in the year 3758, which was December 13, 4 BC. (This was the beginning of Hanukkah.)

3. Birth of Yeshua in Bethlehem took place on 1 Tishri 3759 Rosh Hashanah, which was September 11, 3 BC. (Feast of Trumpets)

4. Brit Milah (dedication) at the Temple—(took place on) 8 Tishri 3759, (which was September 18, 3 BC.)

Since 9-11-99 I have since seen that other researchers have also found these codes and others that confirm the times and dates of Yeshua's birth!

I have also discovered another interesting "code" in the Hebrew language that relates to His birth. Remember our discovery of gematria, the mathematical matrix that assigns each Hebrew letter a numerical value? Well, guess what... the Hebrew word for "pregnancy" has the value of 271 which is the number of days for a "normal" gestation of a human baby. The Hebrew word for pregnancy/conception is "herayon" (hey resh yud vav nun). The numerical values are as follows:

hey=5, resh=200, yud=10, vav=6, nun=50; or total=5+200+10+6+50=271

You can do the math, but I'll tell you, it fits!

We are not superstitious, ignorant peasants! Neither are we arrogant, deluded pseudo sophisticates thinking we are the only ones in the Cosmos, right? We are using both sides of our brains now, correct?

We know that this coming tetrad of lunar eclipses with another solar eclipse occuring in the middle are governed by the laws of astrophysics, but what are the odds of those coming events falling on "Biblical Holy days"? It has been calculated. Perhaps it is the season to consider the option that an intelligent designer designed these events to happen right "now." That before the beginning of the concept of time as a separate dimension, when all the dimensions were still connected, that these events were designed to occur "now."

The software that runs your computer was designed by a software engineer. What about the exponentially more complex software that runs the universe... who designed it? Think about it.

Starynight software is fun and the software program NASA utilizes is incredible, but consider that this software that we have been looking at does not simply track the Cosmos and its trillions of stars, planets, solar systems, universes, and black holes… you get the picture… it designed it and programed it and it would appear that it is still running it!

Well, by now I may have "cleared the room." On one side we have the religious extremeists of all faiths climbing back into their boxes and on the other side we have the agnostic pseudo intellectuals on the scientific fringe of no faith, retreating to the shelter of their preconceived ideas… but in the middle of the room stand the truth seekers, looking a bit dazed and confused but still standing! Take a deep breath and relax. You don't have to believe everything you read you know. In fact you shouldn't until you prove it to yourself with your own search. There is more science, more spirituality, more myth busting and more code breaking and truth just ahead as we consider how we as humans relate to the concept of a Quantum God.

I go to nature to be soothed and healed,
and to have my senses put in order.
~ John Burroughs

Chapter 11
Man's Ability to Conceptualize a Quantum God

Fine! The gloves are off, pal! C'mon, lemme see a little wrath! Smite me, O mighty smiter! You're the one who should be fired! The only one around here not doing his job is You! ANSWER ME!
~ Jim Carrey addressing "God" as Bruce Nolan
in *Bruce Almighty* 2003

As a father of six children and currently eight grandchildren, I am reminded of one of my boys who would run to keep up with Daddy until he just couldn't any more. Then he would maneuver to get in front of me with both hands outstretched and say: "Carry you... Carry you, Daddy?" He was asking for Daddy to carry him. There are so many sweet memories of our children that we cherish forever.

However, that doesn't mean I wouldn't slap the hand of that same sweet innocent young son... if he reached out to touch a campfire knowing that it would burn and disfigure him for life.

We all go through stages of development and there are appropriate rules and regulations for each of those stages. What may seem restrictive and harsh to an uninformed outsider might be just the thing that saves grave damage to a young one who is still naive to the dangers of the world.

But rules change as maturity levels change. It is abnormal to remain in pre-school into your teens. Yet religion, in many cases, has done just that! Ways of relating to God are often passed on from generation to generation without thought, as if they are sovereign truth. This filters the perceptions of our image of God in a severely dysfunctional manner. It puts God in someone else's box and limits the perception of this Magnificent Creator to the perceptions of the original "box maker."

To be free and understand the magnitude of God, we must free the mind. Education at its purest teaches us how to relate, how to think... outside the box. It shows us how to think for ourselves. When it doesn't do that, what used to protect us then traps us. However, it is our choice; we can stand in our "box" or reach to the sky for more information... more freedom. The same is true of our spiritual journey. It is not wise to remain in our boxes for too long or our perceptions become distorted and our growth will become stunted. I believe there is an ultimate truth, an equation of everything, but for now I am in a box that limits my perception. So are you. Our environment, our culture, our schooling, our religion, on and on... the boxes that form our foundations determine our perceptions to a large degree. With any luck and an open mind we will emerge with a great view some day.

> It was six men of Indostan
> To learning much inclined,
> Who went to see the Elephant
> (Though all of them were blind),
> That each by observation
> Might satisfy his mind.
> The First approached the Elephant,
> And happening to fall
> Against his broad and sturdy side,
> At once began to bawl:
> "God bless me! but the Elephant

Is very like a wall!"
The Second, feeling of the tusk
Cried, "Ho! what have we here,
So very round and smooth and sharp?
To me 'tis mighty clear
This wonder of an Elephant
Is very like a spear!"
The Third approached the animal,
And happening to take
The squirming trunk within his hands,
Thus boldly up he spake:
"I see," quoth he, "the Elephant
Is very like a snake!"
The Fourth reached out an eager hand,
And felt about the knee:
"What most this wondrous beast is like
Is mighty plain," quoth he;
"'Tis clear enough the Elephant
Is very like a tree!"
The Fifth, who chanced to touch the ear,
Said: "E'en the blindest man
Can tell what this resembles most;
Deny the fact who can,
This marvel of an Elephant
Is very like a fan!"
The Sixth no sooner had begun
About the beast to grope,
Than, seizing on the swinging tail
That fell within his scope.
"I see," quoth he, "the Elephant
Is very like a rope!"
And so these men of Indostan
Disputed loud and long,
Each in his own opinion
Exceeding stiff and strong,
Though each was partly in the right,
And all were in the wrong!
~ John Godfrey Saxe, 1816-1887

Great word picture, isn't it? We are sure we have it all figured out, and in fact most of us do have a lot of things figured out—at least to a greater degree than when we were young and immature. The question is what boxes are we blind, too? Where have we become frozen in our ice boxes? How has that distorted our views of reality?

We might be stuck in a box of old inaccurate, outdated understandings that have been passed on for generations, but if it is a blind spot how will we know? How do you see a blind spot? Good question! We may have grown up to PhD level in life and academics, but maybe we are still stuck in a kindergarten mindset when it comes to the larger picture of life due to some poor instruction or perhaps some traumatic experiences or events early in life that left a blind spot, a box of constriction. Becoming a lifelong learner is imperative in today's world and that includes our spiritual nature as well.

I believe it is essential that we take time to educate, play, and rest our minds bodies and spirits. Balance in all things is the mantra and that means that ideally we will grow continually throughout our lives in every dimension. How foolish to become a PhD in family matters and business or even emotional maturity, yet stay frozen in time in our relationship to God. It would be like leaving a part of you wrapped up in a box back in kindergarten. Get over yourself, get outside yourself and get moving again, and laugh yes especially at yourself. Nothing will shatter old paradigms and set you free from blind spots and boxes faster!

Obviously, no one can literally fit God into a box. It is our limited perceptions that create a view of God that restrict our understanding of Him to a box of our own making. He clearly is not limited by our understanding, we are. Our limited perceptions must have a range of vision as diverse as the human experience itself, Lots of boxes! Even the atheist has a box for God... it's just empty... Because they need their God, to be absent and nonexistent, while at the other end of the spectrum "we" mystics perceive our God in a box of pure love and light.

I find this interesting because I have spanned this spectrum personally. I like my current position better than where I started.

Our perceptions are incredibly powerful and govern what we see and how we interpret our experiences. Our preconceived ideas and filters have boxes ready for each experience so as to neatly make sense of the chaos and to create a measure of order from our daily disorder. Those who believe in reincarnation—the ultimate recycling program—have a box with a revolving door... sort of like the Eagles song "Hotel California": *You can check out but you can never leave.*

We are so busy shaping and reshaping the boxes we inherited from our family systems or culture or religion of lack thereof that we often will go a lifetime without truly looking outside "our" box to the unseen dimensions and the real world. We even fool ourselves into thinking we left our boxes we inherited behind when all we did was move the furniture around inside the box we are in!

Just because God is seen in a certain way by us doesn't mean he is that way. Over the course of a lifetime we will hopefully see Him and encounter Him in many different forms and roles. Much as we do our own parents and teachers.

I believe the progression to know God... really know Him outside the boxes of our preconceived ideas is a life-long journey of outgrowing one box after another, one paradigm after another, one set of filters after another, growing in understanding with each box shed like a cocoon. We never will become butterflies and stop crawling like caterpillars if we stay in our cocoons, will we?

Our vision of God seems to grow directly out of our deepest inner values. So as our values change, as we mature and hopefully become enlightened, so then, do our perceptions of God. When I was a child I saw and acted as a child... etc. This transition is spoken of by the Biblical teacher Paul. He was an expert at shedding his perceptions of God! He went from a knowledgeable strong arm enforcer of what he perceived to be true to a Mystic with practical applications of his out-of-the-box experiences. He shed the confines of the normal dimensions we all live and operate in. In fact, he managed to be caught up into the "seventh Heaven," seventh being the number of completion. Perhaps he was saying he was able to leave this material world and transition into the other dimensions physicists tell us are out there, into a place that lacks nothing... to a place of completion where he saw "God" as "He" is, no boxes allowed. When he returned he was unable to fully describe those dimensions... just that they were complete and lacked nothing.

Some say that man created God, that God is simply an invention of the ignorant or the simple to answer the questions that they are unable to answer and to lend meaning to their otherwise meaningless lives. They contend that as we grow in understanding, we no longer need the concept of "God" to explain those things that were previously unexplainable. My search actually did the opposite; science guided me toward a higher power not because I was superstitious and uninformed, but because of the amazement that I developed for the complex yet intricate order that exists in science and nature. I agree that as we grow in understanding our relationship, our vision of who God is will change... I hope so! He does not exist in the sand boxes of kindergarten except to relate to those who are there. He is simple, yet complex, understandable to a pre-schooler and a mystery to a genius like Einstein. If we take the time to relate to him, He is relevant and a friend at every stage of our growth, even though His essence is so far beyond where even our greatest scientists have gone so far.

There is a text in the Bible that says it is the glory of God to conceal a matter and the glory of his Kings (us) to reveal (uncover) a matter. He does not want us to sit in a box of ignorance but to grow and discover and uncover those secrets still yet to be found. He designed it that way so we don't get bored.

As our intellects soar and the information we understand increases exponentially, it only makes sense to an enlightened mind that the cosmic mind has been this way before and is happy that we are where we are… although is unimpressed…it's still preschool for Him. What impresses Him is when an individual frees his spirit as well and soars like Einstein did in his imagination, not desiring information only as another god… or box, but wanting to learn to think *like* God in a constant upward progression. We don't outgrow God but we do outgrow simplistic paradigms; kindergarten views of God fade away as we grow spiritually. Just like we no longer believe the moon is made of cheese, simplistic views of who and what God is are outgrown as well. The moon isn't threatened. The moon does not cease to exist! In fact, now we know that there is more to the moon than we ever thought possible. Minerals have been discovered that will be well worth mining for. What a metaphor! Perhaps it is a good one for the relationship with God as well. There are always new truths worth mining for in a relationship with the energy source that creates and sustains it all. If you ask me, He wouldn't have it any other way.

It is important to learn what we must in pre-school, in middle school, high school, college, and beyond because each new level of knowledge and understanding builds a firm foundation. We weren't meant to live in the basement. We were designed for the penthouse! Keep building higher.

In ancient times when the God of Creation, the quantum God, spoke to Moses, He gave instructions on how to convey how things worked in the transitional dimension between Heaven and Earth, where God and man interacted. He said, "Build me a tabernacle, a place to dwell on Earth that follows the Heavenly pattern." These are the dimensions that quantum physicists believe must exist... somewhere. Adam and God are said to have walked together face-to-face in that time before the rebellion. It is my contention that this was possible because we as a human race were accessing at least ten dimensions in our beings but with the rebellion there was a consequence and part of it was the removal of that access to the universe, a house arrest as it were. We were limited to our physical dimensions and domiciled here on Earth alone, with more of the Cosmos existing right next to us in dimensions we can perhaps at times sense, but have yet to access.

The Tabernacle became a place of overlapping dimensions—man's, man/God, and God's dimensions in the form of a place where we could see that God desired to be among us and that there was a way to approach Him even in our rebellious state. It was a place where our dimensions could overlap and we could communicate with each other. The "outer court" was man's, and it represented Earth, man's dimension. "The Holy Place" was the transition zone or place of overlapping dimensions where God could influence and touch emotionally and spiritually His creation... humanity. Then there was His, God's dimension, represented by the "Most Holy Place."

The holidays, three of them especially, that we just looked at, periodically directed the People to come to the tabernacle and interface with God. They pointed to a time when this pattern would be restored to the one before the rebellion when God and man interacted "face to face." As we saw, the hidden messages within each one speaks of the reconciliation of God and man and His plan to become one of us and reconcile man again to God. Like Bruce Nolan as Bruce Almighty prophetically sang, "What if God was one of us?"

It is recorded that at the moment Yeshua died on the cross, an unseen "hand" tore the "indestructible" curtain that separated the Most Holy Place from the Holy Place... from the top to the bottom. There must be a message there, somewhere? Perhaps it said I am out... I am coming for you, no longer limited to My dimension. My spirit will invade the Earth, and for those who desire we no longer are limited to the transition zone but... I will take you higher... to my dimensions, and He does with those who are willing. This is a place where the Mystics dwell—Enoch, Moses, Elijah, John, Paul, and others—throughout history.

This is a place of deep relationship, not found in our pre-school view of God, not in our middle school view of God, not in our high school view of God, not even in our college or post grad view of

God. It's the PhD, tenured professors approach and view of God; that is, one who has truly become a humble life-long learner... who can lead others into enlightenment... the Sifu, the Sensei, the Master's perspective.

It is His intention that His dimension will continue to expand through the transition zone and past it throughout the entire Cosmos, enveloping and swallowing up our dimension, establishing unity again throughout the universe... as the three dimensions—His, ours, and the transition zone—give way for the original order. That is the mystical and magical place called the Garden of Eden where humanity lived in the ten or twelve dimensions that existed before the rebellion. It still exists. Where, you ask? Well, perhaps right beside you in a cosmic Area 51, restricted dimensional airspace. Wherever the lost dimensions are, they will one day reappear and be reconnected.

His Kingdom will continue to expand and there will be no end of it as it reestablishes the proper order to the universe and brings unity again to our world. Throughout the entire Cosmos the duality that has brought such disorder and chaos will be consumed...

Part of the dissolution of duality and the reestablishment of Divine unity occurs each time we foolish humans realize that the gulf between spirituality and science only exists as a grand canyon in our own minds... science and religion are not really opposites but just very different ways of trying to decode the universe. Like non-identical twins. Or perhaps closer to home like the left and right hemisphere of our brains that had a fight over the perception of reality and aren't talking… quite dysfunctional!

Both see a vision that contains the spiritual and the material world, but they seem to have blind spots where the other is concerned. What could possibly reunite our twins, our competing views of reality, living within our own minds?

Maybe a little electroshock therapy? Perhaps it's as simple as backing off for a minute and getting the big picture back before spirituality and science split. If you go back far enough you are faced with the profundity that something had to start something… on a quantum level something had to exist to apply frequencies to "itself" to create matter, the elements, quantum particles, the Higgs field, etc. There has to be an unseen source of creation, because the Cosmos can be traced back only so far before time and space dissolve. And there has to be a place where these two perceived opposites meet. Why? Because statistically and mystically, that's how I see it. Isn't it past time to heal the philosophical lobotomy and the damage it has done to our understanding of true reality?

If we only had a time machine we could settle this in a second! Well, some second, somewhere, would hold the answer, right? Buckle up, folks, we are going to take a trip like Einstein was fond of taking. A trip into the unknown using our imaginations as our means of transportation… for the moment, anyway. We may find something better in a moment, a second, or… well, you get the picture. Time, it is just so relative…

How can we travel through time?

Time travel is hard. Really hard. In fact, in ancient ages, most people believed that it was entirely impossible.

Was I talking to the preschooler in you? Let's step it up a bit. Time was seen as just a linear series of events. Cause and effect—that was the order of things, and it could not be changed. Or could it? Einstein's Theory of Relativity described time and space as fluid things that merge into each other, and what had been the traditional universe since the split of spirituality and science couldn't hold up. Before the split it seems the ancients knew more than we now do, in some areas at least. Once we split science apart from spirit we had to relearn everything, prove it on our own so to speak, but the cool thing is that we are! In the process I believe we will see a healing of our self-induced skitsophrenia.

In *Bruce Almighty,* God tells Bruce that he is going on vacation and makes Bruce God for a week so that he could just fix everything:

> *God (Morgan Freeman) "There are only two rules. You can't tell anybody you're God; believe me you don't want that kind of attention. And you can't mess with free will."*
> *Bruce Nolan (Jim Carrey) "Can I ask why?"*
> *God (Morgan Freeman) "Yes, you can; that's the beauty of it!"*

That's as good as it gets in our present labotimized state. We need both sides of our brains working to ask AND find the answers.

Astronomer Frank Tipler has proposed a means of time travel he calls the "Infinite Cylinder." Infinite? Sounds a bit like spirit, doesn't it?

Here is the theory in a nutshell: This mechanism would allow very advanced civilizations (very, very, very advanced civilizations, or perhaps interdimensional spirit beings) to travel through time.

For this cylinder to work, you will need matter that is roughly ten times the sun's mass (a LOT of matter). But that's easy; that's just frequencies applied to energy, right?

Then you will need to roll this matter into a very long and very dense cylinder. And I mean very dense. This super-dense cylinder would be a bit like a black hole that has passed through a spaghetti factory (so you can imagine the technology that would be needed to create this density… or spirit).

The key to this device is its spin. Tipler argued that a cylinder might produce closed time-like curves if the rotation rate were fast enough—at least a few billion revolutions per minute. Once the cylinder is rotating fast enough, a spaceship nearby (if it follows a very precise spiral around this cylinder) could possibly travel billions of years into the past and several galaxies away.

However, Stephen Hawking proved that time travel would not work with a finite cylinder unless you have negative energy (rather unlikely). But there is hope! It would be possible if the cylinder is infinitely long.

To sum it up:

~You need to essentially create a black hole in the shape of a cylinder.

~You need to make this super massive, super dense object rotate a billion times a second.

~It needs to be infinitely long.

Saying that this theory is going to be difficult to put into practice is a bit of an understatement, at least for us at our present stage of development.

And that is the point, isn't it? Are we in a self-induced state of arrested development? In our ignorance, are we fighting against our selves—the science camp versus the spirituality camp— when what we really need to do is end the schizophrenia and duality and bring harmony and unity to our minds with science and spirituality? Could be!

Perhaps it time to get out of the false paradigm box of science we were taught from preschool on and drop our preschool approach to God and allow a supernatural and scientific healing to take place! Science and spirit both agree healing takes place more easily when the mind-body-spirit is relaxed, so unwind for a minute and remember the first time you saw the movie, *The Lion King*. Remember when one evening Pumbaa, Timon, and Simba, were laying back relaxing in the grass just as the stars come out?

> *Pumbaa: "Hey, Timon, ever wonder what those sparkly dots are up there?"*
> *Timon: "Pumbaa, I don't wonder; I know."*
> *Pumbaa: "Oh. What are they?"*
> *Timon: "They're fireflies. Fireflies that, uh... got stuck up on that big bluish-black thing."*
> *Pumbaa: "Oh, gee. I always thought they were balls of gas burning billions of miles away."*
> *Timon: "Pumbaa, with you, everything's gas. What do you think, Simba?"*
> *Adult Simba: "Well... "*
> *Timon: "Yeah?"*
> *Adult Simba: Somebody once told me that the great kings of the past are up there, watching over us.*
> *Pumbaa: Really?*
> *Timon: You mean a bunch of royal dead guys are watching us?*

Can you spot the boxes?

As college students we used to joke that all PhD stood for was the same stuff just... piled higher and deeper. Perhaps we could reframe that and call it "Placed Higher and Deeper into the things of God and His science," and we might just take a quantum leap!

So with that in mind, let's go higher and deeper into some science as well:

I guess you could say that a Type 1 A supernova is one of those "Royal dead guys up there watching us." But as the movie *The Lion King* also says, there is a "circle of life" and from death comes life at another level. The circle of life can be seen played out above us from the active black holes at the center of some of the galaxies to the Type 1 A supernovas that result from the "death" of one of their two stars; yes, you heard me: two stars. Visualize our solar system with two Suns and no night… A Type 1 A supernova is actually the result of a two-star system where one of the stars dies and draws the life out of the other and explodes, forming a supernova. When it explodes, it sends its raw material trillions and trillions of miles into the universe seeding—in effect—new life. Its iron flows throughout the universe in its elemental form. The larger stars that are more dense and become supernovas give off heavier elements like gold and platinum as they die.

Our sun is scheduled to die out in a few billion years—not sure who set that schedule—but as it goes it will become hotter and expand and most likely engulf our planet and then cool off and become a white dwarf star. It is too small to become a supernova, not that it would make much difference to Earthlings at that point. It will become incredibly dense as it cools off so that a teaspoon of its surface will weigh 5.5 tons on earth; that is, if there still is an Earth…

Interestingly, by mass, iron is the earth's most common element, forming much of the inner and outer core of our planet. Seems we may have done our share collecting from the "circle of life." But it turns out that our place in the solar system is unique in that the larger outer planets deflect and absorb much of the incoming debris from space, so most scientists think that it "came that way"; that is, our iron is indigenous.

When a star dies, the nuclear fusion forces diminish and the forces of gravity become un-balanced and more powerful and begin to pull the star in on itself. When the iron element begins to form in what was once a powerful fusion reactor, it is doomed; the iron triggers the process that ends in an explosion, a nova, a supernova, or a hypernova, depending on the size of the star and the number of the stars. Once there is an iron core, the star then shrinks rapidly and explodes. The blast rips through the outer layers and releases the elements into space. I am told that our sun will release iron when it finally goes after living on as a white dwarf star for a few more million years. If it were a much larger and denser star, it would release the heavier elements like gold, etc. into the Cosmos.

Sometimes there is a shell left after the giant explosion of a supernova. It leaves an interstellar zombie-like star, called a neutron star. The average neutron star is 1.5 times the mass of our Sun… and only 12.5 miles across! Talk about dense. One teaspoon of a neutron star would weigh 100,000,000 tons! Really, who weighed one? I want to know!

Astrophysicists say that a piece as small as a grain of sand would go right through our Earth like a hot knife through butter. Its gravitational pull is so strong that if a marshmallow wandered by

(Really, a marshmallow? Stay with me here; let's exercise your imagination), it would be pulled in and strike the surface of the star with the force of a 1000 hydrogen bombs! Some of these critters spin so fast that they blast open on the north and south poles and shoot gamma-rays off into space; spinning like rotating beacons on an airplane, they are called Pulsars.

The first Pulsar was discovered by Jocelyn Burnell and Anthony Hewish in 1967. They found it in the center of the Crab Nebula.

When a larger class of star explodes—say thirty times the size of our sun—they can sometimes leave behind a core, too, and if they do, they become something called a Magnetar, emitting powerful magnetic pulses into space. They are fairly rare; in fact astronomers have only identified ten in our Milky Way Galaxy. These magnetars are even weirder than the Pulsars. They generate massive magnetic fields, powerful enough to suck the hemoglobin right out of your blood from inside a space ship thousands of miles away from its orbit.

Sometimes a supernova of the hypernova magnitude leaves behind such damage that it crushes the time/space dimension and creates a black hole, which distorts the very fabric of space! Scientists have now found that every galaxy has a black hole in some state of existence at its center. Some are actively sucking in raw material and creating new stars and planets, and others seem to be dormant like ours in our Milky Way Galaxy. These stars are one hundred times the size of our sun and when they explode the resulting nuclear explosions are so large it creates something called a hypernova... a bigger supernova but with different results... the formation of a black hole.

A hypernova or hypernovae (plural) nearly started WWIII. Did I get your attention? No, this is not part of your imaginary trip; this really happened! In 1963 the US and the USSR agreed to ban certain nuclear weapons tests and had placed satellites in orbit to monitor each other's compliance with the agreement. In 1979 one of the US satellites detected a series of large nuclear explosions in a remote location over the Indian Ocean. It turned out to be a series of supernovae explosions of the hypernova magnitude. Before that was finally understood, both sides of the cold war grew very hot as the US immediately suspected that the Russians were secretly testing nuclear space weapons and everyone went on high alert. The scientists went to work and saved the day and the world from nuclear war by discovering the phenomena of exploding hypernovaes. It wasn't a "religious" or spiritual leader who saved the day that time... or was it?

So engage your imagination again and visualize this: during a "regular" supernovae explosion gravity crushes the core into a neutron star; weird enough, but in a hypernovae the explosion crushes the core into something even stranger... a black hole! A distortion in the time/space dimension!

The black hole immediately begins to devour the dead star but is unable to consume it fast enough and the force feeding results in the black hole regurgitating energy back out in two great streams in opposite directions. Powerful gamma rays produced by the black hole tear through the remains of the star and explode out into space. (Gamma rays are the most energetic form of light—ten thousand to ten million times more powerful than visible light.)

Astronomer Michelle Thaller says these gamma ray bursts are the most violent events that they have ever recorded in our universe. (I guess they haven't seen my cat and dog get into it.)

The gamma ray bursts are so energetic that every point in the universe will eventually be lit up with their explosion. They typically last for about 100 seconds at a time but some may last for hours. They are the brightest thing in the known universe. To see it in perspective, a typical (if there is one) supernovae explosion will emit as much light as a star like our sun would in ten billion years!

Imagine: a gamma ray burst is 100 million times more brilliant than a supernova! It is without a doubt the brightest of the bright! If a gamma ray burst were to hit the Earth, it would destroy our atmosphere in seconds! Here's a comforting thought... NASA's Swift satellite observes roughly 100 gamma ray bursts every year! The nearest candidate to Earth where this might occur is Eta Carinae. It is 7,500 light years away; not far enough for me!

Eta Carinae suffered a giant outburst about 160 years ago when it became one of the brightest stars in the southern sky. Though the star released as much visible light as a supernova explosion, it survived the outburst. The explosion produced two lobes and a large, thin equatorial disk, all moving outward at about 1 million kilometers per hour.

It appears to be a highly unstable like I am beginning to feel. But it is not the worst neighbor we have. Professor Michio Kaku puts it like this: "We are staring down the gun barrel" of the WR 104 which stands for Wolf-Rayet, discovered by Peter Tuthill in 1998. WR 104 is the big Kahuna, the dying double-star formation that can form a black hole and blast us with gamma rays. WR-104 sits in the constellation Sagittarius about 8000 light years from Earth.

We could be sitting right in the downrange trajectory of those gamma ray bursts when it does go super duper nova (new scientific term). Another astronomer said the good news is that we won't see it coming... it would wipe us out instantaneously. In our wildest science fiction epics, we have no answer for this. All we can do is hope that when the two stars do go hypernovae that the resulting black hole will redirect the gamma ray bursts away from our little planet... that now sits in its crosshairs.

We survived a supernova in 1987 but it was 168,000 light years from Earth! Eta Carinae and WR 104 are much, much closer than supernova 1987.

While studying the supernova in 1987, scientists were able to confirm what was only a theory until then. They discovered that neutrinos existed and that they contained the immeasurable 99 percent of the energy that was necessary for a star to explode. They finally had proof of their math. Now we know that roughly sixty-five billion neutrinos of solar origin pass through every square centimeter of the Earth's surface that is perpendicular to the sun every second! We have come so far since then. What science knows and understands and can prove is exploding like a supernova every day. It is nearly impossible to keep up with the increase of knowledge. As you have read this paragraph you have been hit with literally trillions of neutrinos. Fortunately for us, neutrinos are such weakly interacting particles that they can pass right through you and travel deep into the Earth without hitting other particles. Tiny yet powerful little critters! It's good to be transparent, at least when you have the energy of the stars passing right through you! Literally the energy of the Big Bang flowing right through you and me and every one of us!

Did you know that a man named Fred Hoyle coined the term Big Bang? It turns out he did not even believe in the theory that came to be known by the name he gave it in 1940.

Sir Fred Hoyle's Cambridge years, 1945–1973, saw him rise to the top of world astrophysics theory, grounded on a startling originality of ideas covering a very wide range of topics. In 1958, Hoyle was appointed to the illustrious Plumian Professor of Astronomy and Experimental Philosophy at Cambridge University. In 1967, he became the founding director of the Institute of

Theoretical Astronomy (subsequently renamed the Institute of Astronomy, Cambridge) where Hoyle's innovative leadership quickly lead to this institution becoming one of the premier groups in the world for theoretical astrophysics.

In the 1950s, Hoyle was the leader of a group of very talented experimental and theoretical physicists, with William Alfred Fowler, Margaret Burbidge, and Geoffrey Burbidge. This group realized and postulated the basic ideas of how all the chemical elements in our universe were manufactured. This new field was called nucleosynthesis. Famously, in 1957, this group produced the cornerstone B2FH paper (known for the initials of the four authors) in which the field of nucleosynthesis was defined and the large picture solved.

An early paper of Hoyle's made an interesting use of the anthropic principle. In trying to work out the routes of stellar nucleosynthesis, he observed that one particular nuclear reaction, the triple-alpha process, which generates carbon, would require the carbon nucleus to have a very specific resonance energy for it to work. The large amount of carbon in the universe, which makes it possible for carbon-based life-forms of any kind to exist, demonstrated that this nuclear reaction must work. Based on this notion, he made a prediction of the energy levels in the carbon nucleus that was later borne out by experiment.

These energy levels, while needed to produce carbon in large quantities, were statistically very unlikely. Hoyle later wrote:

Would you not say to yourself, "Some super-calculating intellect must have designed the properties of the carbon atom, otherwise the chance of my finding such an atom through the blind forces of nature would be utterly minuscule. A common sense interpretation of the facts suggests that a super intellect has monkeyed with physics, as well as with chemistry and biology, and that there are no blind forces worth speaking about in nature. The numbers one calculates from the facts seem to me so overwhelming as to put this conclusion almost beyond question." [Hoyle, F. 1982. The Universe: Past and Present Reflections. *Annual Review of Astronomy and Astrophysics*: 20:16]

I respect him for telling the truth and letting the chips fall where they may. That is, after all the heart of true science… and spirituality!

It is considerably past time to reunite the twins seemingly separated at birth.

We owe nothing but honor to those who have gone before us in the honest pursuit of truth and disdain to all those who have clung to preconceived ideas proven to be wrong yet still taught as though true.

Truth is the goal and the guide in both science and spirituality. When it is not, humanity's progression to enlightenment is hindered at best and halted at worst. Knowledge is increasing dramatically, but wisdom is not always keeping up with facts that are whizzing by at an ever increasing rate. We need knowledge, yes, but we also need the wisdom to process the facts once we get them. You can have Wiz-dumb or Wisdom… your choice. Choose wisely!

Double star Type 1 a supernovaes like WR 104 that has us in its sights have been found to always explode once the white dwarf star reaches 1.4 the mass of our sun. They also share another constant; their explosions always release exactly the same amount of light. One has to ask "How could this be"? Regardless, this does make them the perfect celestial measuring sticks, to measure distance in space. This has allowed astronomers to measure the expansion rate of the universe and to their shock, they discovered instead of slowing down as the physics of the Big Bang would predict, it was instead speeding up! In 1998 they made this remarkable discovery! This completely changed the way scientists have viewed the Universe. New truth! But what is causing this? They have postulated that it is something called "Dark Energy." Wow, exploding stars, dark energy, black holes starting to sound more like Star Wars all the time, isn't it?

Professor Kaku says: "The Bible says 'from dust to dust.' We say from 'Stardust to Stardust.'" I can live with that, for without a doubt an intelligent caring consciousness is using the supernovae to support and accelerate His creation. We here on Earth are just a speck in the Milky Way galaxy and as luck, chance, or a superior intellect would have it, we are fortuitously placed in the "Goldilocks zone," tucked away in our own little corner of the universe, part of an ever-expanding Cosmos, yet everything is designed specifically for our carbon-based life form to live and thrive in. On Earth, we are protected by our large guardian outer ring planets that absorb much of the incoming assaults of matter and energy, and are safely warmed by our sun, a thankfully slow-burning single star expected to go on for a few billion years more.

There is no room for error in what can be a hostile and very violent neighborhood. Somehow 99 percent of the massive amounts of energy that contact our planet daily come in the form of neutrinos, not gamma-rays or other forms of energy that could wipe out a carbon-based life form like you and me. Isn't it sweet that our bodies and our planet are both constructed to allow these highly energized particles to cruise right through without resistance? Think of it—99 percent of the destructive power of a supernova explosion passes harmlessly right through us and our planet!

Statistically, it is highly improbable that this set of circumstances could have randomly evolved without direction. I think honest scientists and honest spiritual people agree on that. So it is clear to me that both of our estranged twins, spirit and science, have dysfunctional relationships. It is time to get them and ourselves some therapy and reunite the two camps. We know that our brains have certain tendencies or specialties. One side is the creative and spiritual side and the other the more pragmatic or scientific side, and unfortunately our education system has become highly dysfunctional and either pursues one or the other. They need to be reunited and our system overhauled.

Physically our left and right brain are connected by the corpus callosum (Latin: tough body), also known as the colossal commissure, a wide, flat bundle of neural fibers beneath the cortex at the longitudinal fissure. It connects the left and right cerebral hemispheres and facilitates interhemispheric communication. It is the largest white matter structure in the brain, consisting of 200–250 million contralateral axonal projections.

I have seen and dissected this area myself; I know it's there and I think it is high time that we start using it! For us to heal our minds and reunite the scientific and spiritual, we will need to expose and dispose of our preconceived ideas, our boxes, our inherited and learned lies…

In therapy the therapist helps you identify and get past your inaccurate or false perceptions of reality, usually by assisting you in discovering the filters through which you see and often distort life. Often people find they have mother issues or authority issues or father issues, etc. This is also true and even more magnified when we relate to a higher power God, etc. All of our issues come up and separate us from reality. But especially our "father issues" since God is most often seen as a father figure. To put it mildly, if you have unresolved issues with your natural father, they will be magnified as you try and relate to the Father of it all.

To reconnect our spiritual and scientific natures it would be wise to remove those issues blocking the reconciliation. Don't feel bad; the spiritual giants of the past all had father issues, too. Consider the powerful prophet, Elijah. He went toe-to-toe with the followers of the Nephilum worshipping false prophets. These are the descendants and followers of the ancient aliens... the fallen angels and Lucifer himself and their perverted priesthood that routinely killed babies in ritual sacrifice and other deviant practices considered "normal" to them. I have stood on the spot on Mt. Carmel where Elijah confronted the powers of evil in his nation and won a giant supernatural victory. He even called for and received supernatural fire from another dimension that materialized and consumed his rock altar and part of the mountain, while those who followed a false spiritual system stood in amazement, then turned and tried to kill him. He won with the sword and Divine protection... but shortly after this giant victory he was found depressed, dejected, and seemingly fatherless, doubting the God who had just fought and won a supernatural victory on his behalf.

He had issues and for him to progress and pass on a holistic complete legacy he needed healing... don't we all? True science and knowledge educate and inform us, sometimes as to what a mess we are in. True spirituality heals us. We need both.

In the interest of reuniting our spiritual and scientific natures, permit me to tell you the story as I see it.

I Kings 19:8-13

8 So he arose, and ate and drank; and he went in the strength of that food forty days and forty nights as far as Horeb, the mountain of God.

9 And there he went into a cave, and spent the night in that place; and behold, the word of the LORD came to him, and He said to him, "What are you doing here, Elijah?"

10 So he said, "I have been very zealous for the LORD God of hosts; for the children of Israel have forsaken Your covenant, torn down Your altars, and killed Your prophets with the sword. I alone am left; and they seek to take my life."

11 Then He said, "Go out, and stand on the mountain before the LORD." And behold, the LORD passed by, and a great and strong wind tore into the mountains and broke the rocks in pieces before the LORD, but the LORD was not in the wind; and after the wind an earthquake, but the LORD was not in the earthquake;

12 And after the earthquake a fire, but the LORD was not in the fire; and after the fire a still small voice.

13 So it was, when Elijah heard it, that he wrapped his face in his mantle and went out and stood in the entrance of the cave. Suddenly a voice came to him, and said, "What are you doing here, Elijah?"

(NKJ)

After the all the commotion and activity and fire there was finally a still small voice. Behind all the doing was a being, and God the father reached out to him, not in the activity, but in the still small voice of relationship.

After all the busy-ness there was peace. Peace in relationship, not religion.

Religion with the Father, instead of relationship with the Father, creates distance. Emotional distance creates issues of intimacy; Father issues in this case. When there is a lack of emotional intimacy with the Father there is a resulting inability to maintain intimacy in all our other relationships. The greater our Father issues, as expressed in our busyness, our doing instead of being, the further we are from the Father and the greater our anxiety. Anxiety creates over activity (to prevent intimacy), which results eventually in depression, which will eventually cause you to withdraw from the activity, and insulate yourself into a cave like Elijah, where all the unfinished business of your life, all the unresolved father issues will overwhelm you, and you will ask to die.

The activity may be a Godly one, yet draw us away from God the Father, Himself. Religion is a poor substitute for relationship. Doing is a poor substitute for being.

Proverbs 12:25 says:

"Anxiety in the heart of man causes depression, but a good word makes it glad. God the Father reaches out to us with a good word in the still small voice of relationship with Him."

Elijah had just led a great battle between the true religion and the false religion, and He had won! But somehow He still felt empty and anxious! Now He sits in the same place, perhaps the same cave where Moses went after His battle on behalf of the true religion of God against the golden calf that Aaron had built. Victorious in religion but bankrupt in relationship, they both retreated to the mountain of the Father.

In the text above we see Elijah sitting on the mountain where Moses had his personal encounter with the Father. Once again the Father reaches down this time to another son, Elijah, seeking to eliminate religion and establish relationship. Resolving the Father issues by closing the distance between them, He eventually speaks to Elijah in the still small non-threatening voice of restoration. With the Father-son relationship restored, He then sends His son, Elijah, out to become a Father, to his spiritual son, Elisha, just as he sent Moses back to be a father to Joshua, etc.

I Kings 19:12-16

12 and after the earthquake a fire, but the LORD was not in the fire; and after the fire a still small voice.

13 So it was, when Elijah heard it, that he wrapped his face in his mantle and went out and stood in the entrance of the cave.

(When you hear the still small voice of the Father in restoration, it will bring you out of your place of depression, and you will weep tears of joy inside His calling for you. Inside is relationship outside is religion. Inside relationship the mantle connects you; outside relationship it separates you even as you do His work.) Suddenly a voice came to him, and said, "What are you doing here, Elijah?" (When your Father issues are resolved, and the relationship is restored, you will hear His voice say," what are you doing here in this distant place of depression, this isn't you?! You are my son, now go become a father and advance our kingdom!")

14 And he said, "I have been very zealous for the LORD God of hosts; because the children of Israel have forsaken Your covenant, torn down Your altars, and killed Your prophets with the sword. I alone am left; and they seek to take my life."

15 Then the LORD said to him: "Go, return on your way to the Wilderness of Damascus; and when you arrive, anoint Hazael as king over Syria."

16 "Also you shall anoint Jehu the son of Nimshi as king over Israel. And Elisha the son of Shaphat of Abel Meholah you shall anoint as prophet in your place."

(NKJ)

The Father responds, okay, go back through the wilderness of Damascus until our relationship overwhelms what is left of your religion. There is no need to perform to please Papa, Abba, Father anymore; we are in relationship. This is the same road where Saul became Paul, the religion in him died, and he was born again as a son in relationship with the Father. Sooner or later, we will all walk this road or die in the wilderness! Some even "saved" and in a religion, but not entering into the Kingdom! Never arriving! Having a form of godliness but denying the power of it, etc.

Rev 3:15-22

15 I know your works, that you are neither cold nor hot. I could wish you were cold or hot. (I am familiar with your busyness, but your relationship with me is lukewarm at best.)

16 So then, because you are lukewarm, and neither cold nor hot, I will vomit you out of My mouth.

17 Because you say, 'I am rich, have become wealthy, and have need of nothing'—and do not know that you are wretched, miserable, poor, blind, and naked—(yes, in the name of religion you have done mighty works but when it comes to intimacy, relationship with me, you are uncovered.)

18 "I counsel you to buy from Me gold refined in the fire, that you may be rich; and white garments, that you may be clothed, that the shame of your nakedness may not be revealed; and anoint your eyes with eye salve, that you may see. (Let me put in terms you can understand now, if you are going to work, work at our relationship not your religion! Let me give you spiritual eye salve to open your spiritual eyes to see your need for relationship with

Me. With these eyes you will have: In to ME see: Intimacy with Me, your Father)

19 "As many as I love, I rebuke and chasten. Therefore be zealous and repent. (The Greek word here means, "change your mind." It implies action not an overly emotional response in this case, etc.)

20 "Behold, I stand at the door and knock. If anyone hears My voice and opens the door, I will come in to him and dine with him, and he with Me."

21 "To him who overcomes I will grant to sit with Me on My throne, as I also overcame and sat down with My Father on His throne." (Now that's relationship, the marriage supper of the lamb, and sitting on Papa's lap on the throne!)

22 He who has an ear, let him hear what the Spirit says to the churches.

(NKJ) (Open your spiritual eyes and ears!)

Proverbs 20:12-17

12 The hearing ear and the seeing eye, the LORD has made them both.

That's the goal—intimacy—internal and external. Functional unity of all the parts working as designed!

We approach God in different ways at different seasons in our life, and that is normal. It is part of a healthy growing progress.

The preschool view of God is normal in preschool... just like the preschool view of science is normal at that age as well. What is abnormal is to have grown to the level of advanced learning in one area of your life and still be stuck in a preschool relationship in another area of your life. Sometimes we must go back for a moment to correct our course in the interest of balance:

Adult Simba: I know what I have to do. But going back means I'll have to face my past. I've been running from it for so long.

[Rafiki hits Simba on the head with his staff]

Adult Simba: Ow! Jeez, what was that for?

Rafiki: It doesn't matter. It's in the past.

[laughs]

Adult Simba: Yeah, but it still hurts.

Rafiki: Oh yes, the past can hurt. But from the way I see it, you can either run from it, or... learn from it.

[swings his staff again at Simba, who ducks out of the way]

Rafiki: Ha. You see? So what are you going to do?

Adult Simba: First, I'm gonna take your stick.

[Simba snatches Rafiki's staff and throws it and Rafiki runs to grab it]

Rafiki: No, no, no, no, not the stick! Hey, where are you going?

Adult Simba: I'm going back!

Rafiki: Good! Go on! Get out of here!

Simba finally admits that he is out of balance and even though fully grown and out of school in part of his life, he is still stuck in a preschool level relationship in another part of his life. But he learns from the prophet monkey and alters his relationship with the past, then gains balance and sets off on the road to his destiny.

It's amazing what you can learn from some Disney cartoons, isn't it? It's even more amazing the universal truths and therapeutic principals you can find there as well, as long as you don't give up hope and are paying attention… like Simba was.

It seems that there is hope for growth, not only in the creative side of our brains like Disney represents so well, but also in the science, when our Corpus Callosum is engaged! A lot of old paradigms are being destroyed with new information and deeper understandings of the complexity of the external and internal universe around us. Even scientists have to come up for air now and then, and as they do they are finding that the boxes they have been in are too small. Many with open minds are ready to, if not embrace, at least consider new explanations for the intricate well-ordered universe they are discovering more about every day. If this progression to maturity continues, we might even see the healing of the self-inflicted lobotomy that has symbolically shut down free communication between left and right brains of spirit and science!

In studying our beginnings in the Big Bang, scientists have discovered what a long shot it was for matter to take shape the way it did. Physicists calculated that for life to exist, gravity and the other forces of nature needed to be just right or our universe couldn't exist. Had the expansion rate been slightly weaker, gravity would have pulled all matter back into a "big crunch."

We're not talking about merely a 1 or 2 percent reduction in the universe's expansion rate. The proud agnostic Stephen Hawking writes, "If the rate of expansion one second after the Big Bang had been smaller by even one part in a hundred thousand million million, the universe would have re-collapsed before it ever reached its present size." [*The Illustrated A Brief History of Time*, New York: Bantam, p. 156.]

On the flip side, if the expansion rate had been a mere fraction greater than it was, galaxies, stars, and planets could never have formed, and we wouldn't be here.

This new understanding of how miraculous human life is in our universe led the agnostic astronomer George Greenstein to ask, "Is it possible that suddenly, without intending to, we have stumbled upon the scientific proof of the existence of a Supreme Being?" [*The Symbiotic Universe*, New York: William Morrow, p. 27.]

Another agnostic, George Smoot, the Nobel Prize winning scientist in charge of the COBE experiment, also admits to the parallel. "There is no doubt that a parallel exists between the Big Bang as an event and the Christian notion of creation from nothing." [*Wrinkles in Time*, p. 17.]

I think we are watching a healing in progress!

There was never a night or a problem
that could defeat sunrise or hope.
~ Bernard Williams

Chapter 12
Black Holes, Ten Dimensions, Old Codes, New Codes, Duality Dies

Pure mathematics is, in its way, the poetry of logical ideas.
~ Albert Einstein

Since the dawn of civilization man has gazed in awe at the stars, wondering what they are and how they got there. On a clear night the unaided human eye can see about 6,000 stars. The Hubble and other powerful telescopes indicate there are trillions of them clustered in over 100 billion galaxies. Our sun is like one grain of sand amidst the world's beaches. It was Edwin Hubble himself who discovered the universe is expanding. Rewinding the process mathematically, he calculated that everything in the universe, including matter, energy, space and even time itself, actually had a beginning. Many scientists, including Einstein, fought the notion at first. Later Einstein termed it one of the biggest blunders of his life. Eventually the math led him and others to agree. All hail the all-powerful math, it would seem.

Perhaps math is the scaffolding of life and the framework of the universe on which everything else is built. We saw some interesting clues through the book so far. For instance, the Greek and Hebrew languages have mathematical values for each letter tying written communication with math and creating the ability for micro codes—messages within messages.

Then we found that there are mathematical constants hidden within the verses Gen. 1:1 in the Old Testament and in John 1:1 in the beginning of the New Testament. Notice that in the surface text, both of these verses announce the sovereignty of a Supreme creative being. The mathematical constant of Pi in the Old and the mathematical constant and naperian logarithm in the New. Old math in the Old and new math in the New?

We found that there are innumerable codes using gematria decoding the numerical values of the Hebrew letters and we found a seemingly impossible little book within the book, the hidden "bible codes" in which some believe is a record of all human events, from a perspective outside of time itself.

Interesting how science is incorporated into what seems to be the domain of simply spiritual words. Perhaps the words of the Bible are more holistic than we now know. Perhaps there are more scientific truths about life waiting to be unmasked in this Book? Perhaps it has something to contribute to the Big TOE of science, the Theory Of Everything? (T O E)

Some believe that our consciousness creates our own reality; I agree at least in part. They say that matter is a reflection of our intention applied to energy. As Einstein postulated: Different matter is created by the application of different frequencies upon energy.

One might say that on a larger scale the "source" of all energy decided that it wanted to experience a universe, or maybe a multiverse with a multitude of galaxies, with black holes at their centers like hearts. An entire magnificent Cosmos with our little Earth tucked away in the corner of the Milky Way galaxy. There was a big bang and the vibrational frequencies acting on the energy that was itself, manifested matter in the appropriate shapes and forms.

We also learned about the novas, supernovas, and hypernovas and the life span of stars. What an amazing place, our universe.

Or is it all just a virtual reality based on mathematical equations, and we are all just part of a giant hologram? Is the universe a visual projection of a mathematical structure that supports the matrix that is the visual and material expression of energy as matter… or is the universe simply math itself? Oh, I fear we are being drawn into the rabbit hole again!

Is the universe actually made of math? Is it the set of blueprints, the framework upon which the Cosmos is fabricated… or is it the very universe itself?

Pretend for a minute that you are a TSA screener and I must pass through your line before heading to my flight. Lucky me, I am picked to go through your head-to-toe body scan. As you view my skeleton with a large radiograph you can see everything there is to see about me. The question is, though, are you watching me or my blueprint?

I recently read an interesting interview with cosmologist Max Tegmark. He has a unique viewpoint on math. He says mathematical formulas create reality.

He begins with something more basic... the external reality hypothesis... which is the assumption that there is a reality out there independent of us. I think most physicists would agree with this idea. In fact, what he is saying is that our preconceived ideas (boxes) filter our perceptions of reality. To avoid the human baggage, he turns to math. Max is not the first to look to the structure of math for answers. In the 1960s, physicist Eugene Wigner, in his essay, "The Unreasonable Effectiveness of Mathematics in the Natural Sciences" asked the question why is nature so accurately described by math? Before him, the legendary Galileo poetically wrote that Nature was a grand book that was written in the language of mathematicas. And then there was the ancient Greek philospher Plato who said that the objects of mathematics really exist and, of course, Pythagoras, who shared the idea that the universe was built on mathematics. But Dr. Max Tegmark takes it a step further. He believes that the reason why mathematics is so effective at describing reality is that it is reality. That is the mathematical universe hypothesis: mathematical things actually exist, and they are actually physical reality.

Doesn't that just excite you? Your very essence is an expression of the class you hated in high school. It would explain why in the modern age "nerds" run the world. Seriously, Max believes that all mathematical structures are abstract, immutable entities. The integers and their relations to each other; all these things exist outside of time. (Like where the quantum God would exist?) But that time does exist inside some of the equations. Max says to understand the concept, you have to distinguish between two ways of viewing reality. The first is from the outside, like the overview of a physicist studying its mathematical structure. Second is the inside view of an observer living in the structure.

From the perspective of the observer/physicist, there is Einstein relativity, all of time already exists. All events, including your entire life, already exist as the mathematical structure called space-time. In space-time, nothing happens or changes because it contains all time at once. But from my perspective—a humble $2 + 2 = 4$—in one of the equations it appears that time is flowing, but that is just an illusion. A stubbornly persistent one, as Einstein said.

Max puts it this way: "You can think of a frog living in the landscape as the inside view and a high-flying bird surveying the landscape as the outside view. These two perspectives are connected to each other through time. From the frog's perspective, it appears that time is flowing, but that is just an illusion. The frog looks out and sees the moon in space, orbiting around Earth. But from the bird's perspective, the moon's orbit is a static spiral in space-time." [Adam Frank, 6-16-08 *Discover* magazine, "Is the Universe actually made of Math."]

Math as a matrix for life! That doesn't sound all that random, does it? In fact, it's quite the opposite. If randomness does not seem a plausible explanation for the original expression of matter and life, what does? I keep coming back to that question in my search for the Source.

In the beginning of my search I asked that question regarding DNA and its incredible, even elegant, complexity that we are now aware of, and the assumption that it was the result of a lucky break in the cosmic game of craps seemed more than ludicrous!

It is simply not statistically plausible or mathematically reasonable. But a designer, a cosmic consciousness, an intelligent energy source, a master mathematician releasing a frequency upon a rich field of potentiality, like the Higgs field, made more sense to me. Different frequencies applied to energy resulting in different forms of matter. I also began to wrap my mind around the concept that I had been taught as a child, that "God" was without beginning and without end... and in our finite frame of reference on this planet, in our matrix that our beliefs have created, that seemed impossible as well. (From the viewpoint of Dr. Max Tegmark's frog, at least.) That concept had shut me down so many years ago and caused me to disbelieve the entire "Higher Power" story. I wrote it off as a myth. I could see everything has a beginning and an ending, or at least I thought I could see that, having the perspective of the "frog." What I needed and what I did was to fly like an eagle and get the bird's perspective for a "moment." Suddenly that new perspective emerged right before my eyes!

Now as I explored the incredible world of quantum physics and the quantum world within our own bodies, our complex universe within, our DNA, etc., it made more sense. When some scientists now say there is no matter per se, but only an expression of energy as matter in a temporary state, I find that it intriguing and at least quite plausible.

I was already wondering about a dream/vision I had while meditating, where I rode a beam of light back in "time" past man's history and out into space, to a place where the Earth did not exist, to a "place" and "time" where there was nothing accept a void with an incredible energy source residing in the middle of darkness! Then I watched as this energy source became all that we see today and more. To my knowledge, that was not a mathematical event but rather an event where my consciousness was touched by a field of higher consciousness and I travelled to a place that offered an explanation for my questions. Was that God or was it simply my imagination?

There are those seeking an equation for the theory of everything who would say that my experience was indeed a mathematical event, of course, and that it could be explained by overlapping fields with a consciousness, including one my imagination itself projects. So, where if anywhere is God in all this? Is He simply a myth? Is He like the all-knowing all-seeing

Wizard of Oz, or is He the kindly old man behind the curtain, the designer and operator of the Great Oz? Is He simply the architect of a mathematical cosmic computer operating a holographic simulation that you and I are a part of? Perhaps. Did He speak, as the Bible says, and all things were created? Perhaps!

There is a good possibility that we will find more theories, more math on how the frequencies of light and sound, acting on energy creates matter... all sorts of matter. No matter (pun intended) which direction we take, I now believe God will be in the middle of wherever we end up. It seems "He" is an energy source that can manifest Himself as anything. It seems to me that within the Source of our energy there is and has always been a consciousness we can only hope to imagine. Do I believe that "He" is just a spirit, a source of energy then? Take away the "just" and yes, "He" is that, but he certainly could have been and still be the human being known as "Jesus of Nazareth" as well. All that exists, as matter or energy, is an expression of "Him," the Source. As one of those forms of matter, we human beings are making incredible strides in understanding the "laws" of nature and the math of it all. There is no doubt in my mind that we will continue to discover more and more secrets, more rules of how it all works. I believe that they have been hidden like codes for us to uncover... at predetermined times. Visualize this: out of darkness, the emptiness, the void, the entity we call God, that supernatural source of conscious energy "spoke," applied frequencies to transform energy—"Himself"—into the matter that forms our internal and external universes today. Along the way this supernatural field of energy and consciousness and pure potentiality left clues for us—codes if you will—to show "He" was behind it all. Hidden somewhere in each of the operating systems of nature that we have discovered so far, we can "see" His signature at one level or another.

What about dark matter and dark energy and its relationship with black holes, the heart of every galaxy? Is it possible it is a result of the fracture in dimensions that I postulated occurred at the time Christians referred to as the "fall of man"? Did we, the entire Cosmos, exist in ten or more dimensions before that event, and was this separation or appearance of dark matter, etc., a result of that event? At that point in "time" were the other dimensions removed from or hidden from man, kind of a dimensional Area 51? Was man restricted from their use, until a time of reunification? Perhaps that was one of the reasons this Source in human form came to this planet to live among us and effect a healing of that dimensional tear? Just a thought!

If the Bible is true, and if scientists are correct that there is a large amount of unaccounted for matter out there, perhaps the matter the Source created and called angels could account for that. In the Bible, we are told that both rebellious and loyal angels exist, though to what extent and in what numbers we are not told. Another thought.

When one is looking for the truth, it is wise not to write anything off until it can be disproven or explained in a more accurate fashion.

As you know by now, I believe we have committed a terrible mistake by creating an artificial dimensional rift of our own design between science and spirituality. To solve the mysteries of the universe we need both sides of our brains, the questioning, creative, intuitive, and spiritual field as well as the logical, rational side of our being that demands proof! Both sides deserve to be heard. Undoubtedly, neither side will get all that it "wants" in this imaginary negotiation but in the interaction of the whole brain, truth will emerge! Isn't that what we as whole beings really desire?

That only works if we are honestly after the truth and not simply working to prove our own pet theories, no matter, (pun intended), how good they are!

Perhaps there are an infinite number of parallel universes or perhaps the math will be satisfied with reunifying the "parallel" and "lost" dimensions, along with the inclusion of the Higgs field, as a universal field of pure potentiality containing every particle in every location, and a consciousness so that anything can manifest anywhere, anytime without the "need" for "travel." Imagine if a particle enters in one spot but the intention is for it to be sent to another location ten light years away. The moment it is sent it arrives as if through a wormhole. Is it a wormhole or is it the consciousness in the field honoring the intention and manifesting it in the new location from its completely "stocked" field that exists throughout all energy/matter? Food for thought, as my grandfather used to say. Be free to let your imagination run unfettered. Also be free to prove it with the math or find someone who can. The only stupid questions are the ones we don't ask!

I have recently read that Albert Einstein used to use his imagination to do just that. He would visualize himself riding a beam of light out into space and time, observing every minute detail, then "come back" and turn it into math. I guess we do have some things in common after all… many times while studying all these deep subjects I was convinced I was an alien orphan dropped off here upon birth from the planet dumb and dumber.

Speaking of aliens: Are they the dark matter? Are they the invisible race called angels? Except for rare sightings, they remain invisible, at least in "our" dimensions. Scientists say that for now dark matter appears to be invisible. So what does a black hole and dark energy and dark matter look like? We don't know.

Maybe this is what it would look like if we could see it. What you're "seeing" is a galaxy with a black hole in the center. Why is it so bright? Those jets coming out of both sides of the tunnel in the center are reported to be beams of gamma rays, but the same people who named that white spot a black hole told us that, so take it with a grain of salt.

NASA's Wilkinson Microwave Anisotropy Probe (WMAP) provided a true watershed moment in humanity's quest to understand the Cosmos. Its findings calculated the age of the universe and plotted the curvature of space. It mapped the cosmic microwave background radiation, and in a shocking turn of events, revealed that atoms make up only 4.6 percent of the universe.

The rest of the universe is far from empty, however. Dark matter accounts for 23.3 percent of the Cosmos, and dark energy fills in 72.1 percent [source: NASA]. Together, these materials make up a whopping 95.4 percent of the universe, so no wonder we're still trying to figure out exactly what dark matter and dark energy actually are.

WMAP launched in 2001, but the dark energy problem presented itself before—back in 1998 when the Hubble Space Telescope observed three very curious supernovae. The most distant of these cosmic blasts occurred 7.7 billion years ago, more than halfway back to the Big Bang itself [source: Hubblesite]. This insight into the ancient Cosmos revealed that the expansion of the universe hasn't been slowing, but rather, accelerating. That threw astronomers for a loop, most of whom had assumed before this revelation that the expansion had slowed over time due to gravity.

Scientists attribute this accelerating expansion to dark energy, so called because its exact nature remains a mystery, but something must fill the vast reaches of space to account for the accelerating expansion.

We might not know what dark energy is just yet, but scientists have a few leading theories. Some experts believe it to be a property of space itself, which agrees with one of Einstein's earlier gravity theories. In this, dark energy would be a cosmological constant and therefore wouldn't dilute as space expands. Another partially disproven theory defines dark energy as a new type of matter. Dubbed "quintessence," this substance would fill the universe like a fluid and exhibit negative gravitational mass [source: NASA]. Other theories involve the possibilities that dark energy doesn't occur uniformly, or that our current theory of gravity is incorrect.

Dark matter, by comparison, is far better understood. It doesn't emit or reflect light, but scientists can estimate where it is based on its gravitational effects on surrounding matter. Scientists use a technique called gravitational lensing to accomplish this, observing the way dark matter's gravitational pull bends and distorts light from distant galaxies.

These observations rule out stars, antimatter, dark clouds, or any form of normal matter. Some scientists consider supermassive black holes a potential candidate for dark matter, while others favor either MACHOs (massive compact halo objects) and Wimps (weakly interacting massive particles). MACHOs include brown dwarfs, weak stars, that exert a gravitational pull but emit no light. WIMPs, on the other hand, would constitute a radically different form of matter left over from the Big Bang.

Research into the exact nature of dark matter and dark energy continues. Eventually, scientists hope to discern a clearer understanding of these two glaring (or dark) cosmic unknowns.

Whether you're examining a super massive or a regular black hole, they all seem to share one constant. They always have a mass of ½ of 1 percent of the total galaxy mass, no matter the mass of the galaxy; it would seem that there is a direct relationship between the black hole at the center of our and every other galaxy and the galaxy itself. It's fascinating, almost as if it is the heart of the galaxy… black hole size and galaxy mass are related! Seems like the math and perhaps some geometry from the rabbit hole are showing up way out here! There is also a correlation between the orbital speed of the stars even at the outer edge of a galaxy and the size of the black hole. The larger the black hole the faster the orbital speed of the stars on the edge of the galaxy. In my imagination, I see this like a whirlpool at the center of the galaxy you're observing.

So how do we get a new galaxy from a cloud of gas floating in space? That sounds like a question for Simba's friends, Timon, and Pumbaa.

Scientists think that perhaps the center of a gas cloud collapses into a black hole, which immediately feeds on the gas around it, creating a brilliant quasar. The energy from the quasar creates super intense temperature changes to the gas surrounding the black hole, which could cause the gas around the black hole to condense into stars. The energy from the quasar forces the stars out away from the black hole with an interstellar wind, and with only the energy from the quasar within its reach, the black hole swallows it up and stops "feeding" and remains dormant at the center of the new galaxy… and voila, a galaxy is born. All this from a word, a frequency from a creative energy source that said 'let there be…' and matter appeared and continues to appear according to the frequency of what He spoke and still/continues to speak. Could be!

Rest your brain for a moment and let me share some completely random information. While channel surfing a while back, I stumbled across a documentary on George Lucas. It seems that when the original *Star Wars* films came out, many scientists at the time thought that it was ludicrous to suggest there was an invisible energy that permeated the whole universe. George called this "The Force"! Now, however, we just accept that an invisible energy is out there, and most of us are open to the concept of a universal "force." I just love how un-fictional science fiction can really be.

So what is this dark matter stuff anyway? The name gives a fairly accurate explanation of what it is, believe it or not. This is what the dictionary says!

> *Dark:*
> *With little or no light: it's too dark to see much.*
> *Hidden from knowledge; mysterious.*
>
> *Matter:*
> *A physical substance in general, as distinct from mind and spirit; (in physics) that which occupies space and possesses rest mass, esp. as distinct from energy.*

So dark matter is nothing more than a non-light emitting substance with a rest mass energy. And just to clarify, when we use the term "light" what we are actually referring to is a photon. This means that dark matter doesn't emit anything detectable from the lowest part of the spectrum (radio waves) to the highest part (gamma rays).

So the first question you might ask is… if we can't see it, how do we know it exists?

So far the only method that we've actually been able to use to detect dark matter is through its influence on physical matter through gravity. In this way it's sort of like the wind—looking out of a window we can see the leaves and trees moving, but we can't see the air blowing against it.

Now when astronomers look carefully at a galaxy, they can measure how fast the stars within it are moving. The motions of the stars are the result of the gravitational forces from all the other matter in the galaxy. But here is the key problem: When astronomers add up all the matter in all the stars and gas and dust visible with all different types of telescopes, it doesn't total nearly enough to explain the motions they observe. The stars are moving around much faster than they should be! In other words, all the matter we can see is not enough to produce the gravity that is pulling things around. This problem shows up over and over again almost wherever we look in the universe. Not only do stars in galaxies move around faster than expected, but galaxies within groups of galaxies do too. In all cases, there must be something else there, something we can't see, something we now call dark matter.

This mismatch between what we see and what we know must be there may seem very mysterious, but it is not hard to imagine. You know that people can't float in mid-air, so if you saw what looked like a man doing just that, you would know right away that there must be wires holding him up, even if you couldn't see them.

The detection of high energy particles also hints at the potential detection of dark matter. High energy x-rays have detected something at the energies 130 GeV (Max Plank Institute for Physics), 620 GeV and 820 GeV (Calorimetric Electron Telescope). To give you a bit of an idea as to the mass of 620 GeV, it equates to about thirty-seven times heavier than water.

Although the 130 GeV that was detected was put as a potential for dark matter, even more recently it has changed hands and been dubbed the Higgs boson! (Higgs boson is more accurately put at 125 GeV). That is the exciting thing with science; always so much more to learn, and then relearn!

There is so much more that could be said about dark matter. It is currently virtually undetectable, but we can see its effects because of its gravitational influence. It is everywhere in the universe because it affects not only our galaxy but every other galaxy (detectable because of gravity). We don't quite know what it is but we have several potential candidates.

Theories are constantly being proposed to explain what dark matter is. My personal favorite explanation for dark matter (simply because it's cool) is that dark matter is actually gravity leaking between different dimensions—as if they had been torn apart and separated at some point in time! So, dark matter halos could be said to be galaxy-like objects—or at least very large, gravitationally bound objects—in other dimensions. As far as I'm aware, such a theory is currently untestable, so this new explanation ranks a little higher in the realm of being a good hypothesis. But it is just that—a hypothesis.

For several years now, physicists have also been looking at the standard model of particle physics, specifically supersymmetry, for explanations of dark matter. Supersymmetry is an idea that elementary particles with a spin of "one" have a corresponding heavy superpartner whose spin differs by half. Scientists have yet to discover any direct evidence for supersymmetry, but it's interesting that supersymmetry continuously pops up as a solution to many of our problems. It seems like that math Matrix likes it!

There are those attempting to devise methods to test these theories. They are working just as hard as the folks who were looking for proof of the Higgs field were at the LHC back in Switzerland. Remember, to "prove" the Higgs field theory they needed to find a corresponding particle, the Higgs boson. In this particular case, Are Raklev of the University of Oslo proposes a hypothesis that both explains dark matter and gives us a method to discover particles making up dark matter experimentally. This is where gravitinos come in.

Now, a gravitino is the superpartner of the graviton—the force carrier of gravity… hypothetically. It has not yet been identified. So what we have is a hypothetical super partner to a hypothetical particle called a graviton. Okay, that works for me… I think.

Raklev puts it best when he says, "The gravitino is the hypothetical, supersymmetric partner of the hypothetical particle graviton, so it is also impossible to predict a more hypothetical particle than this." He goes on to say, "A graviton is the particle we believe mediates gravitational force, just like a photon, the light particle, mediates electromagnetic force. While gravitons do not weigh anything at all, gravitinos may weigh a great deal. If nature is supersymmetric and gravitons exist, then gravitinos also exist. And vice versa. This is pure mathematics." [Yngve Vogt, *Science Daily*, 1-24-13 "Revolutionary Theory of Dark Matter."]

So, what's the catch? You're probably thinking 'wait, they are talking about using a hypothetical symmetry for the hypothetical superpartner of a hypothetical particle and that isn't the catch? This must be a trick question.' Nope, this isn't a trick question. The catch is physicists are unable to demonstrate the relationship between gravitinos and gravitons (you know, by using math) without unifying the forces of nature. That's right, now enters the need for the grand unification, the Big TOE (Theory of Everything).

Scientists are already three-quarters of the way there. In the mid-twentieth century, electricity and magnetism were unified to form the electromagnetic force. Likewise, in the 70s, electromagnetism was unified with the strong and weak nuclear forces forming the standard model. Now we just need to unify the standard model with gravity and we'll be able to describe every possible (and imaginary) interaction between any possible particle in nature—no pressure. This theory is referred to as the Grand Unification Theory or the Theory of Everything (usually the latter). Or as I call it… The Big TOE.

In order to achieve unification, we need to understand how gravity works at the quantum level. This basically means we need to find the graviton a home within the atomic nucleus. Of course, finding the graviton first would be a big help.

According to Raklev, supersymmetry simplifies everything. If the TOE theory exists, in other words, if it is possible to unify the four forces of nature, then gravitinos must exist."

When I started, I said that this theory was testable, but how do you test the existence of a hypothetical superpartner of a hypothetical particle in a hyperthetical state of nature called supersymmetry when you first need a hypothetical theory to unify the forces of nature? The cool thing about math is we can still test this theory, even with all of that hypothetical-ness. You can see why Max Tegmark likes his 'math is everything' theory! Here we go.

Shortly after the Big Bang, there was basically a large soup of particles colliding with each other. When gluons (the carriers of the strong nuclear force) collide with other gluons, they emit gravitinos. This is when and how most of the gravitinos in the universe were created.

For a long time physicists predicted there were too many gravitinos, which was a problem. So they attempted to create models and theories that didn't require the existence of these troublesome particles. By unifying supersymmetry and dark matter with gravitinos, we create a situation where dark matter is not stable; it simply has a long life span (in contrast to other models which say dark matter has no lifespan). In a universe where dark matter has a lifespan, it means the particles that make up dark matter (in this case, gravitinos) must eventually be converted into something else—either by colliding with each other or by decaying.

Enter the experiment. If gravitinos collide, they should convert to photons or antimatter. Unfortunately, it seems like gravitinos either don't collide or collide very, very rarely. Good drivers! The second observational part of this experiment is to observe the decay of gravitinos. Using mathematical predictions, when they decay, these particles should emit a gamma ray. That sounds familiar and it has potentially been observed. Right?

The Fermi-LAT space probe has picked up a 'small, suspicious surplus of gamma rays from the center of our galaxy.' These initial observations go on to give the model some credence since these numbers both match the hypothesis and are exactly what you would hope to see when gravitinos decay.

So, let's get this right. We have a hypothetical system of symmetry, a hypothetical supersymmetric partner particle to another hypothetical particle, interacting with each other in a hypothetical unifying theory... the Big TOE, and the Fermi-LAT space probe just might help us find the "foot" it goes to.

As a collective species, we contemplate the existence of extra-terrestrial civilizations living in the far reaches of the universe, and we imagine that they have mind-boggling technology that we can't even begin to drum up using our imagination. So far, though, there have been no clear indicators (well, depending on who you ask) that there is anything beyond homo sapiens, which is equal parts depressing and terrifying. After all, if aliens were real, surely there would be some signs, right? Well, there are many theories put forth in the Fermi paradox that postulate why there may be no signs... everything ranging from our technology being so basic that we are unable to pick up whatever signals they have sent out into the abyss, to ETs knowing we are here but choosing not to reach out to us to not hinder our progress. However, a new theory has been put forth that, frankly, makes all of the alternatives seem kind of lame.

Just recently, astronomers announced a colossal find (quite literally, colossal): a series of 'ultra-massive' black holes at the center of many distant galaxies. Each of these black holes is more than ten times the size of our solar system, with event horizons stretching out more than five times beyond the orbit of Pluto. Such black holes are far larger than anything ever predicted before. One of the largest, which lies at the center of an egg-shaped galaxy more than 335 million light-years distant (called NGC 4889), has the mass of more than 21 billion suns. Another of these behemoths is at the galactic center of NGC 3842, which is 331 million light-years away. This one contains the mass of 9.7 billion suns. In comparison, the supermassive black hole at the heart of the Milky Way, Sagittarius A, contains the mass of about 4.1 million solar masses, with a surface area of no more than 17 light-hours (120 AU).

Besides being unexpected, these black holes presented some interesting questions. Namely, how in the heck did they become so large? As we learned already, typically, black holes are formed of the collapsing core of a massive star, but it is postulated that they can become significantly larger from consuming stars and other interstellar materials. And then there are galactic collisions, where two galaxies collide and the central black holes of each also collide and merge.

Some scientists think that the surface of a black hole becomes less extreme the larger the black hole is (in surface area, instead of mass). So hypothetically, if we were able to find a supermassive black hole the size of our solar system, it would be possible for there to be so-called 'stable' areas within the event horizon that may allow stars or planets to orbit the central singularity without being torn apart into a flurry of subatomic particles.

In particular, there is a certain type of black hole that is ideal for this sort of thing. The inner workings of Reissner-Nordström (or charged and rotating) black holes have been studied by

Vyacheslav Dokuchaey, a Russian cosmologist from Moscow's Institute for Nuclear Research of the Russian Academy of Sciences. According to him, not only could a planet remain in a stable orbit within the active galactic nuclei or the 'inner Cauchy horizon' of the black hole (where the fabric of space-time becomes somewhat 'normal' again), but also "living inside the eternal black holes is possible in principle, if these black holes are rotating or charged and massive enough for weakening the tidal forces and radiation of gravitational waves to an acceptable level."

When I originally read this story, the first thought that crept up into my mind was concerning energy. As you all know (or at least I hope you do), the sun is a primary source of our energy. Without it, our plants would be unable to undergo photosynthesis, killing most of the plants on our planet before ultimately killing us all when we succumb to starvation. So where would an advanced civilization living within the confines of a black hole derive its energy from?

According to Dokuchaev, "The naked central singularity illuminates the orbiting internal planets and provides the energy supply for supporting life," he adds. "Some additional highlighting during the night time comes from eternally circulating photons." So any civilization capable of doing so, which would probably rank as a type III advanced civilizations on the Kardashev scale (we haven't made it to type I yet), would derive light and heat from orbiting photons and energy from the singularity itself.

More interestingly, such a civilization would be completely closed off to the rest of the universe beyond the event horizon. Sounds like a spiffy hiding spot, if you ask me. Pretty peaceful, at least, except for the radiation from the stars and other interstellar materials falling in.

So what do you think? Are these intragalactic hideouts a little bit of heaven or a dark corner of hell? Are they the secret to reconnecting the disconnected missing dimensions? It seems that whatever we do, wherever we go, whatever we study, the question of duality is one that remains. Whether you choose to be religious or scientific, spiritual or deist, agnostic or atheist... there clearly is duality in the universe. Or simply: good and evil. Like particles in a large hydron collider, good and evil smash into each other continually. I have seen it and for me the question is then, do we create this duality without the assistance of a deity, or in spite of one and to what extent do we have the power to alter the current status quo? Is there a powerful extraterrestrial lurking in some black hole in the center of some galaxy ready to bring his rebellion back to prime-time here on Earth at any minute? Perhaps there is, instead a benevolent loving quantum Creator God waiting just beyond that event horizon. Who or what is there? The renegade band of intergalactic rebels that once ravaged Earth, or a kind, quantum watchmaker or architect who started it all by applying frequencies to the energy that was Himself?

Or perhaps it's more like ... in this corner we have the Creator of it all, the heavyweight champion of all time, and the other corner we have the challenger, a rebellious created ruler who has destroyed many and has been trash-talking the Champion for millennia.

I don't know about you, but after grappling with all this cosmic science and the deep, philosophical and spiritual questions that someone must if they are seriously looking for the source, my head starts spinning as fast as a star on the outer edge of a super massive black hole! What was it I came in here for again? Oh yes... I'm looking for the Source... the Source of first life. From the rabbit hole... or was it the black hole... comes a reply: "Lamininininin." It echoes throughout our senses.

So what is laminin? A lost remnant of the missing ten dimensions?

I have an idea. If your head is still spinning like mine, let's make like Einstein and use our imaginations as we explore this new frontier. We will discover some new information and have some fun at the same time.

Close your eyes for a minute and visualize yourself on a bridge of a starship far across the universe on the edge of a super giant black hole. You're the captain of the ship and you're in search of a quantum God. You have just received a partial transmission, a clue that might assist your search... if you can decode it:

"Computer, please locate Laminin."

"Searching: Laminin ... yes, laminin is in you, sir!"

"What? Please explain."

"Yes, sir. Laminins are major proteins that make up the basal lamina of the basement membrane of your cells that make up a protein network, a foundation for your cells, sir."

"Computer, please tell me more."

"Yes, sir. The laminins are an important and biologically active part of the basal lamina, influencing cell differentiation, migration, and adhesion, as well as phenotype and survival. In other words, sir, it is a foundation for biological life... a building block that holds carbon-based life forms such as yourself together!

"Really!"

"Yes, sir. Laminins are trimeric proteins that contain an α-chain, a β-chain, and a γ-chain, found in five, four, and three genetic variants, respectively. The laminin molecules are named according to their chain composition. Thus, laminin-511 contains α5, β1, and γ1 chains. Fourteen other chain combinations have been identified in vivo. The trimeric proteins intersect to form a cross-like structure that can bind to other cell membrane and extracellular matrix molecules. The three shorter arms are particularly good at binding to other laminin molecules, which allows them to form sheets. The long arm is capable of binding to cells, which helps anchor organized tissue cells to the membrane.

The laminin family of glycoproteins are an integral part of the structural scaffolding in almost every tissue of an carbon-based organism like you, sir. They are secreted and incorporated into a cell-associated extracellular matrix. Laminin is vital for the maintenance and survival of tissues."

"The Matrix. I knew it!"

"Excuse me, sir?"

"You said they bond to each other and form a matrix of molecules?"

"Yes, sir."

"You said they form the shape of the cross?"

"Yes, sir, they form a cross-like structure that can bind to other cells."

"Okay, okay, give me a moment, computer."

"Yes, sir."

"Computer, please display a diagram of laminin."

"Yes, sir, displaying it now."

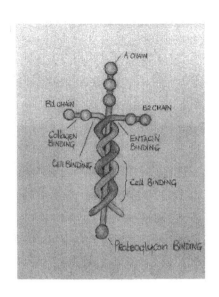

"Really?"

"Excuse me, sir?"

"Nothing; never mind. Computer, do you have any photographs of laminin in Vivo?"

"Yes, sir."

"Please display them."

"Displaying them now, sir. Here is the first one, sir."

Laminin

"Amazing! Do you have any more?"

"Yes, sir."

"Put them up, please."

"Yes, sir, doing so now."

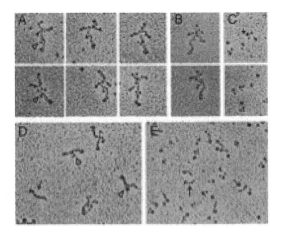

"Very interesting."

"You are looking at a two-dimensional view of the three-dimensional laminin unit. It is dynamic and flexible and moving as it "holds" your carbon-based life form together at the cellular level. This electomicroscopic view shows views from the top, from the side, every concievable perspective, with resultant different viewpoints."

"Yes, yes, computer. I can see that. Thank you. That will be all for now."

In the Bible in Romans 1:20, the mystic Paul makes it clear that we can know God through what He has made. It certainly is possible that a quantum "God" designed the laminin protein and gave it a structure that allows it to perform the function He designated for it, and perhaps slipped it in as another bread crumb in the trail leading back to Himself.

One of the early papers on the structure and function of laminin said this: "Globular and rodlike domains are arranged in an extended four-armed, cruciform shape that is well suited for mediating between distant sites on cells and other components of the extracellular matrix." [K. Beck, I. Hunter, and J. Engel,"Structure and Function of Laminin: Anatomy of a Multidomain Glycoprotein," [*The FASEB Journal* 4 1990:148–160].

In their book, *The Laminins,* authors Peter Elkblom and Rupert Timpl go into more detail about both the importance of laminins and their structure. They describe laminins that, together with other proteins, "hold cells and tissues together." They also say, "Electron microscopy reveals a cross-like shape for all laminins investigated so far," and that in solution the laminin shapes were more like a flower than a cross. The "Rose of Sharon." I recall that is another name for the ONE who hung on the cross 2000 years ago. I think that trail might lead back to the quantum God as well! The strands of laminins do not always stand straight and at right angles, but they do consist of arms, three that are short and one that is long.

Regardless of your belief systems, this is incredibly symbolic, especially in light of this text from the Bible. Is the quantum God the glue that holds us together, with a super glue particle that takes the shape of the cross?

Colossians 1:15-17

"He is the image of the invisible God, the firstborn over all creation. For by him all things were created; things in heaven and on earth, visible and invisible, whether thrones or powers or rulers or authorities; all things were created by him and for him. He is before all things, and in him all things hold together."

I didn't make that up; it's been in print for about 2000 years.

I started my search for the God particle, the Higgs boson—physics answer to the question, 'what is the lowest common denominator?' Could we have found another God particle of sorts?

Well, not really because the Higgs boson is just that—a particle—the lowest common denominator that we have found so far close to the "quanta" itself.

But as the God particle is part of a field that perhaps holds the universe of physics together, I see a parallel at least with this unique biological protein that quite literally holds us together. Like the myofascial system, this microscopic protein holds our internal universe together. For the sake of argument I will nickname it our biological God particle. At the very least it might be another of the signatures of God that we have discovered in this search for the Source. Perhaps this microscopic laminin is another "fingerprint of the quantum God" placed strategically in the very foundation of our carbon-based life form to guide us back to a knowledge of Him when all other beliefs in the Higher power have been destroyed. Perhaps it was destined to be "discovered" at a time when science and spirit would be separated like orphaned twins, blindly attempting to describe and make meaning of the Cosmos, like the men of Indostan!

Laminin may very well hold the key to curing the out-of-balance state we call cancer. We all know the killer that it has become. "Quiescence" is the process by which a biological cell stops growing or dividing. This is the opposite of a cancerous state, in which cell growth and division is often unchecked. Signals from laminin-111, an ECM protein that helps the cell and its ECM stick together, have been linked to cell quiescence but the mechanism was unknown. Mina Bissell and postdoctoral fellow, Virginia Spencer, in Berkeley Lab's Life Sciences Division, have now shown that the addition of laminin-111 leads to quiescence in breast epithelial cells through changes in nuclear actin.

What? You mean it can stop the cell growth of cancer?

A paper detailing the results of this study appears in the *Journal of Cell Science*. The paper is titled "Depletion of nuclear actin is a key mediator of quiescence in epithelial cells." Co-authoring the paper with Bissell and Spencer were Sylvain Costes, Jamie Inman, Ren Xu, James Chen and Michael Hendzel.

Healing from the cross of laminin! That reminds me of a story I heard as a child. The Israelites, wandering around in the desert, were attacked by some poisonous serpents and were dying. Moses went to God and asked what he could do and God told him to make a cross and suspend around it a carving of a serpent. Symbolically, they were to crucify what was killing them. This is where we get our modern symbol for medicine. As the Israelites came and prayed to God before the cross, they were miraculously healed!

Interesting symbolism! Many people miss that story and think the first time Israel was exposed to the cross was under Roman occupation. Certainly the crucifixion of Jesus by the Romans in Jerusalem is the most well-known intersection of Israel and the cross. It appears though that quite possibly the quantum God brought it to them in advance in symbolic form so that some day seekers of truth would see the connection.

Can you handle one more thing before you go off on your own search?

We just saw an interesting shape that appears to literally hold us together discovered by science. Could there be a parallel in the spiritual realm? What could represent that spiritual message in the physical dimension more than the Fabled Ark of the Covenant? After all, this was the place where it is said the quantum God of Creation met with man and symbolically maintained His Earthly presence in the Ark of the Covenant, in the Most Holy Place, in the Tabernacle, at the heart of the encampment of Israel, as they took the journey to maturity in the wilderness.

Dr. Missler told me about some folks with too much time on their hands (thank goodness), who created a geometric layout of what they had found regarding the supersymmetry that the nation of Israel formed as they camped around the Tabernacle in the forty years they wandered in the wilderness. They did the math (recorded in the Bible) and found a geometric shape that revealed a macro code hidden in plain sight, but only visible from a heavenly vantage point, or at least a very high spot like our picture.

One giant laminin molecule holding the nation together!

Even to me it was pretty obvious that both the laminin molecule and the formations that Israel camped in for forty years were in the shape of what we now recognize as the cross. I was shocked! I think it speaks for itself to minds that are open. I sense that was what it was designed to do. This quantum God clearly had a plan before the moment "He" spoke the universe into existence, you know, the Big Bang, when frequencies applied to energy transformed it into to different forms of matter. This quantum God lives outside the dimension of time. He knows the ends from the beginnings and therefore set up sign posts along the way for wayward humanity to take note of and get back on course. In science, in nature, in spirituality, they stand out to open eyes. I am certain that there are many, many more hidden gems waiting to be discovered.

Based on my experience, I would caution you not to search for truth unless you are ready to accept what you find. If you do embark on this journey, don't accept the smooth-talking hucksters selling BS by the barrel and don't fall for the same old beliefs you have been taught. If you really want the truth, you will find it... and it will set you free. Free from what? Well, from false paradigms for starters and false road signs that direct your life off course across the bridge of lies into the wilderness of delusion. Where down is up and up is down... on is off and off is on... and evil is good and good is evil.

This odd war between science and spirit is a futile waste of time... the only place they can truly be separated is in the human mind.

It's your choice; take the red pill and you'll know the truth.

Take the blue pill, you go back to sleep and forget this ever happened.

I only promise you the truth; nothing more, nothing less.

So we fix our eyes not on what is seen, but on what is unseen. For what is seen is temporary, but what is unseen is eternal. ~ 2 Corinthians 4:18

I found that the thoughts conveyed and the codes hidden in the Bible tell us there is more than meets the eye. There is both the seen and the unseen world. Much like a microscope or a telescope, the Bible offers perspectives that we cannot see with our normal eyes, glimpses into unseen dimensions. The Bible gives us perspectives on both the micro and macro levels that help us understand reality in a different way. It contains both micro and macro codes that connect spirituality and science when properly decoded and offer confirmation of both the seen and unseen realms of spirituality and science.

According to scientists, more is "unseen" than is seen with "dark" (unseen) matter and energy, making up 95.4 percent of the universe. It also seems that the Mystics already knew about that... but how did they know? Were they in touch through the unseen realm with the source of both the seen and the unseen? I think yes! And many still are.

Consider the evidence that I have stumbled across in my search so far and imagine for a moment... what if the Creator, the Source of all, has had a plan all along? What if before He initiated "the Creation" or transformation process of His energy into matter, "from the unseen to the seen," He knew the whole story, because that's just how He is. He designed a series of codes and messages in every aspect of human life so as to confirm His unseen presence and His plan to reunite Himself with humanity. From the micro codes in our very DNA signed with His name to the macro codes of the Cosmos, His plan was and is literally written across the sky so that at any given time we could look into the night sky and be reminded we were not alone or forgotten. We would be reminded that He was proceeding with His plan for reunification with humanity. Every major sign of the zodiac and its supporting signs told and still tells a story of rebellion and separation, of the warfare between good versus evil, duality versus unity, and victory for all that is good with an eventual reunification of man with God! Unity reestablished! The lost dimensions found and reconnected again as we see God face to face as Adam did. The contention of duality forever banished from the universe as a "supernatural" unity spreads throughout the Cosmos.

Even now in this age of engagement with the rebels, the Book assures us that we have His "Spirit" dwelling on Earth, implying that there is continuous 'two-way traffic' between the seen and the unseen. There are ground rules for this engagement; God limited Himself so as to give a "fair" opportunity to the rebel Lucifer to prove to the universe that he could lead better, better than the quantum God. Sort of a fight with both hands tied behind His back, God did what he could to allow Lucifer's plans to have a fair exposure and implementation. It would appear that history has proven beyond a shadow of a doubt that it was an unmitigated failure for Lucifer, and according to the celestial agreement recorded in the Book, the time for this contest is nearly up and unity is about to be reestablished. At any time God could have re-assimilated Lucifer and his fellow rebels' very essence, their matter, back into energy and they would have ceased to exist. However, then He would have become what he was already accused of being—a tyrant. The Book says that at some point the Creator will remove his essence from those who do not desire His presence and have proven it through the ages, and He will honor their will. In the process there will be a supernova like none before as matter is recycled into energy and back to its source. The Book describes it as a lake of fire to purify the Earth which He then recreates in an ideal form for those who choose a relationship with Him. A place they can call home forever. A place with the extra dimensions reconnected, and this will not be our only home; we will be free to roam the universe in peace and unity and safety in harmony with all of the expressions of God's creative power. One intention throughout the Cosmos, one heartbeat of unity. You will not lose your individuality, but gain something even more valuable… a never-ending intimate relationship with the Source! Tell me how that's not the best thing you have ever heard! It's goooood! It just could be true. Perhaps now is the time to do your own search and see what you find. My quest continues…

To know that we know what we know, and that we do not know what we do not know, that is true knowledge.
~ Henry David Thoreau

Epilogue

Physicists have just discovered a real gem! A jewel-like geometric object that dramatically simplifies calculations of particle interactions and challenges the notion that space and time are fundamental components of reality.

"This is completely new and very much simpler than anything that has been done before," said Andrew Hodges, a mathematical physicist at Oxford University who has been following the work. [Natalie Wolchover, 9-17-13, *Quanta* Magazine]

The revelation that particle interactions, the most basic events in nature, may be consequences of geometry significantly advances a decades-long effort to reformulate quantum field theory, the body of laws describing elementary particles and their interactions. Interactions that were previously calculated with mathematical formulas thousands of terms long can now be described by computing the volume of the corresponding jewel-like "amplituhedron," which yields an equivalent one-term expression. I think I can grasp a vision of how that might work. Can't you? In Chapter Twelve we discovered how the quantum God has used the shape of things—geometry—to point us in His direction. It would make sense that His sacred geometry might reoccur intertwined with the structure of math and physics as we approach the Big TOE.

"The degree of efficiency is mind-boggling," said Jacob Bourjaily, a theoretical physicist at Harvard University and one of the researchers who developed the new idea. "You can easily do, on paper, computations that were infeasible even with a computer before."

The new geometric version of quantum field theory could also facilitate the search for a theory of quantum gravity that would seamlessly connect the large- and small-scale pictures of the universe. Attempts thus far to incorporate gravity into the laws of physics at the quantum scale have run up against nonsensical infinities and deep paradoxes. Where are those gravitons and gravatinos? The Amplituhedron, or a similar geometric object, could also help by removing two deeply rooted principles of physics: locality and unitarity.

"Both are hard-wired in the usual way we think about things," said Nima Arkani-Hamed, a professor of physics at the Institute for Advanced Study in Princeton, New Jersey, and the lead author of the new work, which he is presenting in talks and in a forthcoming paper. "Both are suspect."

As we saw earlier, locality is the notion that particles can interact only from adjoining positions in space and time. And unitarity holds that the probabilities of all possible outcomes of a quantum mechanical interaction must add up to one. The concepts are the central pillars of quantum field theory in its original form, but in certain situations involving gravity, both break down, suggesting neither is a fundamental aspect of nature.

In keeping with this idea, the new geometric approach to particle interactions removes locality and unitarity from its starting assumptions. The amplituhedron is not built out of space-time and probabilities; these properties merely arise as consequences of the jewel's geometry. The usual picture of space and time, and particles moving around in them, is a construct.

"It's a better formulation that makes you think about everything in a completely different way," said David Skinner, a theoretical physicist at Cambridge University.

The seemingly irreconcilable conflict between gravity and quantum field theory enters crisis mode in black holes. We have seen that black holes pack a huge amount of mass into an extremely small space, making gravity a major player at the quantum scale, where it can usually be ignored.

String theory, a framework that treats particles as invisibly small vibrating strings, is one candidate for a theory of quantum gravity that seems to hold up in black hole situations, but its relationship to reality is unproven—or at least confusing. Recently, a strange duality has been found between string theory and quantum field theory, indicating that the former (which includes gravity) is actually mathematically equivalent to the latter (which does not) when the two theories describe the same event as if it is taking place in "different numbers of dimensions." No one knows quite what to make of this discovery. But the new amplituhedron research suggests space-time, and therefore those dimensions, may be an illusion anyway.

"Beyond making calculations easier or possibly leading the way to quantum gravity, the discovery of the amplituhedron could cause an even more profound shift," Arkani-Hamed said. That is, giving up space and time as fundamental constituents of nature and figuring out how the Big Bang and cosmological evolution of the universe arose out of pure geometry.

"In a sense, we would see that change arises from the structure of the object," he said. "But it's not from the object changing. The object is basically timeless."

That sounds a lot like one of the attributes of the quantum God. Is it hype or is it an important discovery that will open the flood gates of understanding? Can you feel the duality dissolving? What a great time to be searching for the quantum God.

There are yet people who say there is no God.
But what really makes me angry
is that they quote me for the support of such views.
~ Albert Einstein

Bibliography

Ralph P, Coop G (2013) The Geography of Recent Genetic Ancestry across Europe. PLoS Biol 11(5): e1001555.

Gregg Braden, *The God Code*

Bruce H. Lipton Ph.D. *The Biology of Belief: Unleashing the Power of Consciousness, Matter, & Miracles.* 2005.

http://biblia.com/bible/esv/Gen

http://creation.com/noah-and-genetics#end

http://discovermagazine.com/2008/jul/16-is-the-universe-actually-made-of-math#. URPaYGfdGSo

http://news.bbc.co.uk/2/hi/7399661.stm

http://science.howstuffworks.com/dictionary/astronomy-terms/big-bang-theory.htm

http://usatoday30.usatoday.com/tech/science/discoveries/2005-01-29-turin_x.htmhttp://www.asis.com/users/stag/zodiac.html

http://en.wikipedia.org/wiki/History_of_the_Shroud_of_Turin

http://en.wikipedia.org/wiki/Jinn

http://en.wikipedia.org/wiki/Laminin

http://en.wikipedia.org/wiki/Poor_Clare_Nuns

http://en.wikipedia.org/wiki/Sack_of_Constantinople

http://en.wikipedia.org/wiki/Witness_accounts_of_the_Roswell_UFO_incident

http://www.christianpost.com/news/shroud-of-turin-claims-of-authenticity-backed-by-new-research-92886/

http://www.imdb.com/name/nm0000111/?ref_=tt_trv_qu

http://www.khouse.org/articles/2003/482/

http://www.simonsfoundation.org/quanta/20130917-a-jewel-at-the-heart-of-quantum-physics/

About the Author

Dr. Luckey is a third-generation California native living and practicing dentistry in Southern California's wine country. He graduated from Loma Linda School of Dentistry in 1981. He is a father to six children—two girls and four boys—and grandpa to eight: seven boys and one girl. Besides his interest in science, John is an accomplished pilot and athlete with interests from martial arts and weight lifting to tennis and backpacking. He plans to build a unique resort spa and wellness center with a mind-body-spirit approach to wellness soon.